Smugglers' Woods

RUTGERS UNIVERSITY PRESS

New Brunswick · New Jersey

Smugglers' Woods

Jaunts and Journeys
in Colonial and Revolutionary New Jersey

ARTHUR D. PIERCE

CONTENTS

INTRODUCTION

Smugglers' Woods is a book about New Jersey during the American Revolution and the cold war that preceded it. While emphasis is placed upon special aspects of New Jersey's contribution to American independence—a contribution too often overlooked—these chapters are, in so far as practical, laid against the general background of the colonial struggle. Much of the documentary matter they contain has not been published previously.

New Jersey was small in area, population and resources. Yet its destiny was to serve as the stage for many of the Revolution's most dramatic events, and also to tie together in common effort the northern, central and southern colonies during some of the war's darkest hours. Everyone knows of the Christmas Battle of Trenton; many people are aware that important engagements were fought at Princeton and Monmouth Courthouse, now Freehold. But few realize that both the Patriot and British armies had more of their forces in New Jersey more of the time than in any comparable area elsewhere in America, save New York.

It was not in terms of land warfare, however, that New Jersey made its own larger contribution to independence, but in terms of economic and maritime warfare, which have been less often explored. American victory in the Revolution has been a fascinating puzzle over the years. By statistical reckoning, England should have won hands down. On its face the American challenge was sheer impudence. Here were thirteen colonies united more in theory than in practice. They were "governed" by a Congress which was usually broke and frequently confused. When they declared war, the patriots had no standing army and no navy. The armies they managed to raise often melted away like April snow. Many of the troops that remained in service were ill-housed, ill-clad and ill-fed. Arms were scarce, ammunition short, and behind the lines were little more than primitive industrial resources.

England, on the other hand, had emerged from its wars with France as the dominant power of its day. Its navy "ruled the waves." Its army was made up of professionals, boasting long training and wide experience. To assure an overwhelming advantage in manpower, Hessians and other European contingents were hired from German princes. Behind all that lay the vast economic strength of the British Empire. Its industrial resources commanded world respect; and indeed the Americans were fighting the very country upon which they had long depended for many necessities of civilized living. The British pound was the world's standard, while Continental currency at times was worth little more than the paper upon which it was printed.

Finally, the colonists stood divided among themselves, three ways: patriots, loyalists, neutrals. And although shifts took place among these groups over the war years, it is doubtful whether the patriot cause at its peak enjoyed more than 50 per cent active support.

A more unequal contest, in measurable terms, could scarcely be imagined. Yet the patriots won, and Great Britain lost. And, while there is no single pat explanation for that phenomenon, the ensuing chapters will explore three influential factors which commonly receive little attention in conventional accounts.

First, there was the factor of economic warfare, beginning with the chapter on smuggling during the cold war, carrying along through the almost clandestine existence of the glassworks at Wistarberg, the wartime stimulus to shipbuilding, and erection of a chain of saltworks along the New Jersey coast. Today economic warfare is a well-planned aspect of over-all strategy in international struggle, in time of nonwar as well as of war. That was not the case in the eighteenth century.

Second, there was privateering, a form of private enterprise warfare on a scale so large that it engaged almost as many men and counted almost as many prisoners as all the Revolutionary land operations together. Americans proved remarkably adept at this type of maritime operation. Some, it will be seen, proved equally adept at profiteering, another phase of the Revolution which has not had much attention.

Third, there was the deep spirit of dedication at all levels of patriot endeavor. The story of Philip Vickers Fithian exemplifies one aspect of that devotion, and others, notably among the humbler people, are found in various chapters including the two on New Jersey's colonial taverns. Finally, came the transformation of many neutrals and some loyalists into active patriots, in most cases as a consequence of loyalist and Hessian excesses, chronicled here as part of the story of Joshua Huddy's murder.

In *The War for Independence: A Military History*—a book which should be required reading in our schools—Howard Peckham cites other factors responsible for the patriot victory, most of which are beyond the scope of this book. There remains, however, the overriding fact that, as Peckham says, "America had George Washington as commander of its military forces," a man who possessed "in abundance . . . a patriotism running pure and deep that dedicated him to his duties, a courage and patience that upheld him against despair, and a sense of honor: an image of how he must act to gain his own approval and that of upright men."

So if this book, in addition to informing and entertaining, should help refresh the reader with examples set by our human, often fallible, but dedicated and sacrificing forefathers, the author will be doubly rewarded. Finally, if there be any hint of bias in *Smugglers' Woods*, the author makes no apology for it. It is a bias in favor of the men who made this country free and the leaders who made it great.

Often the acknowledgments in a book consist of cold lists of institutions and individuals, as perfunctory as a telephone directory. To me it is a pleasure to thank, in print, the many persons who have helped in making this book, and those institutions which have so generously provided access to their manuscript and other resources. Every author—including those who endeavor, as I do, to work chiefly from original sources—must rely in some part upon the past labors of other authors. While these are noted in the bibliography, special mention should be made of Dr. K. Braddock-Rogers, a keen and probing pioneer, and those New Jersey historians of earlier generations: General William S. Stryker, Charles S. Boyer, George De Cou, Frank S. Stewart, Edwin O. Salter, Joseph S. Sickler and Alfred M. Heston.

For the pleasure of rummaging for treasure through countless early manuscripts—some albeit by photostat—I have to thank Miss Lynette Adcock, Archivist of Colonial Williamsburg; Alexander P. Clark, Curator of Manuscripts of the Princeton University Library; Dorothy Hammond, librarian of the New Jersey Teachers College at Glassboro, who guided me through the Frank H. Stewart collection; and particularly Howard H. Peckham, Director of the William L. Clements Library in Ann Arbor, Michigan. All extended courtesies beyond that mere "line of duty." And thanks to the welcome extended by R. Norris Williams, 2d, Raymond L. Sutcliffe, J. Harcourt Givens and their staffs, the Historical Society of Pennsylvania seemed at times like a second home during the research for Smugglers' Woods.

The author is grateful no less to Mrs. Catherine Wetterling and her charming staff at the Burlington County Library; Frances Moltenbery, of the Library of the College of William and Mary; Donald Sinclair, Curator of Special Collections for the Library of Rutgers, The State University; John L. Lochead, Librarian of The Mariners Museum; and Robert W. Hill, Keeper of Manuscripts of the New York Public Library. Mrs. Rae Hatch, Curator of the Vineland Historical Society, Mrs. Sarah Sheppard Hancock and Newlin Watson lent valuable aid on the Greenwich and Fithian chapters.

My friend, Captain Charles I. Wilson, head of the Delaware River Port Authority Police, contributed generously to several chapters, and his name appears on the dedication page. My thanks to Howard R. Kemble for data on taverns from his voluminous files, his helpful suggestions and encouragement; to Joseph J. Truncer, General Manager of the Wharton Tract for the New Jersey Department of Conservation and Economic Development, for helpful notes on General Greene and Colonel Cox; and to Mrs. J. Manderson Castle, Mrs. T. Charlton Henry, Raymond and Mary Baker, M. Virginia Regenthal, Alice Weber, Watson Buck, John D. F. Morgan, Edward Walton, Jr., and Dr. Harry Weiss, for their cooperation and suggestions. It is modesty, of course, which impels an author to leave his wife's name until last. So with my own wife, Margaret. Yet since *Smugglers' Woods* is as much her book as it is mine, I can only thank her for the gift of her share in the enterprise.

ARTHUR D. PIERCE

Medford Lakes, New Jersey
January 15, 1960

Smugglers' Woods

SMUGGLERS' WOODS

There is a pleasure in the pathless woods,
There is a rapture on the lovely shore,
There is society, where none intrudes,
By the deep sea, and music in its roar.
—Byron: *Childe Harold*, IV, 1818

Eyren Haven, the Dutch called it. Harbor of Eggs! And there were eggs indeed, literally thousands and thousands of them, the eggs of gulls, and sandpipers, and other birds of the sea. Eggs were strewn far and wide upon the sandy beaches, eggs of all sizes, most beyond reach of the encroaching tides. These were first impressions. Fresh ones soon followed as Dutch skippers cautiously explored the coastal bays and inlets of what was to become *Nova Caesarea*, or New Jersey. Following the lead of Henry Hudson, they maneuvered through treacherous channels amid the sand bars; and yet they still had time to sense the depth of the beauty around them.

When the famous Dutch vessel *Half Moon* was sailing toward Eyren Haven early in September of 1609, the mate, one Robert Juet, put this down in his journal: "The Sunne arose, and we steered away North againe, and saw the Land from the West by North, to the North-west by North, all like broken Ilands . . . and our soundings were eleven fathoms and ten fathoms. Then wee looft in for the shoare, and faire by the shoare, we had seven fathoms." [1]

Before them the river wound gracefully through marshy corridors; and as its course led inland from the sea the shining sands of the "broken Ilands" gave way to great forests which only the river seemed to penetrate, forests so dense, lofty, and lush that the eye might easily mistake their dark green for a mysterious black. There was then, and still is, a fascination in that vista. It is not surprising that Mate Juet also wrote in his journal: "This is a very good Land to fall with, and a pleasant Land to see."

By mid-nineteenth century many of the birds and their eggs were no more to be found. Yet, past mid-twentieth century many other charms of Eyren Haven remain. Few sights can surpass in simple majesty the view at sunset from the bridge that carries the Garden State Parkway high above the Little Egg Harbor River, or the Mullica, as it is now called.

As in past ages, the Mullica River estuary curves sinuously through the marshes—eastward to the Atlantic, and westward through a still-wooded horizon—on beyond its junctions with various pineland streams, past historic and still-quaint villages, to halt only after its course has traversed two thirds of the way across New Jersey toward the Delaware River. There is history roundabout the area of the bridge. During the American Revolution a major base for privateers was there, and it was the scene of a battle. Still earlier history of another sort was made at Eyren Haven and far beyond, in the forests to the westward and to the south. For this was Smugglers' Woods.

The forests themselves bespoke mystery and adventure. Today's pines and oaks are dwarfs beside their ancestors of those days. The cedars in particular were incredibly thick, often entangled with other wild growths and encrusted at their bases with strange and colorful mosses. Human existence at first was almost as strange. The earliest settlers are

said to have lived in caves, and some years passed before
they started to cut down some of the great trees in order to
build cabins. These for the most part were squatters; and
so vast were the lands of the New Jersey proprietors that
many such squatters lived out their lives officially unnoticed.
No bother for them with deeds or title searches; their pre-
occupations were of a different kind: food, the Indians, and
wild animals. Most of the Indians were friendly, but not
all. By fishing and hunting—agriculture came later—the food
question was solved, simply if not elegantly.

Wild animals remained a problem for years; as late as
1753 official bounties were being paid for the heads of
panthers and wolves. George May, founder of Mays Landing, collected a pound for a wolf's head. Heads of wild
panthers came cheaper, a mere 15 shillings.[2] Other free-
roaming beasts were bears, red deer, wildcats, and foxes,
not to forget an abundance of hedgehogs, rabbits, pheasant,
grouse, and quail.

Smugglers' Woods grew from these early beginnings along
the New Jersey seaboard, and even into Delaware Bay, and
bred a hardy race of seafarers, traders, trappers, and hunters; while deeper in the forests developed what appear to
have been the considerably less civilized "Swamp Angels"
or "Swamp Men," a curious breed which may be distantly
related to latter-day "Pineys."

These Swamp Angels were, in the late sixteen-hundreds
at least, a rough, tough bunch of thieves who cut down
other folks' timber and sold it, manufactured tar and turpentine, and carried on their operations deep in the recesses
of the forests by day and "removed their plunder by night
to be sold to persons no better than themselves at half the
legitimate value."

One mysterious character named Jonas Tow had built a
shop in a thick swamp far behind his home. In it he kept

"strange sea-faring gear under constant lock and key."
Neighbors suspected that Tow was engaged in some shady
business, but "even after his death nothing incriminating
was brought to light." [3] In the early 1770's that sharp ob-
server, the Rev. Philip Vickers Fithian, wrote in his *Journals* [4] of meeting "many straggling, impertinent, vociferous
Swamp Men" in his travels through Eyren Haven and
Smugglers' Woods. Fithian adds, however: "They used me
with great civility."

Earlier, during the first half of the eighteenth century,
there had been substantial migration into the area of families from New England who brought with them a reputation
of being shrewd traders, and the ability to prove it. Thus
when the incentive to smuggling appeared, the men and
the means were right at hand. Eyren Haven—or Little Egg
Harbor, as it now must be called—was an ideal port for
skippers on illicit missions, being far removed from any
customhouse or regular official observation. The Mullica
River was navigable for miles, all the way to "The Forks"
for vessels of lighter draft. Roads, rough but adequate, had
been cut through the pinelands. There was a trade established between the shore and Philadelphia early in colonial
history.

Goods were conveyed by heavy wagons, fitted for travel
through the sandy roads, and the wagons were driven by
Negro and Indian slaves and redemptioners. Thus contraband cargoes could be quietly hauled overland to Mount
Holly, Haddonfield, Burlington or Cooper's Ferry, and
Philadelphia. And early accounts tell how Egg Harbor farmers who lacked wagons would load produce in bags, throw
them over the backs of their horses, and with their wives
make long, lonely trips to market.

Chances are that any reader with prosperous ancestors
who came to America before 1755 will find a smuggler some-

where in his family tree. From early days—in England as well as in the thirteen colonies—smuggling was a custom. It was against the law; but His Majesty's government smiled tolerantly if not benignly for centuries while smuggling developed into a respectable business. It was engaged in by many of the best people in America. Not only was the law against smuggling largely unenforced, it was "universally considered a dead letter." [5]

Colonial smugglers actually were the grandfathers and great-grandfathers of the Revolution. They never envisaged such an outcome from their activities; yet once the British government decided to end its traditionally apathetic attitude toward smuggling and launched serious efforts to collect American customs duties—from that moment on the smugglers became engaged in the first phase of the long cold war with the mother country. Little notice has been given hitherto to New Jersey's important role in that economic warfare; and not enough notice has been paid to the part played by smuggling in the struggle that began when Britain attempted to enforce the Navigation Acts and the statutes against smuggling after the practice had become a part of the colonial economy and way of life.

In Boston the eminent John Hancock was a smuggler, one of the biggest. In Philadelphia the Quaker merchant James Logan defied meeting rules and "occasionally evaded the Navigation Acts." He shipped three tierces of tobacco which were listed as bread (which was not dutiable), and he explained that the "Streightness" of the customs officials at just that time had forced him and others to "resort to this subterfuge." [6] Logan added that "these methods are not very justifiable tho' common."

For obvious reasons smugglers rarely kept records, which is why documentary background is so scarce. Yet it can safely be said that the great bulk of American merchants who were engaged in foreign trade were also smugglers in varying degrees. Fortunes were built upon the traffic. Smuggling played a substantial role in molding the social as well as the economic structure of American colonial life; and the "Smuggling Interest" became "a factor of great political strength in the trading towns of the North." [7]

The colonists also had ample precedent from the mother country. Smuggling had been a time-honored custom in Britain itself; it was a vocation pursued by gentlemen of rank and character. Illicit trade across the English Channel and with Danish ports dates far, far back. In the thirteenth century Edward III put an "exportation tax" on wool, whereupon all the ports of Kent and Sussex were soon engaged in smuggling wool.[8] There was other contraband trade in lace, silk, and brandy. Similar illicit traffic continued over the centuries despite occasional efforts to stop it, particularly by Charles II. Benjamin Franklin pointed to this aspect of British history when he wrote his paper "On Smuggling" in 1770. Poor Richard observed that "the English never hesitated to avoid payment of duties when they could, even though they had made their own laws, as the Americans had not. When I hear them exclaiming against . . . every little infringement on the acts of trade or obstruction given by a petty mob to an officer of our customs . . . calling for vengeance against the whole people as rebels and traitors, I cannot help thinking that there are still those in the world who can see a mote in their brother's eye while they do not discern a beam in their own."

Resistance to customs duties in New Jersey dates at least as far back as 1680. In that year "the people of West Jersey fought the attempt of Governor Andros to impose such duties upon the commerce of the Delaware." [9] It is worth noting that the protest, even then, was based on taxation without representation.

By 1699 pirates as well as smugglers—the two long were kin—were warmly welcomed in Smugglers' Woods. That year Robert Quarry, vice-admiral of Pennsylvania, wrote that with the assistance of Governor Basse of New Jersey he had "apprehended 4 more of the Pyrates at Cape May." Quarry added: "I might have with Ease secured all the rest of them, and the Ship too," had not local officials "Entertain'd the Pyrates, conveyed them from place to place, Furnish'd them with Provisions and Liquors, given them Inteligence and sheltered them from Justice. All the persons that I have employed in searching for and apprehending these Pyrates are abused and affronted and called Enemies to the Country for Disturbing and hindring honest men (as They are pleased to call the Pyrates)." [10]

In New York and New England during that period occasional efforts were made to enforce customs laws, but those efforts were brief and rarely effective. Corruption was rife. Both pirates and smugglers received the sevententh-century equivalent of ticker-tape welcomes from New York's Governor Fletcher, provided, of course, they paid their protection money. Ordinary "protections" were "commonly sold at one hundred dollars a man. For captains and others of high rank, the price was increased, usually involving open bribes of expensive gifts to the Governor and his family." Captain Tew, a notorious pirate, "was one of the Governor's favorite dinner guests and appeared publicly in his coach." [11]

Prior to 1733 smuggling continued with little interference. Molasses then was king. It was the raw material for rum, favored beverage of those days, and John Adams was to say many years later that "molasses was an essential ingredient of our independence."

Smugglers welcomed any salable cargo, but molasses, or sugar, or rum itself, was the best. Because molasses and sugar were from 25 to 40 per cent cheaper in French Guadeloupe, Martinique, and Spanish Santo Domingo than they were in the British West Indies islands, such as Jamaica, Antigua, and Barbados, the profits in sugar trade from the non-British islands were enormous. This in turn led the British West Indies planters, most of whom lived in England, to howl piteously to Parliament. Finally they whipped up enough sentiment to put through the Molasses Act of 1733, which set a prohibitive duty of six cents a gallon on molasses from non-British islands.

British efforts to enforce this Molasses Act merely increased the incentive to smuggling. The smugglers became even craftier. They had many old tricks on hand and soon acquired a lot of new ones. Bribery of officials was one of the simplest and commonest; others included forged clearance papers, partial entries, and mislabeled cargoes. Legal commodities would be used to mask illegal imports. Ships' manifests would be doctored. The captain of the schooner *Mary*, which put into Philadelphia with a cargo of *eighty* hogsheads of rum, produced papers from Nevis, signed by the customs collector there and showing that the duty on this rum had been paid. But close examination of the papers revealed that they had been altered. They originally were for *eight* hogsheads of rum. By adding a "y" to the "eight" it had been made "eighty." And the difference was the duty on 72 gallons of rum. The Philadelphia customs agent who spotted the fakery declared: "We have no doubt the whole cargo was taken on board at St. Croix." [12]

One favorite West Indian port of the molasses smugglers was Monte Christi, on the northern coast of Santo Domingo, and it was used by both French and Spaniards. John Reynell, a Philadelphia Quaker, while denying that he had engaged in the "monte Christo trade," admitted that "it is very profitable and many from here have made great voyages." [13] And British West Indian officials counted from one hundred to one hundred twenty North American vessels at one time off Monte Christi harbor.

When war broke out with France in 1756—the French and Indian War—this smuggling became, legally, treason. But since the rewards grew still greater, smuggling continued. The French needed American provisions and were willing to pay fancy prices for them. When "an investment of ten shillings would ordinarily bring a return of from fifty shillings to three pounds," [14] it is clear that any risks in illegal trade were far outweighed by the profits. There was now more smuggling than ever. Governor Morris of Pennsylvania, aware that many prominent merchants were in cahoots with the smugglers, tried earnestly to tighten up on customs control but, like an overpatched pair of pants, as fast as it was sewn up in one spot it burst wide open in another. Morris even roamed the waterfront night after night, often forcing windows and doors to gain access to suspected storage places. But he could not patrol Smugglers' Woods and, although he appealed for, and was promised, cooperation in export controls from New Jersey's Governor Belcher, little was actually forthcoming.

Before long, customs corruption again became open and barefaced, particularly in New Jersey and the Delaware Valley. Revenue officers again were bought and paid for, such posts being occupied mostly by "needy wretches who found it easier and more profitable not only to wink but to sleep in their beds; the Merchants' pay being more generous than the King's." [15] This was particularly true at Perth Amboy and Cohansey. James Otis said that "a very small office in the customs has raised a man a fortune sooner than a post in Government."

Thomas Penn reported officially in 1759 that the port of Philadelphia was "swarming with shallops [from French ports] unloading illegal cargoes . . . cheating the King of his duty's, besides carrying provisions and ready money to the Enemy." Penn declared that "a very great part of the principal Merchants" were implicated in this "treasonable trade." Even worse, much of it was conducted under "flags of truce, passes for which [Pennsylvania's] Governor Denny scrupled not to sell in blank form at the low price of twenty pounds sterling or under." [16]

Soon changes were to be made. From London. The wars with France had depleted the British Treasury and the plan now was to obtain enough from the colonies to help fill it again. This was a popular and plausible idea in England. Some Britishers had only contempt for their American cousins. General Wolfe sneered that Americans were "in general the dirtiest, most contemptible cowardly dogs that you can conceive." Brigadier General Henry Bouquet declared that he was "obliged to deal with the insulting rudeness of an Assemblyman (from Pennsylvania) who, picked from a dunghill, thinks himself raised to a Being of a Superior nature." [17] These were minority views, but they were fairly prevalent in influential circles.

Also, Britons noted that in the early 1760's the American colonies were enjoying an unprecedented era of prosperity. Wealthy merchants and planters put on lavish entertainments for British officers, who took home vivid accounts of that high hospitality. "Horse racing, jockey clubs and theaters flourished; in once-puritanical Boston the maids exceeded their mistresses in dress . . . and the Boston Mall, modeled upon St. James Park, was crowded with resplendently dressed ladies and gentlemen." [18] Even the exceedingly grave Mr. Fithian, during his stay as a tutor at Nomini Hall in Virginia, noted that the girls of the Old Dominion were "got up in the latest London stays." He remarked of one of them: "I imputed the Flush which was visible in her Face to her being swathed up Body & Soul & Limbs together." [19]

New York also reveled in London styles. Socially sought after was the returned traveler who could "move a minuet after the newest fashion in England; is a perfect connoisseur in dress . . . and has learned those elegant expressions Split me, Madam; By Gad, Dam me; and fails not to use them on all occasions." [20] Even the common people "lived better and drank better" in what James Murray of Massachusetts called "a Land of health, plenty and contentment." [21]

All this seemed to prove the parliamentary point: that there was money to be had in the American colonies to help replenish His Majesty's Treasury. No one was more confident of this than George III, who had come to the British throne in 1760 with the notion that he could rule from it as well as sit on it.

The new king was careful to surround himself with ministers who would take his orders. One of these was an ex-Whig, George Grenville, known as a financier and a tight-fisted businessman. Grenville's administration began in 1763 and, although he was to last only two years in office, he organized and set in motion the policies, methods, and economic forces which drove Americans first to protest, then to resistance, and finally to a war for independence. Grenville also gave new meaning to Smugglers' Woods when he launched his three-point program:

First, he was determined to police American ports to re-establish a British business monopoly based on the Navigation Acts, so that most American commerce, exports as well as imports, would have to pass through Great Britain. This meant a British rake-off on every transaction, with consequently higher prices. The fundamentals of this policy were old, dating as far back as 1651, but the proposed enforcement was new.

Second, most manufacturing was to be virtually outlawed in the colonies, and the royal governors were ordered to report on any industrial enterprises already operating. This measure was another aspect of British economic philosophy long embodied in the Navigation Acts. It was designed to make America's an agricultural economy—George III liked to speak of "his farms" in America!—leaving the colonists heavily dependent upon Britain for manufactured goods, at prices kept high through freedom from competition.

Third, Grenville proposed to enforce the laws against smuggling and get tough about it, even if it meant using the British Fleet.

It had been costing His Majesty's government 8,000 pounds a year to collect 2,000 pounds in customs duties. Grenville also learned that an estimated 700,000 pounds' worth of merchandise was being smuggled annually.[22] Since most of this was in the sugar and molasses trade, he persuaded Parliament to put through a new Sugar Act in 1764.

On the surface this act seemed to be a concession to the colonies, because the duty was reduced from sixpence a gallon to three, and the revenue was not to go into the general British Exchequer but was to be kept separate to pay for maintaining British troops in the colonies. This was no concession in practice, for enforcement of the lower duty on sugar merely meant that merchants would be paying threepence a gallon where before they had paid nothing. As for the maintenance of British troops, the colonists had only one wish: that they be hustled back to England.

At first Grenville's program seemed to be working. The old customs inspectors whom the merchants had "bought" were replaced by "Scotch Laddys" of whom it was said that they seemed content to live on their salaries. One merchant was quoted as lamenting that "the happy days of smuggling are over." While the Sugar Act did bring prosperity for a time to Britain's West Indian planters, it brought depression to the American colonies. The British islands became "so flooded with provisions, horses, lumber, and fish from the Northern Colonies that these commodities fell precipitately in price."

While thus buying American goods cheap, the British planters, now having a monopoly, began to sell their molasses and sugar at such inflated prices that one American observed that "rum would soon be out of the reach of the poorer people except as a medicine." Other trade began to wither. "Farmers lost important markets for their foodstuffs; lumber rotted on the wharves; and colonial merchants began to wind up their affairs.[23]

It is no wonder that Englishmen soon were boasting of the utter dependence of America upon Britain. Said one of them: "The American today is apparelled from head to foot in our manufactures . . . he scarcely drinks, sits, moves, labours or recreates himself without contributing to the mother country." [24]

Then the colonists started to fight back. Grenville's agents might clamp rigid controls on the big ports, Boston, New York, Philadelphia, Charleston, tie them tight with red tape, certificates, affidavits, bonds and warrants. "Scotch Laddys" might extract the last ounce of duty from cargoes moving in or out. The Royal Navy might be standing by, as for a while it did. But along America's coastline there were other ports —innumerable rivers, inlets, bays, and harbors—which Grenville never had heard about. Many of these enjoyed natural security through the difficult channels that led in from the sea, and from protective sand bars and shoals which even His Majesty's Navy would, and did, find troublesome. Soon much of the trade, especially that highly profitable West

Indies commerce in sugar and molasses, was quietly transferred from the sternly policed big ports to the smaller ones
which were not policed at all.

Such is the background of Smugglers' Woods. Such are
the historic and complex factors which made it possible for
men to enrich themselves—some substantially, others mod-
estly—through the trade that came to Little Egg Harbor,
Toms River, Cohansey, Cape May, and other snug havens
backed up by the South Jersey forests. Both its remoteness
and its natural advantages made the Mullica basin a particularly favored harbor for illicit traders, as it was to become the most important New Jersey harbor for privateers
during the Revolution.

Even before the Batsto Iron Works was built in 1766,
The Forks had a reputation for keeping a "candle in the
window" for smugglers. Ships of lighter draft could dock
there and unload "barrels of sugar and molasses, puncheons
of rum, boxes of tea, bags of coffee and other articles of
trade." [25] These would be taken overland through the
woods, and soon the route not only became familiar but
was marked by a convenient chain of taverns. There was
good reason why Lower Bank, Pleasant Mills, Blue Anchor,
Long-a-Coming, and White Horse blossomed forth with
thirst-quenching taverns almost simultaneously about 1740.

There was business in Smugglers' Woods even if records
were rarely kept and nothing could be proved. From 1720
Wading River, first called Leak's Landing, was a small but
busy center at the junction of Wading River and old Tuckerton trail. In some deeds it is called "Leeks," in others "Leks"
Landing, and it was named for Captain John Leak, an Englishman who settled there even before 1720, the date not
definitely known. Originally a seafaring man, Leak became
a surveyor, built some small vessels, and did a bit of land
speculating. Perhaps he had other enterprises, for the tradi-

tion is that he "fared sumptuously every day." [26] Leak's Landing thus grew into a village, and it provided a cozy, offbeat harbor for any watercraft that might need it.

Up the Mullica River a few miles were four other settlements which appear to have been busy places in early days: Clark's Landing, Lower Bank, Mordecai Landing, and Pleasant Mills. Clark's Landing lay on the south side of the stream. Though a ghost town now, in 1718 it boasted a log church, forty cabins, and a population of over two hundred. Within twenty years, significantly, a new church had been built, there were frame houses instead of cabins, a trading post was thriving, and the population had doubled.

Not far from Clark's Landing, on the north side, lay Lower Bank, the traditional homesite of Eric Mullica, the Swede for whom the river is named. Mullica is credited with being the first white settler in the entire region. (Alfred M. Heston has given 1645 as the date when he arrived there, but my research indicates that it was probably in the 1680's.) Lower Bank is a quaint and colorful village today, as it must have been in the long ago when it was famous for having seven taverns and a population of only a hundred. Transient trade of seafarers, however, was heavy; and today boats are still built there, by a firm with the name of "Leek," proud of having been established in 1720. Kinfolk, of course, of old Captain Leak who spelled his name with an "a" when he lived not far away in Wading River.

Mordecai's Landing, also on the north side of the Mullica, dates back well into the eighteenth century, even before the building of the Batsto Iron Works in 1766. Who was Mordecai? The answer seems to be that he was Mordecai Andrews, of Tuckerton, whose father was one of the earliest settlers (1698) in the Little Egg Harbor area. Mordecai Junior bought a large tract of woodland along the Mullica, roughly a mile from the present site of Batsto, and there

conducted fairly extensive lumbering operations. His landing place by the river has borne his name ever since.

Finally, there is lovely Pleasant Mills, where a squatter
colony is recorded from 1707 and where Elijah Clark in
1762 built his mansion, which still stands.

Smuggling—trading was the polite word for it—laid the
basis for the surprising prosperity of those remote villages.

First trader of record in the area was one John Ridgeway,
who owned a seagoing sloop. Not much later, however,
came John Mathis—the Mathis name is still a distinguished
one in shore counties—and soon he was sending his son
Daniel in "a vessel . . . which followed the West India
trade." [27] Young Mathis would carry lumber from the Egg
Harbor area and bring back "products of those islands." The
principal products of "those islands" were molasses, sugar,
and rum; and there was no customhouse anywhere near
Little Egg Harbor in those days.

Old Thomas Clark, of Clark's Landing, also did quite
well for himself with trading. So did his sons Thomas and
David. They set up their own sawmills at Clark's Mills, near
present Port Republic. Elijah Clark had made a small fortune at Pleasant Mills even before he branched out in
privateering.

This prosperity on the Mullica was at its height while
Philadelphia was under rigid customs regulation in the
1760's. There was some risk in hauling smuggled goods
through the forest roads into Delaware Valley towns but
interference was rare. The wagon drivers usually traveled at
night; their contraband was concealed by a load of salt hay
or a shipment of clams, and at the first sign of real trouble
they usually escaped into the woods whose hideaways they
knew better than anyone else.

New Jersey had three legal ports of entry in that period:
Perth Amboy, Cohansey, and Burlington. In 1749 Governor

Belcher had written, almost apologetically, to the Lords of Trade in London that the collectors at these ports were "vigilent and prevent any Clandestine Trade as much as in them lies." [28] New Jersey even then was notorious as a center of illicit trading due to its abundance of creeks and inlets.

By 1763 all masks were off. Charles Read, builder of Batsto, Atsion, Etna, and Taunton furnaces, was also collector of customs at Burlington, a post he had held many years. His official report then was that "many Vessels trading to Plantations not belonging to the King of Great Britain, returning with cargoes of Rum, Sugar and Molasses, have found means to smuggle the same into His Majesty's Plantations, without paying the King's Duty." [29] Read knew what was going on in Smugglers' Woods; he was even charged with being sympathetic to the very parties he had been talking about. But Read himself was no smuggler; had he been, he might have averted the bankruptcy that led to his flight from the state.

Strict enforcement of Grenville's laws against smuggling did not last much longer than did strict enforcement of the American prohibition laws a hundred seventy-five years later. For a while it hurt. New Jersey's Governor William Franklin, in 1764, reported to the Lords of Trade that "at present there are great murmurings among the merchants and others, on account of the Stop put to the trade with the foreign West Indies." [30] Shortly afterward, however, Franklin wrote that the situation had changed. Now, he said, customs officers had entered into a deal with the merchants, by whom they were paid a dollar a hogshead for sugar and molasses "in lieu of the Duties imposed by Act of Parliament." He added ruefully that he had no knowledge that the money the customs officers were taking was "ever remitted to England." [31]

Even as enforcement of his Sugar Act was breaking down, Grenville pushed through the hated Stamp Act. This measure was designed to squeeze more money from the colonists by forcing them to pay for a tax stamp on newspapers, on marriage licenses, on legal papers, customs clearances, etc. When the colonists defied this levy too, British exasperation reached a new high; and the officials can hardly be blamed for suspecting sabotage from Smugglers' Woods when in September, 1765, the ship *Faithful Steward,* loaded with stamps and stamp tax paper, was wrecked on Absecon beach. It may have been a storm, miscalculation, or just bad luck; but it had been an old trick of wreckers along the coast to erect misleading beacons so as to lure vessels on the rocks or sand bars where they could be seized and their cargoes looted and sold. One wrecker is said to have even arranged a lantern on a mule and walked it in circles to give ships at sea the impression of flashing from a lighthouse.

By 1766, customs enforcement having broken down again, Britain took new steps. An American Board of Commissioners of Customs was created. This agency was given broad powers: it could appoint searchers, collectors, surveyors, clerks, and informers. Changes in other laws now made it theoretically easier to obtain convictions in customs cases. On paper it appeared as if every loophole had been closed. But that was on paper. Prospective candidates for searchers and informers were intimidated by their neighbors, and most declined the jobs. When cases came up in court, witnesses suffered complete loss of memory; and even when crown witnesses did remember, juries usually would refuse to vote for conviction. As a result of all this, the merchants, their skippers, crews, and hirelings soon turned from secrecy and subterfuge to open defiance.

That same year the Boston customhouse officials were resisted in broad daylight when they attempted to inspect the house of a notorious smuggler, and in Rhode Island customs officers were frankly afraid to take any action against "the powerful clique of illicit traders." [32] When John Hancock's ship *Liberty* was seized in Boston harbor in 1768 by customs officers who literally caught the skipper with the goods, Bostonians rallied en masse to the Hancock cause. Mobs overcame the customs officers and landed the illegal cargo. They then marched on the house of the comptroller of customs, Benjamin Hallowell. His windows were smashed and he was lucky to escape to safety in Castle William, the British harbor fort. Then Hallowell's official barge was pulled ashore, dragged through the streets, and "burned joyously" on Boston Common in front of Hancock's house. British officials decreed a fine of 100,000 pounds for Hancock—it was never collected, and the legal case against him collapsed.[33]

Soon violence was spreading. In October, 1769, an unidentified Jerseyman who had been spying on a Little Egg Harbor shallop in Smugglers' Woods showed up in Philadelphia to give information to the customs officials there. Soon after this he was seized by a group of sailors, tarred and feathered from head to foot, then paraded through the street, first in front of the customhouse, then before the home of the collector. After that he was put in the pillory, and finally ducked in the mud beside the dock, after which he was "let go in peace, to sin no more." [34]

That was only a beginning. Smugglers' Woods embraced much of the Delaware Bay shoreline as well as the coastal strip from the Mullica southward. Countless illicit cargoes had been sailed up the Great Egg Harbor River to Mays Landing. Sugar Hill acquired its name from the large quantities of sugar and molasses unloaded at that point. Cohansey (now Greenwich) was another favorite port for the connois-

seurs of contraband. It was at Cape May, however, that
violence was to burst forth next.

Francis Hopkinson had been appointed in 1763 as collector of customs for Cohansey, which district included
Cape May. His early reports mention that "smuggling was
prevalent, chiefly in sugar and molasses." [35] But Hopkinson
seems not to have become excited about it, an attitude explained perhaps by the fact that thirteen years later he
was to become one of the signers of the Declaration of Independence. Incidentally Hopkinson is regarded by some as
the actual designer of the first American flag, an honor
credited by legend to Betsy Ross.

Four years later a man named John Hatton was appointed
customs collector in Hopkinson's place. From the British
point of view no choice could have been more unfortunate.
Hatton not only was determined to halt illicit trade in
Smugglers' Woods, he was so cantankerous and quarrelsome
that he turned many in Salem, Cumberland, and Cape May
counties against the crown. "Petty, overbearing and insolent" was what one fellow townsman called him. In 1768
Hatton charged two Salem men, Grant Gibbon and Edward
Test, with obstructing his enforcement of customs collection. This case created a stir but was settled peaceably.
Governor Franklin threw out Hatton's accusations.

Fireworks started in November, 1770, however, when
Hatton moved into Cape May to crack down on the smuggling there. Already he had written the commissioners of
customs that the Common Pleas justices at Cape May,
specifically Thomas Leaming, John Leonard, and James
Whilden, were in league with the smugglers. He insisted
that they were partners in a conspiracy with "certain Philadelphia merchants to smuggle goods through the Cape";
that "several thousand pounds worth of goods had recently
been landed illegally," and that a wagonload of smuggled

goods had passed his own door in broad daylight and under the escort of armed men who challenged him to seize them.[36]

Soon after Hatton arrived at Cape May a ship, the *Prince of Wales,* came into the bay and was met by several pilot boats, who immediately set to unload her. Hatton, with his son and a Negro aide, rowed down to her and saw them throw over "a great quantity of Bales and Casks of Clarett." When Hatton maneuvered his boat close, "they called out to me and bid me stand off or they would sink me, and they manned their sides with Swivels, Guns, Peteraroes, Blunderbusses and Musketts, and declared they would murder us." Hatton retreated, but decided to attack one of the smugglers' other boats. This time he got aboard, found her full of goods, and legally seized her.

By then the smugglers were set to counterattack. Soon they had captured Hatton, his son and the Negro aide. Says Hatton: "They took our guns . . . and with swords and axes beat us in a most inhuman manner, riffling our Pocketts, taking from me one riffle Pistol, four dollars and my Shoe buckles and other trifles." After that the smugglers put the bruised Hatton, his son, and his aide ashore and went about their business.

Hatton was not a man to let bad enough alone. Learning that at least some of the illicit cargoes had been taken to Philadelphia from the Cape, he sent his son to the Quaker City. With more nerve than judgment young Hatton prowled the waterfront, spotted one of the leaders of the smugglers, and finally located one of the boats. Reporting this to John Swift, collector of customs in Philadelphia, the latter sent his son along with Hatton to see what could be done. They soon found out—the hard way. Swift describes the riot that followed in a letter to the British commissioners of customs:

They met the pilot who own'd the boat . . . and he pretended to be very sorry for what had pass'd, and told him he might take the Boat and do as he pleased with her and artfully engaged him in conversation for near half an hour till he [the pilot] observed seven or eight Sailors arm'd with Clubbs, close upon them; he then told him to take care of himself for they were coming after him, upon which young Hatton and my son took to their Heels, and the Sailors after them. My son was fortunate to get into a House where he was known & protected. Young Hatton likewise got into another House, but the Sailors follow'd & dragged him out, and drove him about from place to place, and with more than savage barbarity tore off the dressing from the Wounds on his head and arm and pour'd a pot of Tar upon his Head, and then feather'd him. The mob gathered as they drove him with sticks from Street to Street. They had a rope round his body, and when he would not walk or run, they drag'd him; they put him in the Pillory, and when they were tired of that, they drove him to the River and duck'd him. Then they put him into a Boat and row'd him across the River to the Jersey shore & there landed him. . . .

I am much at a loss what steps to take in this matter. Many people here say they are sorry for what has happen'd, tho' I believe most in their hearts approve of it. Not a man interposed to prevent it, neither Magistrate or Citizen. . . . If these riots are permitted with impunity it will be impossible for any Custom House Officer to do his duty in this Port. There are not less than a thousand seamen here at this time, and they are always ready to do any mischief that their Captains or Owners set them upon.[37]

Once again Hatton took his case to Governor Franklin.

And once again the governor threw it out. Franklin's report on the appeal mentions Hatton's "very unhappy, violent temper, sometimes bordering on Madness, so that it is impossible that he can live long with his neighbours." Despite this, British authorities kept Hatton on the job. He accomplished virtually nothing, however; and, finally catching on, he moved away from Salem, reportedly to Swedesboro, where he was an active Tory throughout the Revolution.[38]

There is a double significance in the Hatton case. Unstable the man may have been, but was he altogether wrong in his conviction that virtually everybody was against him? His neighbors, the governor, the Courts of Common Pleas, as well as Supreme Court Justice Charles Read, of whom he said: "Mr. Read's actions are as formerly: which is to distress me and the Service of the Revenue all he can." Even the customs commissioners he considered hostile. It was not imagination. Virtually everybody *was* against Hatton.

What happened to him was a demonstration of the overwhelming support which smuggling enjoyed among the people of New Jersey. That sentiment was the same in New York, Boston, and of course Philadelphia. It was identical in Rhode Island, which cheered the smugglers' burning of the revenue cutter *Gaspee* and the shooting down of its commander. When Eben Richardson, a Treasury agent, was transferred from Boston to Philadelphia in October, 1773, Bradford's *Pennsylvania Journal* first described the man and then suggested that "all lovers of liberty will make diligent search and having found this bird of darkness will produce him tarred and feathered at the Coffee House, there to expiate his sins against his country by a public recantation."

Such blatant and widespread approval of smuggling was

not regarded by the colonists as defiance of law but rather as resistance to unfair and unreasonable restrictions on trade. Freedom of trade was justified as a "natural right" which Parliament had no authority to take away. Defense of that right—illegal as the defense might be—represented the first phase of that economic warfare whose original goal was economic freedom, but which culminated in a war for political independence.

Smuggling is a nasty word today. In those times it was not only the forerunner of active rebellion but a powerful, effective—and respectable—answer to British policies which were designed not alone to collect revenue from the American colonists but to strip from them the political liberties which as Englishmen they had been trained to treasure.

As individuals the men of Smugglers' Woods were not heroes; nor were they paragons of virtue. Some were crude, unsavory characters; others were solid and theologically upright citizens. If most of them were heavily motivated by greed, they were fighting greed on the other side. They were engaged in a rough, tough, all-out struggle, and eventually they won. As for Smugglers' Woods itself, one may still roam with pleasure its "greene countrie" and avow it a "pleasant land to see."

PRIVATEERING —
AND ADVENTURE

Came the Revolution and the men of Smugglers' Woods graduated, *cum laude*. Their diploma was the letter of marque, granted by both Congress and the state. They became privateers. In so doing they made Little Egg Harbor the number one privateering center of New Jersey, and New Jersey itself the most dangerous, to the British, stretch of coastline on the whole Atlantic seaboard.

In terms of the eighteenth century a privateer was a ship privately owned, privately armed and equipped, and bearing a license—the letter of marque—authorizing it to prey on enemy commerce. Any prizes, captured vessels and cargo, would be sold at public auction and the proceeds divided among the owners, the officers, and the crew, with the largest share going to the owners. The risks were great but the profits often were enormous, a fact which led some of the elite to speculate in fitting out privateers and induced many of America's ablest seamen to risk their skins in such a dangerous game. Even a common sailor might get as much as a thousand dollars out of one cruise in addition to his wages; and nowhere else was there a job which offered the prospect of making so much money in so short a time. One writer has called it "the most profitable racket in the world —so long as you escaped getting your throat cut." [1]

The cynical said that privateering was simply piracy under a government flag; others argued that it prevented formation of an effective navy during the Revolution; and still others charged that it siphoned off the very manpower, bold and adventurous youth, which Washington most needed in his pitifully small army, for at times an estimated thirty thousand men were thus engaged. Yet whatever the moralities and might-have-beens, American privateers made a monumental contribution to victory in the War for Independence. How much they hurt the British is best judged from the testimony of Britons. In February, 1778, Alderman Woodbridge told the House of Lords that "the number of ships lost by capture or destroyed since the beginning of the war was 733 whose cargoes are computed to be worth over $10,000,000." *The* (London) *Times* observed: "It seems fated that the ignorance, incapacity and cowardice of the Americans by land should be continually relieved in point of effect by their successes at sea." [2]

British marine insurance costs more than doubled in the first two years of war, and soared still higher later on. American privateers were not only running at large off the American coast, but also were invading British waters and capturing ships in sight of the British Isles. One American privateer, the *Rattlesnake*, moved into the Baltic and took a million dollars' worth of prizes on one voyage alone. After France entered the war and French ports were wide open to them, the privateers threatened Britain where she was supposedly most powerful and actually most vulnerable: in her sea power, already spread thin for a lifeline to her armies in America. None of the vital British trade routes was safe, certainly not those in the West Indies. Of sixty ships which left Ireland for Grenada in 1778, only twenty-five were ever seen again and some of those lumbered into port with splintered rigging. One English trader in Jamaica wrote: "Within one week upward of fourteen sail of our ships have been carried into Martinique by American privateers."

By 1780 more than four hundred fifty privateers, armed with seven thousand guns, were stalking enemy commerce. Over the years from 1776 to 1782 privateers had captured or sunk an estimated twelve hundred enemy ships. The financial loss to Britain in terms of vessels and cargo alone was over $20,000,000, an enormous sum in those days.[3]

Most important of all, perhaps, was the great number of prisoners taken. During the Revolution the Continental armies captured about twenty thousand prisoners. Over the same period the privateers captured almost as many, sixteen thousand prisoners, including a whole company of Scotch Highlanders with their officers, an entire contingent of British dragoons, a shipload of Hessians, and many assorted groups of British and Hessian officers. What mattered most, however, were the thousands of British seamen taken, for they were the men George III could least afford to lose.

One little-known venture in privateering was that sponsored by Benjamin Franklin. He had no investment interest whatever; his concern was in obtaining prisoners who could be exchanged "for our poor countrymen" in British prisons. Franklin had learned that in the Mill prison at Plymouth and the Forton prison at Portsmouth many American captives were being told that they were neglected by Congress, that the British had about won the war, and that it was to their interest to accept the king's pardon and enter on board a man-of-war.

Three ships were authorized for this venture: the *Black Prince*, *Black Princess*, and *Fearnot*. Manned by crews of Irish smugglers, the *Black Prince* captured thirty-five prizes; the *Black Princess*, forty-three; the two cruising in consort, twenty; and the *Fearnot*, sixteen. Grand total: "one hundred and fourteen British vessels . . . burned, scuttled or destroyed." Prisoners taken totaled one hundred sixty-one.[4]

All sorts of ships were turned into privateers when, as James Warren wrote Samuel Adams in 1776, "the whole country [went] privateering mad." In the early days of the war any watercraft capable of being mounted with cannon was turned into a privateer. Later the profits financed the building of bigger, finer, and faster vessels designed especially for raiding service. Yet even the larger privateers were tiny ships by today's standards. Few were more than seventy feet long or over a hundred tons in capacity, and many were much smaller than that. Some, used only for coastal activity, were mere open boats, often whaleboats, equipped with a few swivel guns, which were "small portable cannon or blunderbusses turning freely on a pivot, and mounted in a socket on the ship's rail."[5] Oceangoing privateers were equipped with larger guns but rarely anything more than nine-pounders, and most were of smaller size. Some vessels would venture to sea with only two cannons, and several daring skippers supplemented them with wooden dummies to make their ships appear much more formidable than they actually were. Generally, however, a privateer battery would run from six to twelve guns, and a few carried as many as twenty. Hand weapons included muskets, pistols, hand grenades, boarding pikes, cutlasses, and tomahawks.

Actually privateering was a natural outgrowth of colonial maritime traditions. Americans were shipbuilders and sailors from way back. As early as 1676 more than seven hundred ships had been built in Massachusetts alone and at the outbreak of the Revolution a third of the 7,694 vessels engaged in worldwide British commerce were American-built.[6] Privateering itself harked back to the early seventeen-hundreds; and after 1776 the British were merely being paid off in their own coin, for they had promoted and encouraged American privateering, especially during the wars with France and Spain. In the spring of 1743 two privateers "brought 60,000 pieces of eight to the port of Philadelphia, one of them returning again in October with a Spanish prize valued at 30,000 pounds sterling." [7] In 1748 the *Bethel,* out of Boston, captured a Spanish treasure ship of twenty-four guns and "the better part of 100,000 pounds sterling." [8] It is scarcely surprising, then, that when the colonies rose in revolt they promptly moved to profit by these precedents and even improved on some of the British maritime techniques.

New Jersey's important share in all this has been singularly neglected by historians, for several reasons. New Jersey has long been a forgotten state, obscured and crowded between New York and Philadelphia. In Revolutionary times most of the highly articulate political leaders and intellectuals were in Boston, New York, Philadelphia, and Williamsburg. Furthermore, historical source materials relating to New Jersey have often been inaccessible, very often scattered, and in some instances wantonly destroyed. In so far as privateering is concerned, the neglect of New Jersey is due to the fact that many of its privateers, although owned and manned by Jerseymen and operated out of Jersey ports, were commissioned of record in Philadelphia. In Maclay's excellent *History of American Privateers* only one ship is listed for New Jersey, the schooner *Enterprise,* which made a series of exciting captures in 1776: first the British vessel *Lancaster;* then the *Black Snake,* with a rich cargo of rum and sugar; the *James,* with twenty-three men and a similar cargo; while on July 22 of that year the *Enterprise* took two ships in one day, the *Earl of Errol,* mounting six guns and having a cargo worth $100,000, and the *Nevis,* which surrendered after an hour's gun battle.[9]

Just as the New Jersey coast was a natural haven for smugglers, so did its harbors and their tricky approaches make ideal bases for privateers. Chestnut Neck, at Little Egg Harbor, was best of all because of its difficult entrance channel, protective sand bars, and remote havens up the river in Smugglers' Woods, where many smaller craft could take refuge in an emergency. In 1745, when he was collector of customs at Burlington, Charles Read made the following inquiry to officials in Philadelphia: "Application was this day made to His Excellency for a Commission for a Privateer, and as there are no precedents of that kind here, I must beg you will take the trouble of informing me in what manner they grant these Commissions in Philadelphia." [10]

Pre-Revolutionary privateering in New Jersey was probably limited because smuggling then was so widespread and profitable. War clouds changed matters. By October, 1775, seizures of British vessels had begun off the Jersey coast. In January, 1776, a British ship loaded with supplies for the army in Boston was captured off Sandy Hook and taken into Elizabeth-Town to be sold at auction.[11] By the following June "privateers were unloading rich booty at Little Egg Harbor."

Considerable duplication will be encountered in the names of privateers. Just as some names are popular with parents in naming their offspring, so it was with the owners of privateers who were not usually sentimental in other ways. Sometimes American and British ships would have identical names, a fact which leads to some confusion in dealing with accounts in contemporary newspapers. There

were four named *Nancy,* one of them British; four named
Hazard, one British, one Tory, and two American; also three
named *Liberty,* one British. *Polly* was a favorite American
name, there were five of them, and *Speedwell* another. At
least four privateers were named *Chance,* and two or more
were called *Enterprise, Revenge, Alliance, Terrible, Teaser,*
and *Vixen,* to name only a few. There were even two ships
with the name of *Holker,** both brigantines, both commissioned in Pennsylvania, both owned in part by New Jersey
interests, both sailing out of Jersey ports, and both with ten
guns. One, however, carried forty-eight men, the other
thirty-five.

A curious story concerns one *Holker,* a story which suggests further why service on privateers, for all its perils, was
more attractive than being a private in the Continental Army.
Elijah Clark, long owner of the Pleasant Mills plantation on
the Little Egg Harbor River and a colonel in the militia,
made a written agreement through his son, Lardner, with
an indentured servant named James Vaulone. The deal was
that Vaulone, who once had been a watch finisher in England, should take service in the crew of the brig *Holker,* for
her current cruise of five or six weeks, and pay in return for
his freedom eleven-sixteenths of any prize money he received.[12] If that seems like a callous sort of pact, it may be
imagined that Vaulone welcomed the opportunity it afforded. No doubt he did well for himself: on that particular
trip, in April, 1779, the sixteen-gun *Holker* captured a ten-
gun schooner and two armed sloops.

On her next cruise the *Holker* was less fortunate. Although she succeeded in capturing a sixteen-gun brigantine,
there was a ninety-minute gun battle in which six Americans were killed and sixteen wounded, including the cap-

* Jean Holker was a French merchant who furnished supplies to the American Army before France became a formal ally.

tain, M. Lawler, and his first mate. British losses were six dead and twenty wounded.[13] Whether Vaulone was aboard on that trip is not known. As for Elijah Clark, who made one fortune in Smugglers' Woods, he became both owner of and speculator in other privateers.

Privateering off the New Jersey coast often resembled the guerrilla warfare the Continentals were waging on land. There were the same hit-and-run tactics, the same elements of surprise, the same violations of formal rules of warfare then fashionable in Europe. Above all, there was the same boldness—sheer impertinence, from the British point of view—which so often permitted numerically inferior forces to defeat, rout, and even capture larger enemy forces.

Inevitably this type of warfare bred leaders of great daring and resourcefulness, and among the privateersmen of New Jersey the name of Captain Adam Hyler ranks second to none. Hyler's home was in New Brunswick and his maritime haven the Raritan River. Operating much of the time in supposedly British-controlled waters and especially under the noses of the loyalists in their fortified headquarters at Sandy Hook Light, Captain Hyler seized prizes and prisoners wholesale, to the mounting anger and embarrassment of Tories and British alike.

Hyler's brilliant raids depended quite as much upon skillful organization as upon personal bravery. While some of his expeditions were carried out by sailboats alone, his favorite technique was to use a combination of one sailing gunboat and two whaleboats, actually large barges rowed by crews of expert oarsmen. Most of Hyler's whaleboats were kept at New Brunswick, but some would be moored in secret anchorages in the smaller streams emptying into Raritan Bay.[14] One of Hyler's raids is well described in a contemporary newspaper:

October 7, 1781. On Friday last, Captain Adam Hyler, from New Brunswick, with one gunboat and two whale-boats, within a quarter of a mile of the guardship at Sandy Hook, attacked five vessels, and after a smart conflict of fifteen minutes, carried them. Two of them were armed, one mounting four six-pounders, and one six swivels and one three-pounder. The hands made their escape with their long boats, and took refuge in a small fort, in which were mounted twelve swivel guns. From this they kept up a constant firing, notwithstanding which he boarded them all without the loss of a man. On board one of them was 250 bushels of wheat and a quantity of cheese belonging to Captain Lippencott, bound to New York. He took from [the others] fifty bushels of wheat, a quantity of cheese, several swivels, a number of fuses, one cask of powder and some dry-goods, and stripped them of their sails and rigging, not being able to bring the vessels into port in consequence of a contrary wind and tide; after which he set fire to all save one, on board of which was a woman and four small children, which prevented her from sharing a similar fate.

Only a week or so later Captain Hyler, with the same gunboat and two whaleboats, boarded a sloop and two schooners anchored in the very shadows of the Tory fort at Sandy Hook. Only two persons had been left aboard these three vessels. Hyler and his men seized them all. One, being a "dull starter," was set on fire three miles from the fort; another, running aground, was stripped and abandoned; while the third, "a remarkably fine, fast-sailing Virginia-built pilot, mounted with four-pounders," was brought with the two prisoners safely to the home base.

Other raids followed in rapid succession. On November 14, 1781, Hyler and his men, cruising the Narrows, captured the *Father's Desire* and its crew of fourteen. Hyler got his prisoners safely ashore along with twenty hogsheads of rum and thirty barrels of pork. A month later he seized two Tory sloops which had on board six hundred pounds in specie. Adding insult to injury, Hyler soon afterward actually raided the Tory fort itself—not once but twice—carrying off six prisoners the first time, and on the second occasion capturing the captain of the guard and all his men.[15]

It is not surprising that over in Manhattan British exasperation rose about as fast as British patience diminished. In January of 1782 an expedition was organized for the specific purpose of capturing Adam Hyler and destroying his whaleboat fleet. A Philadelphia newspaper offers the following report of the expedition:

> A party of the British lately made an incursion to New Brunswick with the design, it is said, of carrying off the boats of the celebrated partisan, Captain Adam Hyler. They landed at New Brunswick and plundered two houses but were gallantly opposed by the neighboring militia, and the enemy were driven off with some loss. Further accounts say there were some 200 refugees and British, and that they succeeded in destroying the whaleboats. No Americans were killed, but five were wounded and six taken prisoners. Several Tories were killed—four known to be, and several were seen to be carried off. The British made the attack about five o'clock A.M., just before daylight . . . and the Tories held the town for about an hour. The British regulars were detachments from the 40th and 42nd regiments, under command of Captain Beckwith, in six boats, and they took away all of Hyler's boats. The British alleged that Captain Hyler was a deserter from the Royalists.

The British did not capture Hyler. Nor did they, despite this confused news report, seize all his whaleboats. Soon he was back in business, and one of his most audacious exploits took place the following May. In an open boat he boarded a large cutter, ready for sea, which was lying near a man-of-war, the *Lion,* boasting sixty-four guns. The cutter itself had a dozen eighteen-pounders, and "was commanded by one White, formerly of Philadelphia, who had turned apostate." After taking off some forty prisoners, Hyler blew up the cutter within sight of the British warship, headed for home, and on his way seized an enemy sloop which was "ransomed for 400 pounds."

Following is a newspaper account of Hyler's methods:

> He has none but picked and tried men. They are taught to be particularly expert at the oar, and to row with such silence and dexterity as not to be heard at the smallest distance, even though three or four boats be together, and go at the rate of twelve miles an hour. Their captures are made chiefly by surprise or stratagem; and most of the crews that have hitherto been taken by these boats declare they never knew anything of an enemy being at hand till they saw the pistol or cutlass at their throats.

Hyler's career, unfortunately, was not to last much longer. A man who might well have become one of the later builders of a United States Navy, he died in 1782, on September 6, in New Brunswick. And he died in bed.[16]

Scarcely less daring was another New Brunswick privateersman, Captain William Marriner. He is famous for his attempt to kidnap the Tory mayor of New York, Daniel Matthews, often dubbed the "Tormentor General" for his cruelties to American prisoners. The attempt failed. Matthews was out when his visitors arrived. But Marriner did seize six men, including a British officer, and carried them back to New Brunswick.

Marriner's most dramatic adventure of all took place in April of 1778. The American privateer *Blacksnake* had been captured by the British. With nine men Marriner set out in a whaleboat, retook the *Blacksnake*, then put to sea in her and encountered a British ship, the *Morning Star*, which had six swivel guns and carried thirty-three men. After a fight in which the British lost three killed and five wounded, the *Morning Star* surrendered, and Marriner took both his prizes into Little Egg Harbor.[17]

The Garden State Parkway is a landlubbers' link between New Jersey's privateering bases of yesterday. From the great arched span over the Raritan one can see the waters where Hyler, Marriner, and others sailed their raiding craft seaward in those days when the area was not under British occupation. True, it takes imagination to blot out the smoke and factory grime and to visualize the once-lovely wooded shores where the whaleboats were concealed in coves, ready for instant action. It is an impressive vista withal; and heading southward one soon approaches the next privateer port, Toms River.

Toms River still has a faint flavor of the past; and it is still primarily a town looking outward toward the Atlantic rather than inland. Toms River marks the head of navigation on the stream of the same name. To recapture some feeling of the old days one should scan the waterfront and then take a drive past Pelican Island over the seven-mile road to Seaside Heights. Almost opposite the point where the Toms River empties into Barnegat Bay there was once an open channel from the ocean called Cranberry Inlet. It has long since been closed by ocean currents but privateer traffic through it was fairly heavy in Revolutionary days. However, because the channel was shallower and narrower than that at

Little Egg Harbor it was used chiefly by smaller privateers, particularly the specialists with whaleboats.

For over a century whaling had been a major occupation of coastal dwellers in the Toms River area, and with the outbreak of the Revolution it was a simple step to fit their boats with small cannon, stock up on pistols and pikes, run out through Cranberry Inlet, and get their share of the lucrative privateering business. Given a good sea, the whaleboaters could row faster than many of the small, slower sailers from the West Indies; and carrying more men than their prey, they hauled many a prize into Toms River. Among these were the sloop *Fanny*, taken in January, 1779; the schooner *Hope*, laden with "pitch, tarr, and salt"; the brig *Dove* with 140 puncheons of rum; the sloop *Blackjack*; and a great many more. In some cases a captured vessel could not be floated through the inlet; it would be sold as is on the beach. One such was the *Success*, loaded with molasses, coffee, cocoa, and rum. She hit the shore in a snowstorm early in March, 1779. Boarded by the militia, her cargo was auctioned on April 7 of that year.[18]

Much of the privateer warfare along the upper coast—notably in Toms River and the New Brunswick area—was waged against the Tories quite as much as the British, especially those New Jersey Tories engaged in contraband trade with His Majesty's headquarters in New York. Shrewsbury was long a haven for these people, sometimes called refugees or picaroons, the latter term deriving from the Spanish for rogue, or pirate.[19] There were certainly profits to be made in smuggling foodstuffs out of New Jersey and smuggling back into the state silks, satins, and a wide variety of other goods requisite to gracious living. With wartime austerity these luxuries were obtainable only from British merchants in New York, and more than a few ardent patriots were among the customers for such goods, with no questions asked.

A specialist in this type of smuggling was William Dillon, who lived on what then was called Dillon's Island, now Island Heights. For some time Dillon played a successful double role, proclaiming himself to be either a patriot or a loyalist as suited his immediate purpose. Actually his heart belonged to His Majesty, and in addition to his smuggling Dillon was a useful British spy.

In August, 1778, the British ship *Love and Unity*—strange name for a vessel in American waters then—ran aground near Toms River. Legends have it that she was deliberately grounded by secret patriot sympathizers on board. Soon a crew of veteran privateers boarded the craft and floated her inside Cranberry Inlet. The *Love and Unity* was a rich prize. Taken off her were eighty hogsheads of loaf sugar, several thousand bottles of London porter, Bristol beer and wines, as well as cider, salt, flour, cheese, queen's ware, delft, fine wineglasses, tumblers, and other luxuries. On August 31 the ship itself and part of the cargo were sold by Marshal John Stokes at Toms River, while the balance of the cargo was auctioned two days later at Manasquan. The purchaser of the vessel renamed her the *Washington*.

At that point William Dillon entered the picture. He passed the word to his British friends in New York and they sent four ships from Sandy Hook to Cranberry Inlet. At daybreak on September 19 seven armed boats, guided by Dillon, moved swiftly through the inlet, recaptured the *Washington*, and seized two American sloops lying at anchor. The captain and crew of the *Washington* escaped, but the men on board the two sloops were taken prisoner. Four years later Dillon was still in business. He then served as pilot and general informer for the British expedition which captured the Toms River blockhouse and burned much of the town.[20]

Dillon, however, was a gentleman compared to Captain John Bacon. Bloody John was a merited nickname. Bacon's first killing was that of Captain Joshua Studson, a patriot privateersman. Studson had captured two enemy craft, the schooner *John* and the sloop *Catharine,* in the fall of 1780. In company with other Tories Bacon moved into Cranberry Inlet after dark on December 1. The Tories were among those engaged in the smuggling trade to New York. Local militia got wind of the expedition, set out to head off the smugglers, and Studson stood up in the boat, calling upon the Tories to surrender. Without a word of warning Bacon fired. Studson fell dead. In the resulting confusion the smugglers escaped.

Monmouth County annals include a long list of Bacon's plunderings and brutalities. His blackest moment, however, was the night of the Long Beach Massacre. On October 25, 1782, Captain Andrew Steelman of Cape May and twenty-five men on the privateer *Alligator* captured a British cutter from Ostend headed for St. Thomas. This vessel, apparently far off course, had run aground on Barnegat Shoals. Steelman and his men labored the whole day to unload her cargo on Long Beach. By nightfall all hands were dead-tired and curled up among the dunes to rest. In the dead of night Bacon and his followers sailed over from the mainland, crept up on the Americans, and slew them while they slept. Captain Steelman and a number of his men were killed instantly; those who attempted to rise were hacked with bayonets; and of the twenty-five in Steelman's crew only five managed, somehow, to escape alive. Such butchery, coming as it did when the war was virtually over, intensified public hatred for the loyalists.

Hero's Revenge was the singularly inappropriate name

for the boat used by Bacon that night. But revenge there was to be. As public anger mounted, Governor Livingston offered a reward of fifty pounds for Bacon, dead or alive. Headed by John Stewart of Arneytown, a posse of six set out to track him down. They combed the shore villages and finally found Bacon, separated from his men, at the public house of William Rose, between West Creek and Clamtown (now Tuckerton). After a wild melee Bacon was stabbed by one member of the posse—brother of a man he had killed—and finally, as he attempted to escape through a rear door, was shot dead. This took place on April 3, 1783.[21]

One of Toms River's more successful privateers was Captain Sam Bigelow. Early in 1780 he seized the *Betsey,* a ship owned by British sympathizers in Delaware. Laden with supplies for New York the *Betsey* stranded on Long Beach and before she could get free her cargo had been seized and the vessel itself taken as a prize. In December of that year Bigelow had another lucky strike. The *Dove,* a British brig, bound from Tortola for New York with a cargo of 140 puncheons of rum, ran astray off Long Beach. The captain, named Hannek, through some error in navigation thought he was off British-held Long Island. Being short of water and provisions, he sent four men in a boat to seek supplies ashore. They virtually walked into Captain Bigelow's arms. After taking the four as prisoners, he and his crew set out in a couple of whaleboats, took possession of the *Dove,* and brought her into Toms River. Other British vessels captured off Long Beach in those years included the *Polly, Dillylatta, Hope, Fancy, Fanny, Diamond,* and *Dolphin.* Most of their cargoes were sold at vendues in Toms River, Freehold, and Allentown.

"Nest of Rebel pirates!" That is what the British called Little Egg Harbor, most important of New Jersey's privateer ports. The Little Egg Harbor of history is not one place but two. Tuckerton is just a short run of creek from Little Egg Harbor Bay. Usually called Clamtown, but Little Egg Harbor as well, it had its share of privateer visitors. Much more important in the naval war, however, was Chestnut Neck, which is not on Little Egg Harbor at all but a couple of bends upriver from Great Bay. True, the inlet has shifted since Revolutionary days, but the snaky windings of the Mullica were much the same. As a community Chestnut Neck amounted to little. But protected by sand bars and intricate channels, quite unmarked in those days, it was a perfect harbor for privateers; and often upward of thirty ships, some raiders and some prizes, could be seen at anchor there.

Chestnut Neck in 1777 consisted of a dozen dwellings, George Payne's tavern, some storehouses for captured goods, and John Adams' Landing. For a time a second tavern is said to have been located there, kept by Daniel Mathis, who later ran the Franklin Inn near the dam at Port Republic. Yet even two inns in that little village were probably hard put to handle the peak wartime traffic in privateersmen and prisoners. The houses were occupied by the families of men whose names for the most part are still familiar in those parts: Jeremiah Adams, John Adams, Edward Bowen, Henry Davis, James Giberson, Jeremiah Higbee, Joseph Johnson, John Mathis, John Smith, Micajah Smith, Robert Smith, and Joseph Sooy.[22]

Some of these men were privateer captains; others were engaged in the transport of captured prizes and prisoners overland through the pineland trails to Philadelphia. After the Quaker City was occupied by the British, they made their way over other trails to Burlington and to Dunk's Ferry (now Riverton, N.J.), whence the precious cargoes often found their way to Washington at Valley Forge.[23]

The Chestnut Neck fort was built in June of 1777. It followed the first British thrust in that area, a raid which has
been overlooked in most accounts. On July 10, 1777, "a
Brig appeared off Little Egg Harbor Inlet, and made a
signal for a pilot." Colonels John Cox, of Batsto, and
Elijah Clark, of Pleasant Mills, wrote jointly to the Council
of Safety (a letter that was never delivered):

> Joseph Sowey, with his brother and two boys, went off
> to conduct her into port, and were taken on board and
> carried off. Immediately on taking them on board the
> brig proceeded to the mouth of Great Egg Harbor Inlet,
> where she again threw out a signal for a pilot; on which
> Mr Golder went off with his boat, and on approaching
> near enough finding she was a vessel of force, he imme-
> diately put about, and pushed for shore, the enemy's boat
> pursuing, with only two men showing themselves. On
> coming within 100 yards, a number of men showed them-
> selves and fired on Golder and crew, who with some diffi-
> culty gained the shore, but were obliged to quit their
> boat which fell into the hands of the enemy. As Sowey
> is one of our best pilots, we doubt not that he will be
> made use of by the enemy to bring in their tenders and
> pilot them up the bay and river [Mullica].

Two days later this forecast was justified. The enemy
appeared off Chestnut Neck. Another letter, from Colonel
Cox to Charles Pettit, tells what occurred:

> A Brig of 16 a sloop of 12 a schooner of 8 & a Pilot Boat
> of 6 guns were Piloted over the Bar & are now at the
> Foxburroughs [a section of Chestnut Neck] & in posses-
> sion of a Brig in which I am Concerned just ready for
> Sea and a very fine vessel belonging to Wilmington & I
> take it for granted will continue there as there are some
> vessels hourly expected from sea.[24]

This British expedition was entirely naval and apparently disinclined to tarry, because the minutes of the Council of Safety show that it did not wait for those expected vessels. The minutes also note that "the Enemy's Ships of War entered Little Egg Harbor Inlet and seized two brigs . . . & carried them off with a considerable quantity of stock."

The Chestnut Neck fort was built as a result of this raid. Cox, up to his neck in privateering and also anxious to guard his ironworks at Batsto, added in his letter to Pettit: "I shall go down to Chestnut Neck tomorrow with a number of Men in order to Erect a small Fortification of 8 or 10 guns to protect them if possible from penetrating the County." Cox was as good as his word. The fort was built on a piece of high ground almost surrounded with marsh. It was armed with eight or ten pieces of cannon taken from a beached ship of Timothy Shaler, a privateer captain. Apparently the cost of construction was borne not by Cox but by Richard Wescoat and Elijah Clark, for the following September the Council of Safety voted to reimburse them the sum of 430 pounds, one shilling, threepence, for erecting the fort and buying the cannon.[25]

If prior to that first raid the British had been nettled by privateer activities at Chestnut Neck, they had only begun to fume. For 1778 was to be a rich and busy year for the privateersmen. In May of '78 the *Hazard*, a British sloop loaded with Irish beef and pork for British troops in New York, was captured by Captain Peter Anderson and a crew of sixteen. In June a succession of His Majesty's merchantmen were seized and hauled into Chestnut Neck. These included the 150-ton brigantine *Industry*, with 1,700 bushels of the "best Turks Island salt"; the fifty-ton sloop *Speedwell*, loaded with rice and tobacco; *Polly's Adventure*, a thirty-ton sloop carrying 150 barrels of flour; the *Carolina Packet*, a 150-ton brig; the *Prince Frederick*, of 230 tons;

and the sloops *Jenny, Canaster,* and *Dispatch,* not to forget another ship named *Speedwell,* a 150-ton brigantine. These vessels were sold by public vendue, mostly at Richard Wescoat's tavern at The Forks, although some were put under the hammer in Payne's Tavern in Chestnut Neck.

In July and August of '78 there were more rich prizes: the 110-ton *Governor Henry,* with a cargo of tobacco; the 100-ton dogger *Rising Sun,* with salt in casks; the sloop *William;* the *John and Sally,* loaded with a hundred puncheons of Jamaica spirits and nine tierces of Muscovado sugar; also the schooner *Lovely Nancy,* and the sloops *Duck, Elizabeth, Alexandrine,* and *Chance.* Early that September the privateer *Comet,* Yelverton Taylor commander, seized the schooner *Fame* and brought her to Chestnut Neck; and a few days later the *Comet* also captured the schooner *Hannah,* which proved to be a virtual floating department store, with china, linens, chintzes, diapers, hardware and ironmongery, frying pans, brushes, and a wide assortment of foodstuffs. This cargo was sold at Mays Landing.

By that time easygoing General Howe had been superseded by the crusty Sir Henry Clinton as commander in New York, and such large-scale raiding of supply ships undoubtedly infuriated him, especially the seizure of two very important vessels of the Irish Fleet—the *Major Pearson* and the *Venus.* Capture of the *Venus* has long been attributed to the privateer *Chance,* Captain David Stevens, but testimony in a Gloucester County lawsuit of 1780 shows two privateers involved, the *Chance* and the schooner *Sly,* commanded by Chestnut Neck's own Micajah Smith. Some idea of the great value of these prizes may be gained from the following data on the *Venus.* Her cargo included "fine broadcloths, linens, calicoes, chintzes, silks and sattins, silk and thread stockings, shoes, medicines, books, hardware, beef, pork, butter, cheese and porter." The vessel itself, sold to a syndicate which included Colonel John Cox and Joseph Ball, realized 17,609 pounds, and one of her anchors and cables alone brought 1,500 pounds under the hammer.[26] These captures, Hessian Major Baurmeister wrote, "made Admiral Byron decide upon the destruction of this harbor."

On September 30, 1778, a British expedition left New York. There were nine ships and transports under the command of Captain Henry Collins, R.N., whose flagship was called the *Zebra*. In charge of the military wing of the enterprise was Captain Patrick ("Scotch") Ferguson. He had some three hundred British regulars and about a hundred New Jersey loyalists. This task force had a double objective: first, to "clean out the nest of Rebel pirates" at Chestnut Neck; second, to advance up the Mullica and destroy the Batsto Iron Works and military storehouses at The Forks. The first objective was accomplished; the second was not.

A storm delayed the expedition several days, so it did not arrive off Little Egg Harbor until October 5. American intelligence had informed Governor Livingston of the move. He in turn dispatched quick warnings to Chestnut Neck and also ordered Count Pulaski and his Legion to the rescue. Unfortunately, Pulaski got lost and wound up in Tuckerton instead of Chestnut Neck. Then he sent forty to fifty of his 333 men to set up an outpost on Osborn's Island, where, tired and weary, they were killed in their sleep by the enemy.

It is unfortunate that no detailed account of the Battle of Chestnut Neck from patriot sources has come to light. Official British records, however, are available and may be taken as reasonably accurate. Captain Collins's own account admits loss of the element of surprise and observes that "intelligence of our intentions had reached the rebels several days preceding our arrival which enabled them to get four privateers to sea." Sending some galleys and two tenders from his ships *Nautilus* and *Experiment* to Chestnut Neck, "where the rebels had several vessels and storehouses," Collins continues:

> They ranged themselves in a breastwork they had erected on an eminence, and showed themselves in a battery (which we afterwards found had no guns) . . . but were soon disordered by a well-managed fire from the galleys, the troops landing immediately under the protection of the gunboats, and a cannonade of the galleys soon drove them from their works, and made them disperse to the woods without loss. The vessels at this place, amounting to ten in number, we found were mostly British, which had been seized upon by the rebel cruisers; amongst them was the *Venus*, of London, and others of considerable size, which they could not carry higher up [the river]; as all of them were scuttled and dismantled, and some sunk, it was impossible (notwithstanding my solicitude to recover the property of the King's subjects) to get down here; I therefore ordered them destroyed and fired. The storehouses and settlements here, so particularly adapted to the convenience of this nest of freebooters, I was of the opinion, with the commanding officer of the troops, should also be destroyed; which was accordingly done, also the battery, and the work on the hill.

Scotch Ferguson has left an even more vivid and detailed description of the battle in a report, dated October 10, to Sir Henry Clinton. He confirms all that Captain Collins had to say, but adds quite a bit to the story. Since Ferguson's account, printed in Rivington's *Loyalist Gazette*, has not appeared in print for many years, the exciting essence of it is given here:

Sir—I have the Honour to inform you that the Ships, with the Detachment ordered to this place, arrived off the Bar on the evening of the 5th Instant, when Captain Collins sent in the Galleys, but the Ships could not enter before the 7th.

Three Privateers of six or eight guns, with an armed Pilot-boat, has escaped out of the Harbour before our Arrival, in Consequence of Advice received on the second from Mr. Livingston, warning them of our Destination.

As it was Evident that Preparations had been made against us for several Days, it was determined to allow no further Time, but to push up with our Galleys and small Craft, with what Soldiers could be crowded into them, without waiting for the coming in of the Ships; accordingly, after a very difficult Navigation of twenty miles inland, we came opposite to Chestnut Neck, where there were several Vessels and about a dozen of Houses, with Stores for the Reception of prize Goods and Accomodation for their Privateers' Men.

The Rebels had there erected a Work with Embrasures for six Guns, on a Level with the Water, to rake the Channel, and another upon a commanding Eminence, with a Platform for Guns en barbette, in which, however, it afterwards appeared that they had not as yet placed Artillery.

The banks of the River below the Works being swampy, rendered it necessary for the Boats with the Troops to pass within Musquet Shot, in order to land beyond them, previous to which Captain Collins advanced with the Galleys to cover our Landing, and as he came very close to the Works, and the Guns of the Galleys were remarkably well pointed, the Fire from the Rebels was effectually stifled, and the Detachment, landing with Ease, soon

drove into the Woods the Skulking Banditti that endeavored to oppose it.

The Seamen were employed all that Evening and the
next Day till Noon in destroying ten capital Vessels, and
the Soldiers in demolishing the Village, which was the
principal resort of this nest of Pirates. Had we arrived by
Surprize, we meant to have pushed forwards with Celer-
ity to the Forks, within thirty-five miles of Philadelphia.
But as the alarm had been spread throughout the Country, and the Militia there had been reinforced from
Philadelphia by a detachment of foot, five field pieces and
a body of light horse, our small Detachment could not
pretend to enter twenty miles further into the Country
to reach the Stores and small Craft there; and the shallow-
ness of the Navigation rendered it impracticable for the
Galleys to cooperate with us; it was, therefore, determined to return without loss of Time and endeavour to
employ our Force with Effect elsewhere; but some of our
Vessels having run aground, notwithstanding the very
great Diligence and Activity of Captain Collins, and the
Gentlemen of the Navy, an opportunity offered, without
interrupting our Progress, to make two Descents on the
north side of the River, to penetrate some miles into the
Country, destroy three Salt Works, and raze to the ground
the Stores and Settlements of a Chairman of their Committees, a Captain of Militia, and one or two other viru-
lent Rebels who had Shared in the Prizes brought in here,
and who had all been remarkably active in fomenting
the Rebellion, oppressing the People, and forcing them,
against their Inclination and Better Judgment, to assist
in their Crimes.

One of the vessels that ran aground was Captain Collins's
own flagship, the *Zebra*. The delay encountered in vain at-

tempts to refloat the *Zebra* gave Ferguson the inspiration
for the night massacre of Pulaski's troops on Osborn's Island.
In another note to Clinton, Captain Ferguson excuses the
slaughter—by 250 British and loyalists against 50 sleeping
Americans—with this bland comment: "It being a night
Attack, little Quarter could, of course, be given, so that
there are only five prisoners." Of the nearly fifty Americans
"cut to pieces," to use Ferguson's own phrase, were a lieutenant colonel, a captain, and an adjutant. In the same note
Ferguson admits that the massacre was inspired by "a
Frenchman named Bromville" and six other deserters from
Pulaski's corps. He further adds that "as a Rebel, Colonel
Proctor was within two miles with a Corps of Artillery . . .
and the Militia of the Country, I thought it hazardous
. . . to attempt anything further."

A monument erected by the Sons of the Cincinnati marks
the site of this massacre; and a tall, imposing shaft, topped
by the figure of a Minuteman, stands on the site of the
Battle of Chestnut Neck, placed there by the Lafayette
Chapter of the Daughters of the American Revolution.

In the Battle of Chestnut Neck, aside from the separate
affair on Osborn's Island, the British actually gained very
little. Not a single American was killed or captured. Not one
American privateer was seized or destroyed. The only ships
burned were British ships. Although all but one of the
houses in the village were put to the torch, the early warnings had permitted the privateersmen to get four ships to
sea and to run their smaller craft far up the Mullica. It is
a safe wager, too, that most of their more valuable stores
and private possessions had been hidden deep in Smugglers' Woods, where the families themselves found refuge
well in advance of the British attack.

It has often been said that Chestnut Neck was never rebuilt, as if that was a measure of His Majesty's triumph. The

statement is not quite correct. Three of the larger land-owners did rebuild their homes: Micajah Smith, John Mathis, and Joseph Sooy.[27] The others erected new homes in Wrangleborough, which is now Port Republic, save Joseph Johnson whose home reputedly was not burned by the British. There are, of course, several modern houses there today, and an active boatyard. But, however Chestnut Neck rated as a *village* after the British sailed away, as a privateering center it was soon as busy as ever.

Only six weeks after the battle the same Captain Stevens who had captured the *Venus* brought in a rich new prize, the armed schooner *Two Friends,* Captain Sion, out of New York, carrying twenty-two men, six guns, and twelve swivels.[28] By May, 1779, Major Baurmeister was writing ruefully to his superiors:

> The rebels at Egg Harbour have sixteen strong new privateers and a frigate there, and four weeks ago unfortunately captured six three- and two-masted ships . . . among them a royal provision ship. The local insurance company has to stand the loss of 80,000 pounds sterling, for these ships were loaded only with English goods and wine. If but a single frigate had been sent along as convoy, everything would have been saved.[29]

There was probably no day of greater rejoicing at Chestnut Neck than the day in September of 1779 when Captain Yelverton Taylor and his fourteen-gun privateer *Mars* brought in the British vessel *Triton,* with an entire company of Hessian troops, a major, lesser officers, and two hundred fourteen privates! These were reinforcements sent from London to Sir Henry Clinton in New York.

This seizure is confirmed by Major Baurmeister. In *Revolution in America* he writes that Major von Stein, of the Knyphausen regiment, on the *Triton* was captured by freebooters with the entire Leib company. Baurmeister also notes another capture not mentioned elsewhere: "On October 1 [1779] Lieutenant Colonel Heymell's sloop was seized and towed into Egg Harbor." [30] No wonder Baurmeister, speaking of Washington's dwindling regiments, exclaimed: "If only their sea force, instead of constantly increasing, were on the decline, too!"

The year 1780 kept up the pace. Among vessels sold that year at Wescoat's Tavern at The Forks were the schooner *Betsey*, with a cargo of turpentine, and the sloop *Revenge*, a fast sailer mounting two guns and four swivels. On June 12 the privateer *Comet*, Captain Charles Harris, "fell in with a convoy of British merchantmen off Sandy Hook and by adroit maneuvering captured eight of them." [31] The *Comet* was owned by Thomas Leaming of Cape May.

One of the most amusing privateer yarns dates from the same year, and it is a yarn which also demonstrates the resourcefulness of the men who went to sea in ships. Edward Giles was cruising his schooner *Shark* off Brigantine when, taken by surprise, he was captured by the British. A prize crew of four of His Majesty's sailors was put aboard to take the *Shark* into New York. Giles, of course, was made a prisoner, but remained the perfect host. At first he swapped yarns with his captors; a bit later, with a knowing wink, he offered them some fine old special liquor which he had hidden in a chest. The offer was accepted, the chest opened, and the bottle brought out. Soon a good time was being had by all, and most of all by the four British sailors. Finally, when the latter were quite drunk, Giles switched roles again, recaptured his ship, ran the *Shark* into Chestnut Neck, and turned in his guests as prisoners.[32]

That both sides could play the game of privateering is shown also by the case of the *Skunk*, a mere open boat mounting two guns and manned by a crew of twelve. The

Skunk had enjoyed a long run of luck, bringing no less than nineteen prizes into Chestnut Neck after starting operations in the latter part of 1779. One fine day her commander, Captain John Golden, spotted what he thought was a big British merchantman off Tucker's Beach. The *Skunk* set out in pursuit. When he got close Golden fired his first shot— and suddenly the supposed merchantman was disclosed as a British "74" man-o'-war. She gave the *Skunk* such a broadside that, as Captain Golden described it, "the water flew around them like ten thousand whale spouts." By hard rowing the *Skunk* managed to escape, while Golden kept urging, "Lay low, boys. Lay low for your lives!" [33]

Little Egg Harbor had no privateer captain more audacious and colorful than William Treen. His first recorded ship was the forty-ton schooner *Rattlesnake*, armed with six two-pounders and six swivels, and carrying a crew of thirty-five. On March 22, 1780, he recaptured the *Hazard*, an American privateer which had been seized by the British. Just a month later he brought in the sloop *Dispatch*. In December, 1780, Treen took over another vessel, the brig *Fame*, with ten guns. He started out well in his new craft, capturing the British schooner *Cock*, bound from New York to the Chesapeake. Then he met disaster, but not from the enemy. On the night of January 22, 1781, the *Fame* was riding at anchor near Little Egg Harbor Inlet. It was bitter cold. The winds were high and snow squalls were sweeping over the decks. Suddenly, at flood tide, the *Fame* capsized. Treen and two other men were on shore at the time. Four members of the crew tried to swim in, but only three made it. And of the twenty-three still unaccounted for, only four were found alive next day, still clinging desperately to the overturned vessel.[34]

Treen crowded his luck on another occasion. Cruising in one of the whaleboats so successful in hit-and-run tactics, he was approached by two of His Majesty's frigates. He ignored the demand to surrender, whereupon the frigates overran his craft and overturned it. Treen and a boy managed to grab the rigging of one of the frigates, thus saving themselves. Then he demanded that the British rescue his other men, who were floundering around in the sea; when they refused Treen roundly denounced them for wanton cruelty.[35] It is not surprising, then, that Treen soon wound up in the horrible *Jersey* prison ship; and it is not surprising either that somehow he made his escape and by early 1782 was back at Chestnut Neck, commanding another whaleboat, the *Unity*, and hauling in still more prizes.

Among the last enemy ships brought into Little Egg Harbor before the war finally ended was the *Betsey*, sold at Chestnut Neck with her cargo of tobacco, salt, coffee, mustard, china, and queen's ware. And one of the most dramatic exploits of those days took place on a Sunday evening in December, 1782, when Captain Jackson, of the *Greyhound*, "with much address, captured within the Hook [Sandy Hook] the schooner *Dolphin* and sloop *Diamond*, bound from New York to Halifax, and brought them into Little Egg Harbour, where they were sold, with their cargoes, for 10,200 pounds."

Chestnut Neck had been overrun, burned, and devastated. But those "rebel pirates" in the "nest" had the last word, and a large share in the final victory. True, its privateersmen never again had it so good. But it was peace, not war, that made a ghost town of the little village on the Mullica which had thrived on adventure, excitement, and profits for seven stirring years.

PRIVATEERING— AND PROFITEERING

On October 17, 1776, John Paul Jones wrote as follows to Robert Morris, in Philadelphia:

> The common class of mankind are actuated by no nobler principle than that of self-interest. This, and this only, determines all adventures in privateers, the owners as well as those they employ. And while this is the case, unless the private enrollment of individuals in our Navy is made superior to that in privateers, it never can be respectable, it will never become formidable; and without a respectable Navy, alas America! [1]

Morris must have blushed a bit when he received this letter. For John Paul Jones could hardly have known that he was addressing one of the foremost privateersmen and one of the top profiteers in America. Financially, Morris would have a deep stake in not promoting the kind of navy Jones wrote about; privateering was said to have "raised his fortune to between 300,000 and 400,000 pounds." [2] Much the same was true of many members of the Congress. Only three months later Morris was writing to another profiteer, Silas Deane:

> I have not received any goods from you. . . . Neither have I heard of any being sent by you either for this place [Philadelphia] or the West Indies. If you have . . . neglected doing it, you may have leisure to repent hereafter that you missed so fine an opportunity of making a fortune. The prices of all imported articles have been enormously high. . . . There is plenty of room to make as much money as you please.[3]

Morris, elected to Congress in 1775, virtually controlled the Secret Committee of Trade,[4] and behind that front, through his firm of Willing and Morris, he used government funds for his own purposes and profit. Thousands of dollars were diverted to various ventures, notably privateering, and some of that money was not repaid.[5] In fairness it must be said that Morris's foreign trading contacts were very useful to the new government, which needed expert help in procurement and possessed scant credit abroad. It was no secret, however, that Morris bought up commodities he knew the Continental Army needed and held them until he got his price and his profit. It is scarcely surprising that he was frequently a target of criticism and a subject for public inquiry.

Deane, who had been made agent in Europe for Congress, never neglected any chance to make some easy money. His speculations became notorious. John Adams spoke of "his ambition, his desire to make a fortune" and the "combinations, copartnerships and associations in trade in which he and his brothers are or have long been supposed to be connected."[6] Among Deane's shadier ventures was his purchase of two vessels with public money, officially for use as warships but which he secretly diverted for privateering.[7]

Yet Silas Deane and Robert Morris were but two of many like-minded gentry in the higher levels of government, in the Army, and in Congress. Some members of Congress seemed more busily engaged in speculating than in prosecution of the war. One of these was Jeremiah Wadsworth, commissary general. Another was New Jersey's John Neilson, whose firm bought salt at Toms River for $15 a bushel and sold it at Morristown, not far away, for $35 a bushel and whose partner was always alert for "something worth speculating in." [8] Another was Congressman James Wilson of Pennsylvania, whose home, dubbed Fort Wilson, was attacked by an armed mob protesting those enormously high prices which Robert Morris mentioned so complacently. Wilson, long considered a man of integrity, was actually a "notorious" speculator.[9] Others gambled in privateers—such men as Joseph Ball, Stephen Girard, Congressman Samuel Chase of Maryland who used official information "to make a secret purchase of grain for the French fleet," Colonels John Cox and Charles Pettit, and even General Nathanael Greene.

A curiously mixed morality colors this picture which appears so downright shocking against the black backdrop of a Continental Army whose men were hungry, ill-clad, ill-housed, and often unshod. It is no wonder Washington cried out against the "monopolizers," wishing that "one of the most attrocious of each State was hung in Gibbets upon a gallows five times as high as the one prepared by Haman." Yet as evidence of the duality of outlook then current, Washington in another letter observed that "a great and lasting war can never be supported on this principle [of patriotism] alone. It must be aided by a prospect of Interest or some reward." [10] Alexander Hamilton, a man of integrity, denounced profiteers as traitors of the most dangerous kind, and yet he seems to have been fooled completely by Robert Morris.

On the other side of the coin are facts which, in fairness, must be given weight. Many of the speculators were genuinely dedicated patriots who fought hard, labored long, and gave unstinting loyalty and devotion to the American cause. Some of them saw nothing wrong in promoting their private interests at the same time that they were fighting a war, especially if the war had hit them hard financially. If the war had taken wealth away, what was wrong with embracing a chance to let the war siphon some back? Some Continental Army officers might justify their "specs" on the ground that they were poorly paid and often not paid at all. John Paul Jones fought five years without getting any pay.[11] And Washington wrote to Joseph Jones in 1780 that "there is no set of Men in the United States . . . that have made the same sacrifices of their interest in support of the common cause as Officers of the American Army." He added that "no officer can live upon his pay."

It is against this ethically complex background that any story of profiteering, through privateering, must be laid. For one thing, a large and important distinction must be made between investing in privateers and speculating in commodities: privateering was legal and officially encouraged; commodity speculation was not. Many of the speculators thus far mentioned were as active in privateering as they were at gambling in goods. Silas Deane and his brothers Barnabas and Simeon were early promoters in both fields and were among the many who played a part in financing the commerce raiders that prowled the New Jersey coast. Robert Morris was officially listed as owning one or more privateers and had a concealed concern in many others.

Leading businessmen actually "braved the heat, the mosquitoes and the poor roads" [12] to attend auctions at The
Forks near Pleasant Mills, Mays Landing, Chestnut Neck,
and Tuckahoe to bid for captured vessels and their cargoes.
Often they would turn the vessels into privateers and meanwhile haul the cargoes back over the pine trails to be sold
wherever the top price was being paid. A few merchants,
such as Stephen Girard, attended personally to arming and
fitting out the ships they had purchased. Others had new
vessels built, usually smaller craft, at some of the boatyards
along the Mullica, Great Egg Harbor, and Cohansey rivers.
The *Governor Livingston,* a schooner with four guns and a
crew of fourteen, was constructed at Cohansey, and among
her owners were the Elmers and Sinnicksons of Salem and
Cumberland County. [13] Quite a few owners never saw the
vessels on which they risked their money, while a number
—such as the Leamings and Fishers of Cape May; Joseph
Ball, Elijah Clark, John Cox and Richard Wescoat of The
Forks—lived so near the harbors from which their vessels
sailed that they could keep close personal check upon their
interests.

So big was much of the business that ownership of larger
privateers was splintered into eight, ten, sixteen, and thirty-
two or more shares; and those shares were bartered and
sold much as shares of stocks are traded today. Where a
privateer was registered in the name of a company, only
insiders knew how many were in the company and who the
shareholders might be. Even those shareholders on occasion
were fronts for bigwigs who feared to have their names
linked even indirectly with wartime speculation, legal as
privateering might be. There also was much buying and
selling of the ships themselves. A privateer might be controlled by one syndicate when she set out to sea and return
to be greeted by a whole new set of owners. The skipper

likely as not would also find a new captain ready and waiting to take over.

Joseph Ball, long manager of the Batsto Iron Works, ranked high among the owners of privateers in New Jersey and was one of the principal speculators in captured vessels and cargoes. Ball had the face of a cherub and a mind as sharp as a steel trap. His fortune—he was to become one of the wealthiest men in the new United States—was founded largely on fast and fat profits from these ventures, profits which in turn were shrewdly invested, particularly in real estate. By virtue of his residence at Batsto, Joseph Ball enjoyed special advantages over other speculators in privateering. It was only a mile or so from the ironworks to The Forks and Richard Wescoat's tavern, where many of the seized ships and cargoes were sold under the hammer. Ball had ample opportunity to make firsthand inspections and appraisals. He knew many of the skippers personally. He could get from them inside information on the speed, stability, and soundness of the vessels coming up for sale. With such valuable knowledge he could bid accordingly. Should the weather be particularly wretched on the day of an auction, boggy stretches would make many of the woodland roads impassable. In that event Ball might find few others showing up to bid against him and thus be able to pick up choice bargains. Best of all, Ball had been able to accumulate enough money to pay for what he wanted; and in Philadelphia he enjoyed excellent connections through which he could sell shares in the vessels he had purchased, reconditioned, armed, and made ready to send to sea as privateers. As for the captured cargoes that he bought, the same connections could turn those over at a tidy profit.

The records suggest that 1778 was Ball's first year in major privateering activity. Three ships he bought at auction in Wescoat's Tavern: the 150-ton brigantine *Industry;*

the fifty-ton sloop *Speedwell;* and a little thirty-tonner with the provocative name of *Polly's Adventure.* He also had a substantial interest in two raiders: the schooner *St. John,* Captain Rice, and the sloop *Susannah.* The *Susannah* was fitted out at Chestnut Neck. She boasted eight guns and carried a crew of thirty-five.

Whereas many a privateer could haul in prize after prize without fight or bloodshed, the *Susannah* ran into trouble almost immediately. Sailing out of Great Bay in August of 1778, under command of Captain Stoeker, she soon encountered the British man-of-war tender *Emerald,* a ten-gun sloop which was convoying two merchantmen. That was on the 29th. During the battle that followed the two merchantmen got safely away, the *Susannah* lost one man killed and a number wounded, and the *Emerald's* captain and several crew members were killed. The *Emerald,* through superior maneuvering, also managed to escape, and the *Susannah* came back empty-handed.[14]

The year 1779 was a much bigger year for Joseph Ball. He owned a third of the schooner *Addition,* a fourth of the sloop *Hornet,* as well as substantial interests in the following ships bought at auction: the brig *Recovery,* the sloops *Clinton* and *George,* another brig, the *Carolina,* and a second ship with the name of *Speedwell.* He also purchased the *Favourite,* a sloop, selling an eighth to Joseph Carson, one of his Philadelphia associates; and then acquired an eighth interest in a privateer, the *Chances Cruize.* From a single voyage of the last-named, in December of 1779, Ball's eighth share of the profits amounted to 382 pounds.

Ball also was a partner in another boat with a similar name, the schooner *Chance,* armed with six guns and carrying a crew of forty. This was the vessel that played a major part in the capture of the *Venus,* richly laden British freighter, whose wreck still lies at the bottom of the Mullica where the British scuttled her during their attack on Chestnut Neck. This *Chance*—there were others with identical name—was a particularly fast and smooth sailer and made a number of profitable voyages to Statia, as the Dutch West Indian colony of St. Eustatius was commonly called. Ball had four listed partners in financing the *Chance:* Colonel John Cox, Charles Pettit, Richard Wescoat, and Captain Timothy Shaler, who skippered some of Ball's ships.[15]

Peak year in Joseph Ball's career as New Jersey prince of privateersmen was 1780. His ships were sailing in and out of the Mullica as if they were engaged in a regatta instead of a war. He was buying new ones and selling others left and right. His fleet that year included the *Yankey Witch* (renamed *Little Molly*), a schooner with two two-pounders and six swivels, Captain Uriah Smith; another schooner named *Molly*, a new Virginia-built boat, and a fine sailer; the schooners *Adventure* and *Fortune* and the sloop *Hazard*, an American boat retaken from the British by the redoubtable Captain Treen. Ball also appears to have controlled two other ships recaptured by Treen: the forty-ton sloop *Rattlesnake*, which had eight guns and a crew of thirty-five, and the thirty-ton *Betsey*, a cargo boat. In addition to all these Ball owned an eighth of the brigantine *Black Snake*, had an undisclosed interest in the privateer *Revenge*, mounting two carriage guns and four swivels, and in the sloop *Lark*. Some of these were boats he purchased, others were boats he soon sold; and still others were in regular raiding service.

Only a crystal ball with hindsight could reveal the full extent of Joseph Ball's maritime interests, how many other ships he owned or controlled and how many shares of prize money he collected or stood to collect on the ships of others. Even his surviving papers (far from complete) indicate that there was much more than met the eye in his formal accounts. For example, there is an agreement dated 1783 and reading as follows:

> I, Nathaniel Lewis of Mount Holly on the 12th January 1782 did insure on behalf of myself and other owners one eighth of the Ship *Admiral Toutman* which . . . I acknowledge to be the property of Joseph Ball and William Stretch.

No doubt there was excellent reason then for such hidden ownership, but the agreement gives no hint of it.

One of Ball's more important Philadelphia partners was Joseph Carson. Nine privateers were commissioned, in that city, by "Joseph Carson & Co."—the *Rattlesnake* and *Chance* (already mentioned), the *Quicktime, Luck & Fortune, Fox, General Maxwell, Fame, Governor Livingston,* and *Black Joke.* Whether Ball was a partner on all these ships does not appear, but a statement of accounts between Ball and Carson covering the period from July, 1778, to November, 1780, reveals the following interesting information:

> Outfitting of the sloop *Chance* cost 4216 pounds.
>
> Cargo of the *Venus,* which the *Chance* captured, sold in December 1779 for 17,609 pounds, plus an extra 1500 pounds paid for one Anchor and Cable belonging to the Ship *Venus* [the hull was scuttled by the British].
>
> One cruise on the *Chance,* in May 1780, netted profits of 3056 pounds; and another cruise in November of that year paid off to the tune of 15,422 pounds.

Other items in the Ball-Carson accounts include a note that the cargo of the sloop *Clinton,* 53 hogsheads of molasses and 19,500 limes, sold for 22,223 pounds, of which the ship's captain, David Stevens, and the crew received 6,000 pounds. Profits on one voyage of the ship *Adventure* ran to 2,448 pounds. Still other items: Colonel John Cox, in October, 1779, was paid 899 pounds for his share of goods in the company; for nine pairs of silk hose, 67 pounds 10 shillings was recorded; by Batsto accounts for 10 Barrels Beef, 750 pounds; and 18 pounds, 17 shillings, sixpence was paid for "one Spy Glass and Dictionary."

Because too few records of such ships have been found or published, the following itemized account of fitting out the privateer galley *Alligator* is of particular value. The *Alligator* was another of Ball's ships, and the captain was his reliable Timothy Shaler. Dated May-June, 1782, it reads:

	£	Sh.	Pence
To 9 Swivel Guns . . . @ 20 Pounds pr. pair	90	—	—
To 3 Musquettes, 3 Bayonets and 3 Cartouches	9	—	—
To Plank and Timber, delivered to Carpenters	30	—	—
To Cash paid Phillips for a Cabouse		7	6
To time and Expences attending Vendue at Cape	3	10	—
To Cash pd. Henry Davis	1	10	—
To do pd. Sharp for Pikes and Rings	2	5	—
To do pd. Lane's Expences from Tom's River to Barney Gatt as a Pilot	1	17	6
To do pd. Mr. Chambers for carrying Swivels and Shott to Trenton from B. pond	2	10	—
To a Mainsail for the Galley	30	—	—
To a Square sail for do.	20	—	—
To 250 Wt. New Rigging	17	—	—
To Capt. Vansant	4	3	4
To Cash pd. Buoy	1	10	—
To do pd. Abraham Davis, for clothing	3	—	—
To do pd. Platt . . . . for Oars	2	5	—
To do pd. The Governor—for Commission, £3, Expenses and Horse hire £	6	—	—
To a Journey to Philadelphia to wait on Congress and the Board of War for two Brass pieces of Ordonance which was promised, and horse hire . . . 8 days	8	—	—
To Cash pd. Dolby for 30 Wt. Pork	1	16	—
To do pd. Saml. Cooper . . . for the Ferriage of 4 Guns and Sundry other Things		17	6
To do pd. Mother Tucker's bill	7	10	—
To 1 large Cheat hammer		7	6

	£	Sh.	Pence
To 1 Gun and Bayonet	2	10	—
To 3 Cutlasses and 2 Bayonetts	2	—	—
To 1 Brass Compass	2	10	—
To Capt. Vincent . . . for ½ piece–Brittanias	2	17	6
To Cash pd. Brush for 3 of my hands Expences	3	—	—
To do pd. Joseph Eshtoll . . . for 51 Meals Victuals for my Carpenter	1	18	3
£	271	7	1

Privateering and profits did not always go hand in hand. That was demonstrated by the brief venture of Stephen Girard. Girard possessed an eagle eye for prospects of monetary gain and a firm grip on pounds, or pieces of eight once they had come his way. An old hand at smuggling, faking customs declarations, doctoring ships' papers, and bribing the right people, he should have been successful in privateering. Girard felt no rush of loyalty to the Continental cause, but he could see the easy money being made by others and wanted to get some too. Word came to him that a two-masted schooner, the *Minerva,* was for sale at Chestnut Neck. It is not clear whether this was the same *Minerva* which, under Captain J. Earle, had made some lucrative captures in the summer of 1778. But she seemed a likely ship even if she did need calking and a general overhaul.

Girard was interested. However, only the year before Chestnut Neck had been destroyed by the British, and he heard that some British cruisers again were patrolling offshore. Cautious as well as covetous, Girard thought twice, probably three times, about risking his capital in buying the *Minerva.* So, as Harry Emerson Wildes writes in his fascinating biography *Lonely Midas,* Girard embarked "upon a highly complicated financial arrangement to win control of the vessel at the least possible personal expense." He formed a syndicate with himself as manager even though his investment as a partner was but one thirty-second of the total.

Reconditioning of the *Minerva* was supervised by Girard personally. After conferences with his syndicate at Margaret Glass's tavern in Philadelphia, he bought a longboat which he painted Prussian blue and red, ordered two coats of Spanish brown paint for the ship itself, then had her "corked" at a cost of $600.

Girard's previous explorations into South Jersey had never gone beyond Mount Holly, where he lived and kept a store during the British occupation of Philadelphia. Now he rented a one-seater carriage and set out boldly over the rugged Pine Barren trails to Chestnut Neck. He wanted to mastermind the *Minerva*'s armament. Says Wildes: "he found his workmen ill; they had been eating too many clams and 'hoisters.'" Girard took charge of their cure, fed them on "milk, eggs, corn, butter, fish, venison and salt."

Soon they had recovered sufficiently to mount the guns on the schooner. There were twelve of these, with 1,065 shot. Other arms included 19 muskets with 852 cartridges, four "blunderbushes," two pistols, thirty "cutlashes," 67 hand grenades, and 18 boarding pikes. Supplied also was a case of amputating instruments and twenty-five pairs of handcuffs for anticipated prisoners. Neither of the latter was to be used. Nor was a single cannon to be fired.

A grand sight it must have been that October day in 1779 when the *Minerva* set sail and moved proudly out through the Mullica estuary from Chestnut Neck. Resplendent on the deck was Arthur Helme, master of the vessel, bedecked in white flannels. There was glamor as well as excitement in the air.

All Helme wanted now was to spot an enemy merchant-man; he spotted a storm instead. It was a sea-churner which drove the *Minerva* far off course. Soon she was found to be

leaking "at every nailhole," despite the costly calking. Off
Cape Fear, as the weather cleared, Helme did spot a
schooner in the distance. He moved toward her. He made
ready for action. He checked his guns and had the "cutlashes" handy. The ship turned out to be a derelict, a Virginia pilotboat, the *Barbary,* with only some dead men and
a cargo of tobacco aboard. Helme put her in charge of a
prize crew and ordered the *Barbary,* under emergency sail,
to Chestnut Neck. It was the *Minerva's* one and only prize.

Another storm came up. The *Minerva's* sails were ripped
to ribbons, and soon she was in such great danger that
Helme dumped overboard eight of her valuable cannon to
lighten ship. Creaking and crippled, the *Minerva* managed
to reach Chincoteague harbor in Maryland, and there
Helme sent a quick distress call to Girard. Meantime the
Minerva's crew, their dreams of prize money gone, stripped
the ship of her rigging and disappeared. By this time Girard
was disgusted, but reluctantly put up a thousand dollars for
repairs. It was throwing good money after bad. Frozen in
for the winter, the *Minerva* was patched up after a fashion;
but when Helme attempted to get her to Philadelphia in
the spring he wrecked her again. She was a total loss.[16]

Despite such a succession of disasters, Girard character-
istically came out even or better financially, thanks chiefly
to sale of that lone prize cargo of tobacco. He also wound
up as owner of the derelict, the *Barbary,* which he reconditioned, renamed the *Whim,* and put into service as a
freighter. Vanished, however, were his dreams of lots of
easy money; and while Girard was persuaded to enter one
further privateering venture—involving the brig *Recovery,*
once owned by Joseph Ball—he again was lucky to get out
with his investment. After that he left commerce raiding
to others.[17]

Other syndicates operating in New Jersey fared better.

One of the biggest of these was Thomas Leaming & Co. While its vessels were formally commissioned in Philadelphia, Thomas was one of the distinguished Cape May Leamings, and some of his partners also were Cape May people. Among the ships owned by Thomas Leaming & Co. were the schooner *Mars,* famed for its capture of the whole boatful of Hessians; the sloops *Comet* and *New Comet;* the *Fly,* which claimed participation in seizure of the *Venus;* and no less than nine other schooners and brigs with a galaxy of bright names: *Enterprise, Hawk, Hector, Hetty, Polly, Sly, Rose, Salem,* and *Sally.*

For the record a list of owners and a list of masters of privateers working out of New Jersey, known to me and not already mentioned in the narrative, are included below. Some of these were Jerseymen, others were Philadelphians, and a few came from as far off as New England. But all of them were concerned in the war off the Jersey coast and used the state's bays, inlets, and rivers, particularly Chestnut Neck; and while most of them were firm patriots, all were keenly interested in profits. Prominence of some of these names suggests the wide public interest in privateering and its general acceptance.

OWNERS OF PRIVATEERS

Thomas Adams, James Ash, Joshua Baker, James Boylan, Samuel Brown, Andrew Bunner, James Craig, Jeremiah Fisher, Joseph C. Fisher (related to and associated with the Leamings), Moses Griffing, Daniel Griggs, Francis Gurney, Jesse Hand, Robert Knox, Blair McClenachan, White Matlack, Charles Miller, John Neilson, George Nixon, James Oellers, George Payne, Joseph Potts, Benjamin Randolph, William Semple, Robert Shewell, Henry Thorne, and John White.

MASTERS OF PRIVATEERS

Charles Allen, James Armitage, John Badcock, John Brice, George Bunner, Thomas Craig, Nathaniel Chew, Peter Day, Francis DuCloss, Joseph Edwards, Phineas Eldredge, Silas Foster, James Forbes, Rufus Gardner, William Grandal, Moses Griffing, Charles Harris, Alexander Holmes, Humphrey Hughes, Joseph Jackways, James Josiah, Nicholas Keen, John King, James Leach, John McCarthy, Henry Murfitts (originally from New London, Conn.), John Ord, James Selover, Robert Snell, Enoch Stillwell, John Stillwell, Joseph Sooy, Joshua Studson, Woolman Sutton, William Tanner, David Thompson, Ebenezer Tucker, John Van Voorhis, Enoch Willits and Hope Willits.

There probably were many more owners and masters who had some connection with New Jersey privateering, but these are all I have been able to gather from sources available. The names of the crewmen do not appear, save in rare instances; there were too many of them. Of the thousands involved at one time or another during the Revolution at least two thousand, and probably more, must have been engaged in the Jersey enterprises, which brought booms, crowds, excitement, and revelry to coastal towns which are such quiet places today.

Speculation in privateers and the shameless profiteering in the necessities of life of the American people was not limited to private citizens, such as Joseph Ball, Stephen Girard, and Benjamin Randolph, or to congressmen and other politicians, such as Wadsworth, Wilson, and Morris. It reached high into the upper levels of the Continental Army command, just short of Washington himself. While standards of public conduct were more relaxed in Revolutionary times than today, the fact that one of the major participants in profiteering shrouded his operations in the greatest secrecy—even to the point of proposing that a code be used in correspondence—suggests that if the details had leaked out there would have been scandal which could have weakened public faith in the military command and possibly have affected the outcome of the war. The men involved in this business were all highly placed and highly esteemed: Nathanael Greene, quartermaster general of the army, and his two assistant quartermasters general, Colonel Charles Pettit and Colonel John Cox.

All three had a speculative interest in Batsto Furnace, although Greene's was carefully hidden. Colonel Cox, of course, having long been owner of Batsto, could continue to operate in the open without causing talk. Pettit, however, was careful not to take title to his share of Batsto until he was shucking off his duties as assistant quartermaster general. The deed of interest to Greene was never even recorded.

All three men—Cox, Pettit, and Greene—had been and remained associated with Joseph Ball, who stayed on as manager of Batsto until the war was about over, engaging in his privateering adventures in spare time. Probably because the Continental Armies were in such desperate need of the cannon, "shott," and mortar shells which Batsto could supply, the spectacle of quartermasters general buying them from a company in which they held a substantial money interest seems not to have caused adverse comment. The American Army needed able men as much as it needed munitions, and there can be no question that Greene, Pettit, and Cox were able men and loyal patriots.

Greene had publicly declared that he did not want the post of quartermaster general. Pettit had said he was not interested in being an assistant. Cox gave much the same impression. Yet Greene conditioned his acceptance of the post upon willingness of Congress to name Pettit and Cox as his aides.[18] Even at the time there were some who felt all this to be a bit odd. But Washington wanted Greene, so Congress approved all three.

During the winter of Valley Forge Greene assumed the heavy responsibility of procuring supplies for an army whose very survival seemed in the balance. Up to that time the job had been mishandled; Greene did much better. He made a comparative success of most things. As a general he was shrewd, skillful, trustworthy, and devoted to Washington. He was rated as America's best after the commander in chief himself, and his southern campaign prior to Yorktown is considered a masterpiece of both strategy and tactics.

A man of fundamentally high character, it is significant that Greene felt uneasy about speculating in wartime, even in privateering. It is not clear, even now, how deeply Greene was involved in speculative ventures by his own two brothers, Jacob and Griffin. The measure of Greene's concern over exposure and perhaps the naggings of his conscience are evident in a letter of April 14, 1779, which he sent to Wadsworth:

> You may remember I wrote you sometime since that I was desirous that this copartnership between Mr. Dean, you and myself should be kept a secret. I must beg leave to impress this matter upon you again; and to request you to enjoin it upon Mr. Dean. . . .
>
> While we continue in the offices we hold, I think it is prudent to appear as little in trade as possible. For however just and upright our conduct might be, the world will have suspicions to our disadvantage.[19]

Evidently Greene was deeply worried, for in another letter to Wadsworth, written on April 30, he says:

I have received your two last letters with the inclosed alphabet of figures to correspond with. The plan is very agreeable which is proposed. But in addition to it will it not be best to take upon us a fictitious name? This will draw another shade of obscurity over the business and render it impossible to find out the connection. The busy world will be prying into the connection and nature of the business; and more especially as a letter of Mr. Deane's has lately been intercepted in which it is pretended great things are discovered and dangerous combinations formed.[20]

A year later, from Morristown on April 11, 1780, Greene wrote:

How stands our 298.37 (company affair) with B.D. [Barnabas Deane]? . . . send the information in one letter and what you say upon it in another.

You Know Who

If "You Know Who" suggests the signature on a childish valentine, and the code seems equally juvenile, they offer some measure of the messy situation in which Greene found himself by that time; a time when he was deep in privateering as well. And this conspiratorial background will help explain and highlight the devious conduct and odd maneuvers in the story which follows. That story is drawn mostly from manuscripts, particularly from letters of the Charles Pettit-Nathanael Greene correspondence in the William L. Clements Library, supplemented by other letters of Pettit, Greene and Cox in the Historical Society of Pennsylvania, Princeton University Library, and Library of Congress.

This particular co-partnership, to use the term then

fashionable, was composed of those three men: Pettit, Cox and Greene. Apparently they speculated in anything—"rum, coffee, tea and dry goods" from a Mr. Irwin; "land in East Jersey"; an "adventure in Molasses"; the iron works at Batsto—but principally in privateers. On various deals at Chestnut Neck and Little Egg Harbor they worked through Joseph Ball. For the most part, however, the set-up seems to have been this: Colonel Cox was the man on the ground in New Jersey, and handled, both directly and through Ball, many of the group's affairs at Batsto and Chestnut Neck; Pettit was the financial manipulator in Philadelphia, who decided which ships were to be bought or sold and financed those transactions while keeping close liaison with Cox; and finally Greene, so far in the background that it is a question whether even Cox knew he was involved in certain of their ventures. Pettit was Greene's front man, and the general appears to have trusted him implicitly; so much so that their letters contain no talk about secrecy and not even a hint of code, assumed names, or other masqueradings.

The Pettit-Cox-Greene fleet of privateers, the ships in which they had varying interest, were the following:

The Hunter

This was a schooner, Captain Douglas, which carried twelve guns and sixty men. The syndicate held a one-sixteenth share.

On April 20, 1779, the *Hunter* "brought in a prize schooner from St. Kitts with 135 hogsheads of rum" after which Captain Douglas was to "proceed immediately again on a cruize." This prize, Pettit wrote Greene, "will about clear the Privateer and will put the rest of the cruise on clover."

The clover wilted. On May 5, 1779, Pettit wrote that the previous Saturday it was reported the Hunter Privateer . . . had taken a Jamaica Ship; but it seems she came off with a Flea in her Ear after an engagement with a ship from Liverpool. She is returned to port and the Captain thinks the Vessel not fit for the purpose. The owners have therefore concluded to sell her; and this moment they consulted me about buying a new Brig for Captain Douglas which will mount 16 guns. To effect this will cost near 80,000 pounds of which the sale of the *Hunter* will produce between 50 and 60 thousand. I have a good opinion of the Captain, of the proposed Brig and of the scheme save that they ask about 20,000 pounds more for the Brig than she cost; but at the present depreciation I do not know whether she could be built for less. She was launched about 3 weeks since and will soon be ready. I gave Mr. Clark [apparently Elijah] the acting owner my opinion against giving so great an advance but told him that as our share was small I would not stand in the way of the rest.

The name of this vessel is not disclosed.

Pettit then added: "I believe I told you I had relinquished the one-fourth I had taken in a new Brig with Mr. B. [Blair] McClenachan. She carried too little cargo in proportion to the value of the vessel to make any Profit."

Two Burnt Frigates

These were wrecks in which Pettit was induced to buy a quarter interest for 12,000 pounds, because one wreck "would serve to repair the other, and Major Eyre tells me they are a good pennyworth." That was in May of 1779. A year later the burnt frigates were still "laid up by their unwieldiness and the timidity of some of the owners and the negligence of some of the others."

It was two full years before Pettit and Greene realized

anything on their 12,000 pounds sunk in these hulks. In the spring of 1781 a "new ship was built on the ruins of the frigates and named *Congress*."

The Congress

The reconstructed vessel was "92 feet keel, 30½ beam, mounted 19 twelve-pounders on her main deck and four brass five-pounders on her Quarter Deck." She set sail on a cruise on May 24, 1781, under command of Captain Geddes, former skipper of the brig *Holker*. Pettit was enthusiastic: "This ship will cost to sea 20,000 pounds specie or upwards—we hold one-sixteenth. So fine a Ship and so good a prospect have tempted me to scruffle hard to maintain this Share for this triumvirate, amidst all my difficulties with the furnace [Batsto]."

No further mention is made of the *Congress* in this correspondence. For a good reason, perhaps. It was the destiny of the *Congress* to make history rather than profits. In one of the most brilliant sea fights of the war in which an American privateer was engaged, the *Congress*, on September 6, 1781, tackled a British war sloop, the *Savage*, Captain Sterling, off Chesapeake Bay. The *Savage* was one of a group of smaller British cruisers assigned to the plundering of estates along rivers of the eastern coast, that of Virginia in particular. It was the *Savage* which sent ashore the expedition which raided Washington's home at Mount Vernon.

At dawn that day Captain Sterling, believing the *Congress* a more powerful ship, hastened to escape. The *Congress* gave chase. By ten-thirty she had caught up and a thunderous broadside duel followed. Although the *Congress* had the advantage in armament, her rigging became so badly shattered that Captain Geddes fell back for repairs. These completed, he returned to the fray and in an hour had reduced the *Savage* to a wreck. It is said that the vessels were so close at times that some of the men were burned by flashes from the enemy cannon and that hand grenades were hurled by the Americans with telling effect. As Geddes prepared to board the shattered ship and finish the fight on her decks, the boatswain of the *Savage* waved his cap in token of surrender. British losses were admitted to be eight killed and twenty-four wounded, one of the dead being Captain Sterling. American losses were thirty dead or wounded.[21]

Unfortunately for the Pettit-Cox-Greene triumvirate, this was a Pyrrhic victory for the *Congress*. Before Captain Geddes could get his prize home, a British frigate captured the badly weakened *Congress* and retook what was left of the *Savage*. Making quick repairs, the British put the *Congress* into service, renaming her *Duchess of Cumberland*. Two weeks later she was wrecked on a deserted island off Newfoundland while transporting American prisoners to St. John's, where a British prison ship was stationed.

"So good a prospect!" Colonel Pettit had written only five months before.

The Revolution

Just when the triumvirate purchased a quarter share of this privateer is not indicated. On January 7, 1780, however, Pettit wrote that "I sold the one-sixteenth (half our share) of the *Revolution*, at a clear advance of 7000 pounds. I have since agreed for the purchase of another 16th at a lower rate" (about £3000). This is a typical example of speculation in ship shares.

Pettit was as optimistic about the *Revolution* as he had been about the *Congress*. In the same letter he told Greene: "I am the better pleased with this Ship as she is gone to Sea and may make her voyage while others remain frozen up. She passed Rheedy Island on her way out last Friday— sails like the wind and bound to Dominique."

Ten days later Pettit was mourning his bargain. He wrote that he had bought the shares of the *Revolution* "on the presumption that the Ship was at Sea and from her fast sailing I don't know but I could have sold out at double first cost or near it, but unfortunately she was caught in the Ice . . . and is now on shore near Cohansie Creek. The Guns and Rigging I hear are got on shore and there is hopes of saving the Cargo and Hull, in which case the savings will be worth near first cost. We have an adventure of six or seven Hhds. [hogsheads] of tobacco on board besides our share of the Cargo and Ship."

It cost nearly a hundred thousand pounds to repair and refit the *Revolution*. Meanwhile the triumvirate's tobacco aboard her was landed and sold. By summer the vessel was again ready and headed for Martinique. This voyage, however, "turned out very poor." In June, 1780, while returning with a cargo of rum, molasses, and coffee, the ship was challenged by a British vessel, the *Galatea*. After many maritime maneuvers in which no shots appear to have been exchanged, the *Revolution* landed her cargo at Matomkin Inlet in the Chesapeake. But she was in rather bad shape and had to be refitted there in preparation for a voyage to Statia. Now Pettit was again enthusiastic: "The ship sails remarkably well—she was chased divers times going out, among others by a copper-bottomed frigate noted for swiftness who chased her into Martinique but did not gain on her."

By August—the last time the *Revolution* is mentioned—Pettit told Greene that she was "yet delayed in Virginia." He was now in a mood to sell out, and gave this enlightening summary of her financial affairs:

Would you choose to sell out as she now is or carry your concern through the voyage? She . . . would now sell for 60,000 pounds or near it for an eighth . . . she stands the owners near 40,000 pounds an eighth as money was at the time of advancing it for disbursements at her departure in April last. Her prize [what prize she took is not recorded] will net the owners about 100,000 pounds. Her voyage, without that, would hardly clear its way.

The Lady Gates

Pettit at times appears to have taken tips on privateers as eagerly as a novice takes tips from touts at a race track. In January of 1780 he was offered an eighth of a ship called the *Lady Gates,* which was then in Boston. A Colonel Hay had made the offer and said his assistant, Major Hale, planned to fit her out with sixteen guns. Pettit noted that he would not make this buy without Greene's approval.

Greene gave his approval and soon was to regret it. Somewhere along the line the eighth share was reduced to a sixteenth. Six months later even that was too much for Pettit. In July, he wrote that he had taken his "first look into her affairs and I was determined not to have occasion for another. After unloading she was sold at vendue for 37,000 pounds, being old and crazy, and so ill conducted that I would rather have given away our part than invested money in a fresh outfit. I have given Col. Cox full remarks on some past management of her that he may give the Gentleman an overhaul as he was the offensive owner."

The Hetty

This privateer was a "fine Bermudian" which had been lengthened and equipped with sixteen guns. She was, noted Pettit, "the large sloop left in Harlem River in 1776, fitted out by the enemy as a privateer or tender, and brot in here as a prize in 1779."

On January 17, 1780, Pettit told Greene that the *Hetty*, under Captain Houghton, was "ready for sea as soon as the Ice permits; we own one-eighth." Actually she did not get to sea until April and then she sailed head on into trouble. She was chased by a British man-of-war, "sprung her masts," and was forced into St. Martin (in the Dutch West Indies) where her cargo brought miserable prices. On her return, after a poor voyage, a quarrel broke out among her owners.

This time Pettit acted quickly. While the other shareholders were arguing, he made a private deal to sell one of them "our one-eighth at the rate of 180,000 pounds for the whole." He was just in time. As a result of the dissension the *Hetty* was "struck off at Vendue at about half that sum."

The Duke of Leinster

From the correspondence it is not clear where Pettit bought a quarter of this ship for his triumvirate. But the colonel regretted the purchase. He admitted to Greene that "I got rather unwarily concerned in it, and have repented it ever since, and have been trying to get quit of it. I sold one-eighth the beginning of June [1780] at first cost and took a ninth of the *Morning Star* at 20,000 pounds in part pay. I have been constantly on the watch to get rid of the rest and believe I shall sell it at 10 pct. advance to be paid in Loan Certificates. . . . I do this to get rid of a foolish bargain—the only one I have found cause to blame myself for making."

The share was sold, for loan certificates, but Pettit was unable to get any real money for those.

The Morning Star

This brigantine was another disappointment to Pettit, and General Greene must, by this time, have grown weary of receiving so much unfavorable news. As noted above, the ninth share of this boat was taken as part payment in the deal to unload the *Duke of Leinster*. Pettit lamented:

"I took the one-ninth at 20,000 pounds (while she was at sea) expecting, and so did the owners, that on safe arrival it would be worth 40,000 pounds. On looking into her affairs I found little chance of profit and some risk of loss. I therefore sold by the hump without either, being determined to be rid of such a concern."

The triumvirate made some minor speculations: in a ship called *Alliance*, Pettit noting "a 600 pound investment in the adventures of Captain Smith"; and in the *Buckskin*, in which the Pettit-Cox-Greene share was "three fourths of one-eightenth, or one twenty-fourth." Neither vessel had either profits or adventure worthy of mention. The three-some also was concerned in the *Chance*, whose exciting career and capture of the *Venus* have already been mentioned.

Of the ships noted some sailed from Jersey ports, some from Philadelphia, and a few from Boston or other places, depending upon the fortunes of war. The triumvirate, however, was also deeply involved in what Pettit called "our Egg Harbour concerns." These were deals worked mostly through Joseph Ball. These ships are not named and it is quite possible neither Pettit nor Greene knew what they were, since Colonel Cox was the go-between and appears to have conducted the transactions singlehanded in the name of the triumvirate. That Pettit and, presumably, Greene were not too happy about them is indicated by these bits from the correspondence. Pettit wrote:

January 5, 1780: I have never yet been able to get either an account or a shilling of money from our last year's concerns at Eggharbour. My name does not appear in the business and therefore I am the more easily put off; and our good friend who represents these concerns has wealth in so many ways that he does not feel the delay. [The "good friend," of course, is Cox.]

January 17, 1780:   That business [at Egg Harbor] has vexed me and I have spoken more fretfully to our Friend Col. Cox than I ever did on any other occasion to induce him to procure a Settlement, as he stands between us and the People who have the management of those affairs.

August 27, 1780:   Our concerns in navigation at Egg-harbour are yet in the clouds as to my view of them, tho' I have some accounts respecting them. They were at first not as profitable as we had expected, and there are some losses to reduce those that afforded profit. I have all along comforted myself with this reflection, that is if I rec'd nothing from them, they began from nothing, having advanced no money originally for them . . .

May 27, 1781:   Our friend Mr. Cox confines himself at Bloomsbury [now the Trent House] in the cultivation of his farm which is in a flourishing way.

Not until 1784 was there even talk of a settlement on the "Eggharbour concerns." Nearly five years was a long time to wait. Worse, the profits themselves proved small—2,000 pounds to be divided three ways. On February 7, 1784, Pettit wrote Greene that "whether he [Cox] will consent to pay this or contend that it shall remain to be settled at the Close of our other Concerns, I am not ascertained. I am clear, however, that he has in his Hands, besides this, at least a full proportion of what has been appropriated by us all . . . even admitting his mode of accounting for what he early took to his own use [presumably for Batsto]." Pettit then added, wryly, that "you are not unacquainted with the Considerations which induced me to yield on many points [presumably in the accounting on the privateers] rather than risk a breach of Friendship. . . . However his opinions may be biased by self-interest, to which Humanity is always liable, I have the fullest confidence that he *means* to do what is right."

Greene appears to have felt that more was due from the Chestnut Neck privateer ventures, and a claim was drawn up. Pettit, however, "after getting him [Cox] and Ball together and talking the matter over . . . saw Reasons which induced me to reduce the claim considerably, but told him I could not answer for your coming to the same Opinion." After some more haggling, Cox convinced Pettit that the profit on their really big prize, the *Venus*, was tied up by rival claims, that there were losses "to a greater amount than the gain on the prize," and that he, Cox, had "not benefitted by all we have lost." Finally, in March, 1884, Pettit reckoned that "there may be 600 or 700 pounds due to each of us."

On that blue note the correspondence closes in so far as the Chestnut Neck interests of the triumvirate are concerned. Nor is there further mention of other privateering ventures; probably all they owned had been liquidated, or sunk, by that time.

From every indication the three partners wound up with very modest profits in exchange for all their risks, their schemings, their secret correspondence, and their headaches. It is true that many others made large gains in privateering; so it is a question whether Pettit was just unlucky, whether he let his optimism befog his judgment, whether he relied too heavily upon the recommendations of others—he was always investigating his ships *after* he had bought them—or whether he and his partners were simply taken in by smarter operators. But if the three men came out badly in privateering, there is every indication that in profiteering on commodities they did rather well.

Inconceivable today is the looseness with which Greene, Pettit, and Cox ran the Quartermaster General's Department. Substantial sums appear to have been diverted from government procurement to their privateering and other speculations. Legally, no doubt, the money could be chalked up as advances against the commissions they were to be paid. In about two years Greene disbursed some eighty million dollars, but his departmental records seem to have been so confused that when Congress sought some accounting none was forthcoming. Greene resented even the request. Inquiries, however, continued and when Congress proposed to reorganize the Quartermaster's Department on a basis which would have excluded Pettit and Cox, Greene angrily resigned, giving Congress but ten days' notice. The resignation was instantly accepted, and only Washington's intervention, on the basis of maintaining military morale, blocked a Congressional probe of Greene's activities.[22]

Evidence of the tangled web woven by Greene, Pettit, and Cox out of government finance may be judged from the following extracts from a private agreement between Greene and Pettit. Dated November 8, 1783, it is an effort to untangle those finances, at least among themselves.

> Whereas the said Nathanael Greene, John Cox and Charles Pettit have at divers times *drawn from the Cash and Effects put into their Hands for the use of the Department of Quarter Master General several sums of Money* on account of . . . Commissions, which stand charged to their respective accts. in the Books of the said Department kept *under the care and direction of the said Charles Pettit,* on which account of the said Nathanael Greene there appears to be a Balance for Monies

appropriated to his use over and besides the monies placed to the credit of his said account, of *one hundred and seventy-five thousand six hundred and sixty-one Continental Dollars or thereabouts* . . .

And whereas also divers sums of money have been drawn from the same source by the said Charles Pettit for and on account of the said Nathanael Greene, John Cox and Charles Pettit *to be invested in Trade and Merchandize* . . .[23]

[The italics are mine. A.D.P.]

Bear in mind that their personal use of the money was not authorized by nor even known to Congress.

How much real money accrued to Greene, Pettit, and Cox when it was all over is difficult even to guess. Greene apparently did well. Colonel Cox, as Pettit once remarked rather enviously, was well heeled and soon able to move in high society. Pettit probably came in a bad third. Of the three, he could best claim mitigating circumstances. In 1781 he had written of his financial "pangs of distress" and declared he was so hard up that the amount of money he was free to spend as he chose "would not pay the wages of one of my clerks." Greene claimed to have sacrificed heavily in the colonial cause, and in its earlier days that probably was the case; later he made up for lost money as well as lost time.

After the decisive defeat of the British at Yorktown, the number of privateers at Chestnut Neck and elsewhere dwindled to the vanishing point. Prospects of peace were taking the profits out of war. Commodities began to become more plentiful. Privateering was to be revived lustily in the War of 1812—but that is another story.

One final word on profiteering is in order. Even before

the new nation was on its feet many of the old speculators made killings when Congress, in 1790, voted to redeem its depreciated wartime certificates of indebtedness at face value. These certificates originally had been used to pay many of the soldiers who fought in the Revolution and the farmers who had furnished supplies to the Continental Army. They had been difficult to dispose of even at fifteen cents on the dollar. But when Hamilton—secretly at first—proposed that the government pay a hundred cents on the dollar for these certificates, the speculators, a number of them Congressmen, swung into action. They rushed scouts to the hinterland and sent fast ships to southern ports to buy up the certificates cheap—before the soldiers and farmers got the news that Congress would redeem them at full value.

Jeremiah Wadsworth, copartner of Greene in wartime "specs," sent out one of the ships and made $9,000,000, according to reports at the time; Robert Morris doubled that, clearing $18,000,000,[24] at the expense of the soldiers and farmers who had fought and sacrificed to win American independence. This remains one of the worst scandals in American history. Nathanael Greene, however, was not a part of it. Having twice refused appointment as secretary of war, he had died in Georgia on June 19, 1786, of sunstroke.*

---

* After the Revolution, Pettit and Ball became leading figures in the financial world. Pettit served as president of the Insurance Company of North America from 1796–98, and 1799–1806, while Ball was one of the original directors of that company, a member of the Pennsylvania House of Representatives, a director of the Bank of the United States, and first president of the Pennsylvania Company for Insurances on Lives and Granting Annuities. Cox and his family were leading figures in post-Revolutionary society, dispensing hospitality from their mansion at Trenton, then called Bloomsbury Court and now the Trent House.

WISTARBERG:
A NEW LOOK

It is best to select a bright day, so that any stray bits of glass will have their chance to twinkle in the sun. The journey will be more cheerful too. Recommended as a place to start is the ancient oak in Salem, said to have passed its four-hundredth birthday; yet whatever its age, it is a landmark of majesty in a fast-changing world.

Traveling eastward along the main street of this colonial community one goes directly to the Bridgeton road. Now it is only three short miles to Quinton—it was Quinton's Bridge in 1778 when a bloody engagement there sent the British into temporary retreat. Quinton also marks the junction of the "Great Road" to Daretown, which swings east by northeast and soon takes one to the village of Alloway, scene of another Revolutionary skirmish.

The word "Alloway" originally was "Allowas" or "Aloes" after a local Indian chief, but people called the town Thompson's Bridge in the days when the British were coming. Later they called it "Allowaystown"; now it is simply Alloway, a clean, neat little crossroads place with a venerable tavern, attractive old houses, and a gracious atmosphere which befits its historic past.

From Alloway the road takes several gently rolling curves past inviting Alloway Lake. A generous half mile farther and it is time to pause. True, there is nothing dramatic here to be seen: a small white farmhouse with a significantly oversized four-pot chimney, a few outbuildings, and open fields on both sides of the road, clay-clogged fields laboriously tilled over long years. Quite a stretch to the left, beyond downsloping terrain, a screen of trees hides the swift-moving Alloway Creek. To the right a vista of rolling farmland is broken only by two or three distant houses and a few small cedars marking boundary lines in the soil.

This was Wistarberg. Most authorities agree that here the glass industry of America had its real beginning. Here, too, legend, misinformation, and history have been compounded into a glamorous mixture. That is why it has been common for passers-by over the years to see men and women digging in the dirt thereabouts. Usually those diggers were farmers, but quite a number could have been identified as antiquarians and glass fanciers hopefully seeking buried examples of Wistar glassware. A very few of the glass hunters have been lucky; most have had to be content with chips and pieces of the history that was fashioned here.

Two lucky ones tramped those fields forty-six years ago. One was Frederick W. Hunter, author of *Stiegel Glass*. The other was his brother-in-law, J. B. Kerfoot, another authority on old glass. Hunter wrote:

> During the summer and fall of 1913 I paid several visits to the site of the Wistarberg works; very thoroughly canvassed the ground; made exploratory excavations; and gathered enough fragments of the glass made and used there, and enough pieces of the factory's finished output to form an excellent and illuminating basis for a determination of the kind of work done, and for a critical sort-

ing out and identification of at least the more markedly characteristic Wistar pieces from the surviving specimens of early American glass.[1]

In his explorations Kerfoot "disinterred numerous pieces of glass . . . and also found fragments of straight-sided bottles on the order of gin bottles of a later period."

Contemplating those tranquil fields today one may regret that exploration of the Wistar lands lacked that archaeological thoroughness which has marked the excavations at Jamestown, on the site of the very first glasshouses in the New World. While those glasshouses were short-lived and relatively unimportant in the history of the American glass industry, we still know more about their plant—the buildings, furnaces and site locations—than we do about the much-larger Wistar works which lasted forty years. Those Jamestown diggings, for example, dispelled the ancient legend of the money beads. A stated major purpose in building those works was to produce glass beads for use as money, especially in trading with the Indians; but despite the most meticulous research not a single bead was found.[2]

At Jamestown the ground was searched systematically. After the ruins themselves had been located, "test trenches were extended out . . . for a distance of about one hundred feet in every direction. The first test trench revealed that nearly a foot of earth had accumulated over the original surface of the ground." Found were the remains of four stone ovens, all built of rounded river boulders imbedded in clay. The size of the main body of the furnace could be determined, and for the recent Jamestown Festival a reasonable approximation of the old glassworks could be reconstructed. The methods used there included accurate recording of the location and depth of every object found, setting out reference stakes to make that possible, screening every shovel of earth excavated, and keeping the material recovered from each unit within the area, and from each soil layer, in separate containers.[3]

The Jamestown method of glass hunting has been given in some detail because nothing approaching it has been done at Wistarberg, which is one reason why the good earth there is still mixed with so much mystery. As Helen and George McKearin noted in their *Two Hundred Years of American Blown Glass,* Hunter (and presumably Kerfoot) "did not differentiate between fragment evidence, local tradition and personal opinion in presenting material. . . . Apparently not even one complete vessel could be reconstructed from the fragments. It is regrettable that they were not catalogued and fully described for other students."

Because legend has played such a large part in substituting for a scientific approach to Wistarberg, nearly everything concerning it has become engulfed in dispute and confusion. Take the name itself: it is spelled Wistarberg in this account because that spelling has come into general use. The Wistars themselves spelled it Wistarburg and also Wistarburgh. In Germany the family name was Würster, although it sometimes is given as Wüster. When Caspar first came to this country he simplified that to Wister. However, when he took the oath of allegiance to the king in 1721, a clerk incorrectly spelled it Wistar, and presumably to make life simpler Caspar adopted that spelling thereafter. Such confusions were common with non-English immigrant families adapting to ways of life in the New World. Similar differences occurred in the maiden name of Wistar's wife and in the names of many of his employees.

Further conflict has surrounded the glassworks itself. Some authorities, including Hunter, credit Wistar with making the first flint glass in America. Flint glass is made from a mixture leavened with lead. Others dispute this, find no evidence of flint glass at Wistarberg, and give the honors in that field to "Baron" Stiegel. Again, some experts list several dozen authenticated pieces of Wistar glass; others say there are only a few, and the McKearins put it flatly: "We do not know of a single piece of glass that can be attributed with certainty to this glass house." There also has been dispute over Wistarberg colors and styles, and even the closing date of the factory is controversial.

It may be asked why, amid all this confusion, one should make a journey to Wistarberg now. The scenery is not that compelling, and only the highly imaginative eye can people those open fields with ghosts of the old glass blowers. The white cottage with the four-pot chimney is said to contain within it a portion of an original Wistarberg house, but it has been basically and extensively remodeled. While the soil in some places still yields glass fragments, prospect for fresh finds of intact Wistarware are dim.

The reason for this chronicle is that there is a story to tell, a story which in large part has never been told before, to the best of my knowledge. Since that story casts some bright, fresh light upon Wistarberg, a visit to the old site serves as a frame of reference and inspiration as well as a pleasant day's outing.

Much of the information that follows is disclosed by manuscript and other records of Caspar Wistar and his glassworks.* Perhaps the narrative will be kept in better

---

* Many of them repose in the Historical Society of Pennsylvania. That society, of which I am a member, has given me permission to make use of them now. Many of these records were written in old German script, which is far from easy to decipher, but they still offer considerably more to the researcher than the farmlands can now be expected to yield to those who would make one more trip "through Wistarberg with trowel and shovel." In addition, there has been recourse to official records, deeds and the like, as well as to the researches of others, which are noted in the text or the bibliography.

perspective if at this point a summary is made of certain indications and conclusions gained from Wistar's records:

1—That the over-all Wistarberg enterprise originally was called the United Glass Company.

2—That under Caspar Wistar and his partners only window and bottle glass were produced commercially.

3—That while the range of products was expanded by Richard Wistar, it was still limited in scope.

4—That under both Caspar and Richard Wistar but three basic colors were available—white, green, and bottle glass—with such shade variations as the raw materials and processing happened to contribute.

5—That any of the fancier pieces attributed to Wistarberg, if actually blown there, were not factory made but were produced for friends and family or to supply local needs, as was the case at many other South Jersey glassworks.

6—Both Wistars seem to have considered their glass enterprise as more or less of a sideline, and at least secondary to their brass-button making business.

Caspar Wistar was born on February 3, 1696, at Hilsbach, near Heidelberg, Germany. His parents were Hans Caspar and Anna Katerina Würster. The father held the fairly important post of *Fürstenjäger,* or chief huntsman, to Prince Carl Theodore of Bavaria. This office was hereditary, and as eldest son Caspar was in line for it.[4] Despite that fact and his father's urgings, he decided to live more adventurously and seek his fortune in America.

On September 16, 1717, Caspar Wistar arrived in Philadelphia. According to family legend, he was very poor, possessed only of "his clothes, a double-barreled gun and a pistareen." However, Caspar was anything but poor in human resources. He had good health, driving ambition, a shrewd mind, and a faculty for holding onto the money he acquired. His very first job was harvesting apples, the pay being all the apples he could eat or carry away; and his first meal, it is told, was bread and apples. His famous grandson, Dr. Caspar Wistar, once commemorated this "menu" by serving bread and apples at one of his socially triumphant Wistar Parties in Philadelphia.[5]

Soon Caspar got another job: wheeling ashes for a soap and candle maker. At this period he apparently ran for some undisclosed local elective office. The opposing candidate sought to ridicule him by hiring a man to wheel ashes near the polling place on election day. Quick to turn any situation to his own advantage, Caspar took off his coat, rolled up his shirtsleeves, approached the man, and said: "You are not doing that right. Here, let me show you!" Whereupon he wheeled the ashes about, to the recorded delight of the crowd that had gathered, and was elected without a dissenting vote.[6]

Within three years Caspar had accumulated enough money to become a partner in building the Colebrookdale iron furnace in eastern Berks County. Leader in that enterprise was the famous ironmaster Thomas Rutter and the other partners were Alexander Woodrop, Samuel Morris, Richard Lewis, and John Mickle.[7] Some of Wistar's savings apparently had come from speculation in real estate in Northampton County, lands which he subdivided and sold to other German immigrants. Five years later Wistar invested in a second iron venture, the building of Pool Forge on Manatawny Creek, also in Berks County. Meanwhile in Philadelphia he had launched upon the most profitable of all his undertakings: a factory for making brass buttons "warranted for seven years." Caspar, indeed, seemed to have the Midas touch.

In the same year that he bought a share of the Pool Forge

Wistar embraced the Quaker faith, no doubt because he intended to wed the attractive Quakeress, Catherine Jansen, daughter of Dirick Jansen of Germantown. (Later the Jansen name was changed to Johnson.) The marriage took place on March 25, 1726, in the Abington Friends Meeting House before a large gathering. Thereafter Wistar moved more and more in Philadelphia Quaker circles, although detailed information on this aspect of his life is scanty.

The following year, 1727, is important in the Wistar saga because June 7 marked the birth of his first son, Richard, who was to succeed him in management of the glassworks. That year, too, he brought his brother John over from Germany, and soon John was making money in the wine business as fast as his brother was making it in brass buttons.[8]

Caspar was fairly active in Philadelphia affairs for a man so preoccupied with business. In 1732 it was announced that he would receive subscriptions for the *Philadelphische Zeitung*, the first German-language newspaper published in America.[9] When the Fellowship Fire Company was organized, March 1, 1738, Caspar and his son both were listed as subscribers (although Richard was but ten years old). That Caspar was an active member is suggested by the fact that five years after his death the fire company was still keeping ladders "at the Widow Wistar's on Market street."[10]

Another measure of Wistar's community interest was his contribution of fifty pounds toward the founding of the Pennsylvania Hospital in 1751, and he also is listed among those present at the first meeting of subscribers. A brief glimpse of his home is given by his purchase, from Joseph Richardson, Philadelphia silversmith, of "4 Porringers, 1 Pepperbox, 1 pair of Salts, 4 buttons and 1 pair Knee Buckles."[11] How much of a library he possessed we do not know, but in 1734 he bought a "Dutch Barclay" bound by Benjamin Franklin, probably a German edition of this book

which then was said to belong in all good Quaker households.[12]

Let no one conclude that Caspar Wistar was an austere
and humorless individual. Quite the contrary. This is illustrated in a tale told by his great-granddaughter, Mary
Wistar Brown. It seems that Caspar was appointed to a
committee with a number of other persons, among whom
was the Rev. Richard Peters, rector of Christ Church in
later years and then secretary of the Governor's Council.
The committee was to deal with an Indian treaty in the
interior of Pennsylvania, and "it being the trout season they
expected to be well provided with that favorite fare. On
arriving at their destination and being summoned to table,
they were exceedingly disappointed in seeing but one small
dish of inferior trout with a single good-sized one placed on
the top. The divine hurried to his seat and sticking the fork
in the only desirable fish, transferred it to his own plate.
This being secured, with closed eyes and uplifted hands,
he said *now* let us pray, and rehearsed the usual form. While
he was thus engrossed his facetious friend [Caspar Wistar]
being seated near him, quietly removed the coveted fish—
and when the surprised dignitary opened his eyes to the
fact, he was thus pleasantly accosted, "Parson Peters, men
ought to *watch* as well as *pray!*" [13]

There is a curious historical affinity between the manufacture of iron and glass. Working with one of the hardest
and toughest of metals seems to have impelled many men
to go to the other extreme and experiment with the most
delicate and fragile product of their times. So with Wistar;
so, too, with Baron Stiegel, who made his money in iron
and lost it in glass. So, also, with many later ironmasters,
including the Richardses of Batsto, who turned to glass
when economic tides began to encroach on the charcoal era
in ironmaking. The use of furnaces was a further common

factor, and glassmaking like iron smelting relied for most
of its raw materials upon neighborhood sources of supply.

In those times there was yet another stimulus to the
manufacture of both glass and iron: that already noted exploitation of the colonies by the mother country and the
colonial trend toward industrialism as well as independence.
The prevailing British mercantile philosophy was that "all
these Colloneys, which are but twigs belonging to the Main
Tree [Britain] ought to be kept entirely dependent upon &
subservient to England, and that can never be if they are
suffered to goe on in the notions they have, that as Englishq-
men, soe they may set up the same manufactures here as
people may do in England." [14] No matter that the British
were not producing enough glass to meet their own domestic needs, let alone for export. No matter that British
factories were relying heavily upon imported Continental
workers! If the Americans wanted glass they could get it
from British merchants who in turn would buy it from the
Continent, adding a nice profit when they shipped it along
to the "Colloneys." If the resulting price of glass was ex-
orbitant, it meant that few in the New World would be
able to afford glass windows in their houses. While the
duties on glass thus unintentionally encouraged colonial
glass manufacture, Wistar had reason to fear that con-
spicuous success in that field might lead British merchants
to demand legislation prohibiting glassmaking in America
along the lines of the 1750 act which prohibited erection
of mills for plating and slitting iron.

The beginning of Wistarberg is traced in family records
to a day when Caspar Wistar was traveling through South
Jersey to promote the sale of brass buttons. Always observ-
ant, he noticed the prevalence of white sand which reminded him of sand used by glassmakers in his native Hilsbach. Soon he realized that South Jersey possessed all the

essential resources for manufacture of glass: the abundant white sand; clay for furnaces and pots; stone for construction; plenty of wood for fuel. Once the decision was made he began buying land in the vicinity of what came to be Wistarberg. His first recorded purchase was in 1738, one hundred acres from Clement Hall. Soon afterward Amos Penton deeded him a thousand acres of woodland, and on April 27, 1739, the tract on which the glasshouses were built was acquired from Amos Hilton.[15] In all, about two thousand acres were assembled. Not only did these lands offer the sand, clay, and fuel for glassmaking, they were traversed by two streams, Deep Run and Alloway Creek, which were navigable for the shallops Wistar was to use in transporting his supplies and finished products.

Wistar himself knew nothing about glass manufacture. So he sent abroad for experts. On December 7, 1738, he reached an agreement with four European glass blowers: Caspar Halter (or Halder); Johan Martin Halter (misspelled "Halton" by both Hunter and McKearin); Johan Wilhelm Wentzel, and Simeon Kreismayer. The spellings here given are those in most of the account books, although even these vary, and Wentzel's name is sometimes spelled Wentzell, while Kreismayer's appears as Simon Kreismeyer, Simeon Breissmayer, and Simon Greismeyer. Worst of all, one of Wistar's own accountants sometimes spelled his name Wister, although its bearer clearly signed it Wistar.

The contract with the four glass blowers provided for paying fifty-eight pounds, eight shillings to Captain James Marshall for their passage to America and included an advance of necessary funds for expenses and promises of land, homes, fuel, and food. Wistar agreed to "furnish all materials for glass-making, including pot-clays, silica and fluxing ingredients . . . also molds, tools, etc." The men were to receive one third of the profits, and they in turn were to teach the secret art of glassmaking to Wistar and his son Richard. Apparently the four men sailed from Rotterdam the day after the contract was made. The nationality of these men is one more disputed point. Hunter says definitely that they were from Holland and speaks of Dutch influence at Wistarberg; in *American Glass,* the McKearins speak of experts from Holland or Germany, and in their *Two Hundred Years of American Blown Glass* they shrewdly avoid the whole issue. The men's names certainly suggest German origin. The important thing is that the men arrived, helped Wistar establish his glassworks, and shared with him the responsibility for making it a success.

Wistarberg, one of the first cooperative ventures in America, swung swiftly into action. By 1740 the factory had been built and put into operation. A company store was in business, and a mansion house and various dwellings were either built or building. First official notice of the new enterprise appeared in the following letter:

To THOMAS HILL, Esq., Secretary to the Lord's Comsrs. for Trade and Plantations.
Sir:
Mr. William Frasor, Collector of the Customs of Salem in West Jersey having informed the Commissioners, that there has lately been erected a Glass Works within Eight miles of that Port by one Caspar Wistar, a Palatine, and is brought to perfection so as to Make Glass: I am directed to give you an account thereof for the Information of the Lords of Trade,

I am Sir

Your most humble Servant
CHAS. CARKESSE [16]

Custom ho. London,
31: July 1740

The Wistarberg store evidently was a busy place. Wistar's "Receipt Book" shows purchases of a barrel of rum on October 7, 1746, for four pounds, seven shillings, other consignments of rum in various quantities; "half a hundred Gunpowder from Thos. Lightfoot" on July 26, 1747, for five pounds, ten shillings; and other purchases of "Indian Blankets," salt, "3 tons of Barr Iron" for eighty-one pounds, iron pots and skillets, molasses, a cask of nails, 7,500 bricks, 2,000 shingles, and one box of pipes. All these purchases presumably were for Wistarberg, although not so stated. Another interesting entry is a receipt by William Holliday "the 29th of July 1747 from Caspar Wistar One box of Glass for Walter Daugherty which I promise to land at Holloways on Duck Creek."

Wistar's contract with his glass blowers seems not to have covered all the important points in establishment of the factory. An extract from his diary in 1741 reads:

This day, I and four glass blowers mutually made a covenant that I assume and take all glass and all debts, whatever they may be, from the beginning till now, and I further pay each one in money the sum of 85 pound. Excepting however their own private bills and what they have had of me and the white glass, potash and other ashes. All other expenses I am to pay to this day.

The text of this covenant has not come to light, but apparently it still did not clarify all points at issue, for on February 4, 1744, the following "Declaration and Explanation" was drawn up:

I, the undersigned, Caspar Wistar do declare and affirm in regard to the four glass blowers, Hans Wilhelm Wentzel, Simeon Breissmayer, Caspar and Martin Halder that mine agreement has always been as now, that at the

expiration of this covenant, they shall receive and hold
the Glass Works as their property, including the furnaces
bought of them by me, and all property, tools and other
things bought by me, not stationary. However, there shall
be divided between me and them the two boilers in the
potash house and all other iron tools bought by the whole
company for the use of the company, provided such tools
are not stationary. Of these the glassblowers shall have
one share and myself two shares. In witness thereof I
have hereunto set my name

                                        CASPAR WISTAR

4, Feby. 1744

The rights of the four glass blowers noted in this declaration raise interesting questions, some of which are answered in the Wistar account books. First, however, it may
be best to see what those books reveal about Wistarberg
and its organization.

One volume is marked "Book G." Edward Otto, who trans-
lated a few portions of it for the Wistar family, suggests
that "it is what in German business houses is called 'Geheim-
buch,' or secret book. In days when safes were not common
. . . business men kept the total results and principal accounts between the partners of a firm in a book accessible
only to them." Scrutiny of Book G tends to support that conclusion. It consists entirely of balance sheets of the financial
relations between Wistar and the four glass blowers, who
were virtual if not actual partners. Unfortunately there is
no record of the company's over-all receipts and expenditures and, save for incidental mention, no list of its customers. Indeed, in this book there is no indication of direct
factory sales in any city except Philadelphia.

From Book G we learn the name of the original Wistar
firm. In 1743 it was called the United Glass Company.

"Factor," or accountant, at that time was another German immigrant, John Stockard. Business manager at the plant from 1741 to nearly the end was Benjamin Thompson, member of an old Salem County family, one of the few non-Europeans on the payroll.

Book G also shows us that the business setup was far from simple. The United Glass Company appears to have been a parent concern, the equivalent of a holding company; and under it were at least four subsidiaries, one for each of the four furnaces whose books were kept independently, with each furnace expected to show a profit. Those books probably have not survived, but this master record speaks frequently of companies within the main company, expenditures of the whole company and also those of a particular company.

In 1741, for example, a statement of Johan Wilhelm Wentzel's account includes such items as "freight for his helper" 10 pounds, 11 shillings; an advance of 4 pounds, 12 shillings; "commission for selling glass in Philadelphia according to agreement" 8 pounds, 10 shillings. His share of expenses of the whole company were down as 27 pounds, 7 shillings, 2 pence.

Wentzel was in charge of the third and fourth furnaces, and the accounting mentions various consignments of glass made by them. For instance, "From the 3rd Furnace 314–8–8; deduct for breakage 27–0–0." Remaining to Wentzel's credit was 287–8–8, which divided by three gave him 95 pounds, 16 shillings, 2½ pence. Added to this was his third of 31–8–10 for glass sold at the store, a net of 10–9–6. The fourth furnace furnished glass in the amount of 365 pounds with a 27-pound deduction for breakage leaving 338 pounds, with Wentzel's third being 112 pounds. The over-all net balance due Wentzel was 236 pounds, 11 shillings, 11 pence. And to the entire account was appended:

To certify these things as above written I have signed
my name, Feby 8, 1744

           JOHANNES WILHELM WENTZEL

Hereby I certify that these things are true.

Feby. 8, 1744   CASPAR WISTAR

Some of the accounts mention payments—probably advances of funds—by Benjamin Thompson. Most, too, list
shipments of glass to Philadelphia, usually to a David Mat-
zinger. In one of Wentzel's accounts there is an item for
bottling glass and note of purchases from a "Pottash Company" which may have been still another Wistar subsidiary.
Breakage was an important factor although identical breakage allowances of 27 pounds each for several furnaces raises
a question whether this may not have been an arbitrary
figure, with actual loss from breakage either more or less.
While the handwriting varies, most of Book G was kept
by Stockard. As an introduction he wrote:

> In as much as there is so far no written evidence con-
> cerning the business and covenant of our Glass Works,
> and whereas the human memory is so frail and weak that
> it cannot be depended upon, which leads to errors and
> misunderstandings, therefore the United Glass Company
> has found it timely and expedient (to avoid misunder-
> standings) to commit to this book their dealings with
> one another, and to this end commenced this book in
> the year (one) seven hundred and forty three.   1743.
>
>   by JOHN STOCKARD, Factor
> The Lord Himself crown our labor and prosper it with
> the blessings of His hands. To Him be given then all the
> praise and glory, for all the love and grace by Him on us.

These comments seem to suggest that the oft-quoted
original contract with the four glass blowers may have been

a verbal one, even though the pact with the ship's captain may have been written. In any case Stockard's fervent prayer was surely answered. Judging from Book G, the United Glass Company enjoyed a lucrative trade, while Wistar himself became a wealthy man, particularly since his brass-button factory also was flourishing. Wistar's partners, the glass blowers, prospered too, if one may judge from these accounts. When Kreismayer (or Breissmayer) died in 1748 his widow, Susannah, received a total of 406 pounds from the company. That was then a substantial sum.

At mid-century Wistarberg was still thriving in spite of stepped-up British exploitation of the American colonies, plus increasingly adverse economic conditions generally. When provincial governors sought to ease the depression of those days by encouraging domestic manufactures in secret defiance of parliamentary policy, some of them suggested building glassworks. In 1747, having heard of Wistarberg, a Bostonian wrote Governor Belcher of New Jersey to ask how to go about starting a similar plant. Belcher in turn made inquiry of Wistar, who gave him no encouragement. Belcher wrote his friend that Wistar had complained that "the Clay for the Furnace Bottoms was but poor and often gave WAY to their great damage and complain'd also that they could not make their Glass so Clear and Strong for want of HELP, their Works being near two hundred miles from any Quantity of it." [17]

How much of the truth was Wistar telling? The two hundred miles was an outrageous exaggeration. But was his business really bad at just that time and the quality of his glass so poor? Or was he intentionally deceiving the New Jersey governor, either to discourage competition or to conceal the prosperity of his plant from a Parliament eager to stifle manufacturing in the colonies? Such deviousness was

common in the pre-Revolutionary period. When Lord Grenville demanded details on manufacturing, in 1768, Benjamin Franklin, a friend of the Wistar family, suggested to
his son, Governor Franklin, that in answering for New
Jersey he report "a Glass house, coarse window glass and
bottles, all the finer goods coming from England." This, of
course, was double-talk. Minimizing the importance of the
Wistar works was intended to pull the wool from parliamentary wigs over parliamentary eyes. The governor took
the hint, and wrote London as follows:

A Glass House was erected about Twenty years ago in
Salem County, which makes Bottles, and a very coarse
Green Glass for windows used only in some of the houses
of the poorer Sort of People. The Profits made by this
Work have not hitherto been sufficient it seems to induce
any Persons to set up more of the like kind in this Colony:
but since the late Act of Parliament laying a Duty on
Glass exported to the Colonies, there has been talk of
erecting others, but I cannot learn that any are yet begun:
It seems probable that notwithstanding the Duty, Fine
Glass can still be imported into America cheaper than it
can be made here.

When Caspar Wistar died, of dropsy, on February 13,
1752, his estate was extensive and considerably larger than
the 3,000 pounds officially estimated. To his son Caspar he
left a plantation in Bucks County, Pennsylvania. His four
daughters received various substantial bequests. To his wife,
Catherine, there went "half of the tools and materials used
in his trade," which was equivalent to a half interest in his
enterprises. Richard, the eldest son, was given the other half
of the brass-button factory in Philadelphia and the glassworks in Salem County. An extract from the will reads:

In case of my death before the time mentioned in an article of agreement between Johan Wilhelm Wentzel, Caspar Halter, Johan Martin Halter and Simeon Kreismeier, and myself, bearing the date the 7th day of December 1738, has expired, I direct my executors to continue the business until my part of the contract shall be fulfilled; afterward they are to be managed by my wife and son Richard.

Richard's legacy contained one stipulation: so long as he ran the glass factory he was to give his brother Caspar, annually, "400 boxes of the best 8 x 10 glass, 400 boxes of the best 7 x 9 glass, 100 boxes of the best 9 x 11 glass, three dozen half gallon case bottles, six dozen pocket bottles, one dozen pint bottles, etc." [18] The executors, incidentally, were his wife, Richard, his wife's brother Richard Johnson (ex-Jansen) and "a kinsman" David Deschler.

Until his death Caspar Wistar had the field of American glassmaking virtually to himself. A few other ventures of hazy scope and brief duration are recorded, but none that compares with his, and the inception of Baron Stiegel's sky-rocketing career in glass was still ten years away. Even a 1752 venture in New York was to wait until Caspar's passing. Native glass, therefore, was still a scarce commodity, and the glass annuity willed to Caspar Wistar, Jr., was of much greater monetary significance then than it may seem today.

How far had Wistarberg come in those first thirteen years? The United Glass Company was a financial success. The little community in Salem County's sandlands had grown, too, swelled by a number of Dutch and German glassworkers, many of them brought over by Wistar himself. In 1748 the Emanuel Lutheran Church had been built nearby at Freasburg (now Friesburg), and many of those

workers were members of the congregation. An advertisement for sale of some land in Salem County, in 1768, mentions that it is about "4 miles from a Glass-house where are
settled many German families." [19] The company store was
doing a substantial business. And all of this had been
achieved within the limitations of the glass factory's output. In Book G, for example, only two kinds of glass are
referred to: window glass and bottles. As for colors, they
were limited to three: white glass, green glass, and bottle
glass. There is not the slightest evidence that flint glass was
made; and when Caspar Wistar, in his will, called himself
a brass-button maker, it is clear that history has attached
much greater importance to his glassworks than he did.

These assorted data support three opinions expressed by
Rhea Mansfield Knittle in her book *Early American Glass:*
that few colors were employed at the Wistar works, that
there is no proof flint glass was made, and that the early
output is supposed to have been coarse and crude. Also
confirmed thus far is the view of the McKearins that there
was no attempt to produce fine wares and that any fancy
glass was turned out by the workers for their own purposes
and was not part of the normal factory output. All evidence
points to the conclusion that Caspar Wistar had the temperament of a businessman rather than that of an artist, the
exact reverse of Baron Stiegel. Wistar was interested in the
kinds of glass that would sell quickest and best, not in
fashioning the masterpieces of craftsmanship and beauty
which delight today's connoisseur. This is not to belittle in
any way Caspar Wistar's role in glass history; it is only to
keep it in proper focus.

Richard Wistar, clearly, had more expansive ideas than
his father. In 1752, not long after Caspar's death, he published this advertisement in the *Pennsylvania Gazette:*

Richard Wistar hereby gives notice that he is removed from his Father's House in Market Street Philadelphia to a house higher up in the same Street next door to the Spinning Wheel almost opposite the Prison. Where may be had Glass 9 x 11, 8 x 10, 7 x 9 and all other sizes of Window Glass and Bottles, wholesale and retail. He likewise carries on the trade of Making Brass Buttons where merchants shop keepers and others may be supplied as usual.

This notice confirms the fact that Wistarberg production was limited to window glass and bottles. The quick change of residence also hints at new ideas; and they were not to wait long.

Richard's expansion program for Wistarberg was launched one year after his father's death. An inventory of the estate of his mother, Catherine, who was to survive him, shows a borrowing schedule made up much like a present-day mortgage amortization table. This dated from March 25, 1753. Payments of principal (listed as rent of the glassworks) and interest were calculated, and over twenty-four years totaled 2,150 pounds. But there were other, and bigger, glass works debts—principal 1,157 pounds, 16 shillings, 10 pence, interest 2,333 pounds, 6 shillings, 3 pence, a total of 3,491 pounds, 3 shillings, 1 pence. It was these borrowings that financed the expansion of Wistarberg and the means for making a considerably wider range of glass products.

Another odd development that followed Caspar Wistar's death was the formation of yet one more company within the company. This is listed as the Wentzel and Halter Company and first appears in the books late in 1752. Whether it included both Halters, Caspar as well as Martin, is not indicated. However, Wentzel died in the latter part of 1759 and the company received 6 pounds, 14 shillings, 3½ pence from his executors. Shortly after that another bit of inside financing took place. Noted is an "abatement agreed with Martin Halter [he seems to have dropped the Johan] for me, Richard Wistar, to take all his Part of the outstanding debt."

However fancy the financing, the effect of Richard Wistar's expenditures upon Wistarberg production was considerable. This is evident by comparing the output advertised by Wistar in 1752 with the wares offered in another of his advertisements, found in the *Pennsylvania Gazette* of September 28, 1769:

> Made at subscriber's Glass Works between 300 and 400 boxes of Window glass consisting of common sizes 10 x 12, 9 x 11, 8 x 10, 7 x 9, 6 x 8. Lamp glasses or any uncommon sizes under 16 x 18 are cut on short notice. Most sort of bottles, gallon, ½ gallon, and quart, full measure ½ gallon cafe bottles, snuff and mustard bottles also electrofying globes and tubes &c. All glass American Manufacture and America ought also encourage her own manufacture.
>
> N.B. He also continues to make the Philadelphia brass buttons noted for their strength and such as were made by his deceased father and warranted for seven years.

In an otherwise similar advertisement in the *Pennsylvania Chronicle*, Wistar varied the phraseology as follows:

> . . . also . . . receivers and retorts of various sizes, also electerising globes and tubes, &c. As the above-mentioned glass is of American manufacture, it is consequently clear of the duties the Americans so justly complain of; and at present it seems peculiarly the interest of America to encourage her own manufactures, more especially those

upon which duties have been imposed for the sole purpose of raising a revenue.

In these announcements there is a markedly wider range of glass products even though the list does not include many items in general use, some of which, such as cream jugs, sugar bowls, wineglasses, tumblers, vinegar cruets, and candlesticks already were being made by Stiegel. Wistar's comments about encouraging American manufactures were in tune with the times. The notorious Townshend Acts put a tax on glass and other commodities as well as on tea, thus forcing up prices. Equally in tune with the times was Wistar's manufacture of "electrofying (or electerising) globes and tubes." A popular wave of electrical experiments, sparked by Benjamin Franklin, had "spread to other cities—New York, Boston, Newport and Charleston—whence came orders for Philadelphia-built equipment." [20]

Despite debts almost as impressive as the Wistar production catalogue, the works appear to have been making money. Available letters of the brothers give no hint of financial worry about Wistarberg; in fact, they do not even mention it. Writing to Richard from New York in 1765, Caspar Jr. tells how "the Sons of Liberty exhibited to the Publick the effigies of Lord C—— Gren—— and Governor Murray, the latter for signing a pass on Stamped Paper, which is the first stamp that has made its odious appearance in this City, and tomorrow the Stamps which are now in the Dungeon here are to be shipped on board the Packet and consigned to Lord Bute by a Sett of enterprising Gentlemen." Other letters mention Caspar Jr. sending "two snuff boxes for thy Sally," with much discussion about the purchase of horseflesh. But not a word about the glassworks. Probably the sons took Wistarberg in stride as had their father.

Martin Halter died in 1769. This would seem to have left one of the original partners of the United Glass Company still in the picture, i.e., Caspar Halter. Yet there is a singular absence of Caspar Halter's name throughout these Wistar books, which invites the question whether he did not die during the earlier years of the enterprise. This could account for frequent mention in Book G of the division of money into thirds rather than fourths. If such was the case, then by 1769 Richard Wistar was entirely on his own in Wistarberg management although quite a few of his father's old employees were still at work there; and, while Richard made his home in Philadelphia, he never was any stranger to the glassworks or in Salem County. He often lived at the mansion, signed letters from there, and was a party to considerable litigation in the Salem County courts. That Richard was socially active in Salem is suggested by the fact that both his wives were "down Jersey" girls. His first marriage, to Sarah Wyatt, took place at Salem on November 27, 1751.[21] And it was on August 4, 1776, that he married Mary Gilbert, a widow and the daughter of John and Elizabeth Bacon of Cumberland County. That wedding took place in the Salem Friends Meeting House.[22]

How exciting it would be to discover a Wistarberg payroll! Not because the wages matter, but because it would provide a welcome list of the names of those glass blowers who sweated and stifled in the terrific heat of the furnaces, who maintained a production pace which in terms of energy expended would scarcely be dreamed of today, and who made not only glass but an industrial tradition. As Helen and George McKearin put it so well, they provided the beginnings of American folk art in glass.

Luckily a partial picture can be pieced together. Records of the old Emanuel Lutheran Church at Freasburg (now Friesburg) supply the family names of some of the glassworkers: Meyer, Hayn (or Hahn), Born, Ridman, Frollinger (or Froehlinger, Trullender, and now Trollenger), Mackassan, Heppel, Ziegler (now Sickler, a notable Salem County name), as well as four families brought over in 1748: Souder, Kneist, Tobal, and Freas (for whom Freasburg was named). In the late 1760's some, if not all, of seven brothers named Stenger (or Stanger) worked at Wistarberg. Solomon and Daniel Stenger were active in the Freasburg church, and Adam and Philip had children baptized there. The three remaining brothers were Francis, Peter, and Jacob. That Jacob was an indentured worker is indicated by a 1770 advertisement stating that he had run away and offering $20 for his return, along with that of another runaway, John Kindiel. Jacob later turned up in Glassboro when his brothers started a glasshouse there. Caspar Wistar brought over some other indentured servants, and while there is no evidence that they ever worked at Wistarberg, their names are given here in the event that some clue thereby may turn up: Jacob Bechtel, Abraham Zimmerman, Melchior Zimmerman, Johan Becker, Anthony Reyffner, Peter Ambas, and Johan Leger.

Best picture of Wistarberg in its latter days comes from Richard Wistar himself in three advertisements, two of them suggesting that glassmakers experienced the same difficulties with indentured labor that was common in the iron plantations of South Jersey.

One notice offers a reward of twelve dollars for return of "a Dutchman named Phillip Jacobs" who wore a "red plush jacket, striped Ticken Trowsers, good shoes with large brass buckles and a Castor Hat about half worn." [23] Jacobs "took with him also a Fiddle, upon which he is much addicted to play." The other advertisement offers ten dollars for the return of Adrian Brust, "who had on when he went away an old Felt Hat, a lightish coloured Upper Jacket with

Brass Buttons . . . Leather Breeches, Gray Yarn Stockings,
a good Shirt, and generally wears the Bosom Part behind." [24] It is inviting to visualize these men—one addicted
to the fiddle, the other with his shirt bosom part behind—
half running, half straggling through the woodlands of
Salem County in search of greener grass somewhere.

The third Wistar advertisement offers the best description we have of the plant itself:

The GLASS MANUFACTORY in Salem County West
Jersey is for sale with 1500 Acres of Land adjoining. It
contains two Furnaces with all the necessary Ovens for
cooling the Glass, drying Wood, etc. Contiguous to
the Manufactory are two flattening Ovens in Separate
Houses, a Storehouse, a Pot-house, a House fitted with
Tables for the cutting of Glass, a Stamping Mill, a rolling
Mill for the preparing of Clay for the making of Pots;
and at a suitable distance are ten Dwelling houses for the
Work men, as likewise a large Mansion House containing Six rooms on a Floor, with Bake-house and wash-
house; Also a convenient Store-house where a well
assorted retail Shop has been kept above 30 years, is as
good a stand for the sale of goods as any in the Country,
being situated one mile and a half from a navigable creek
where shallops load for Philadelphia, eight miles from
the county seat of Salem and half a mile from a good mill.
There are about 250 Acres of cleared Land within fence
100 whereof is mowable meadow, which produces hay
and pasturage sufficient for the large stock of Cattle and
Horses employed by the Manufactory.

There is Stabling sufficient for 60 head of Cattle with
a large Barn, Granery and Waggon House. The unim-
proved Land is well wooded and 200 acres more of
Meadow may be made. The situation and convenience

for the procuring of Materials is equal if not superior to any place in Jersey. For terms of sale apply to the Subscriber in Philadelphia.

RICHARD WISTAR

This advertisement in the *Pennsylvania Journal* of October 11, 1780, indicates that Wistar's factory had diminished in size from earlier years when records tell of four furnaces, whereas now there are only two. And it leads to the final riddle: when did the Wistar works close down?

Hunter interprets this advertisement to mean that the plant was already idle at that time. Not a word is said about labor or whether the ten houses were occupied. Mention of the assorted retail shop is in the past tense. Richard himself died at Rahway the following year, before a sale could be concluded, and some have stated that the works closed then. Other guesses have ranged from early 1780 to the oft-repeated story accepted by Mrs. Knittle, that in 1781 Richard's wife, Sarah, and their son, John, tried to operate the works, but the times were more than they could cope with.

The Wistar records suggest a different ending. Significant are two facts: that Richard's mother survived them both and still had a large measure of control over what was left of Wistarberg; and that, while Richard's debt payments to his mother and other creditors were calculated to the year of her death, 1787, his payments on the glassworks were a sole exception, stopping as of March 25, 1776.

Other bits of straw in the old Wistar fields also point to 1776 or early 1777 (prior to March 25) as the windup time of glassmaking there. Prior to that period quite a few lawsuits were recorded with Richard Wistar as plaintiff; after 1777 his name does not show in the court dockets at all. In 1777, too, the British occupied Philadelphia and gained control of the Delaware. It is unlikely that Wistar's shallops stood much chance of delivering glassware under such conditions, for even if the British facilitated passage, the local militia would have stepped in. There is also a blank spot in the following year. Colonel Mawhood and Major Simcoe were conducting raids in the area, but there is no record that they molested the glassworks or that their foraging parties carried off any Wistarberg livestock.

From this we have a choice of two conclusions: there was little left to seize and molest; or Richard Wistar, being a Quaker, may have been exempted from pillage because, as a noncombatant, he had followed Henry Drinker's example at Atsion where the furnace was closed down to prevent its use by the Continental forces. Both Henry Drinker and Richard Wistar were included in a "sort of Social Register of Philadelphia Quakerdom just before the Revolution." [25]

Actually, if Isaac Jones Wistar is correct in his *Autobiography*, Richard Wistar was an outright British sympathizer whose house in Philadelphia was attacked by a mob after Clinton left town with his army. In this account the Wistar house had been closed and barred; but Richard, who, according to tradition, was of no very submissive temperament, seized a cane and rushed out to remonstrate, probably not in the gentlest tones. He was set upon by the crowd, knocked down, trampled, and beaten and would have been killed on the spot but for a retiring rear guard of the royal troops who charged and dispersed the mob.

This account goes on to say that Richard, for safety, was carried off in a baggage wagon and went with the retreating troops to Rahway, New Jersey, where he died of his injuries on the fourth of August. This, of course, is fiction. Clinton's evacuation took place in 1778 and Richard Wistar was in Philadelphia advertising the glassworks for sale in

1780. And though his death occurred in Rahway, it was in 1781, not 1778.

An interesting letter was written on March 21, 1778, by Colonel Elijah Hand, who shared command of the American militia in Salem and Cumberland counties. Telling Governor Livingston about "the suffering state of our county," he mentioned the fighting that took place in the vicinity of the glassworks and appealed to the governor for more weapons and more men. That letter was written from "Glass Works, Salem County." If Colonel Hand needed men and Wistarberg had been occupied, he could have got some help there and then. But he makes no mention of that, and says not a word about activity at the glassworks.

It has been stated that one reason for closing the Wistar works was the departure of many workers to join the militia. I checked the rolls of the Salem County militia and could find but one name linked with Wistarberg, that of Daniel Wentzell, who was first a lieutenant and then a captain in the Second Battalion. A militia detachment was stationed right by the glassworks itself in 1778, but none of its members is on the list of known glassworkers. Here are the names of the men in that detachment: William Smith, captain; Jacob Hausman, first lieutenant; Samuel King, ensign; Elwell Moore, ensign; Elias Craig, Ephraim Newcomb, John Cain, Lawrence Carney, Cain Dare, Daniel Dare, William McClong, James Demonons, John Hunt, Parsons Lummos, and James Smith.

Official records also show that Jacob Freas had left the glassworks by June, 1777, when he applied for a license to keep a tavern at Alloway. A year later, incidentally, he was tried for high treason, but acquitted. This much, then, may be said: when the British attacked, first at Quinton's Bridge and then at Alloway (Thompson's Bridge), there is no record of the glass blowers rallying to the defense of their own

community. Maybe they were there still trying to make
glass, or just doing nothing. But that is difficult to believe.

Revisiting Wistarberg in the light of the foregoing height-
ens rather than diminishes the aura of excitement which
somehow lingers there even when one realizes that it is a
matter of mind and not of locale. There is a pervading sense
of quiet and almost silent contentment. The occupants of
the little white cottage offer a gracious greeting: lucky souls
who sense only faintly the dormant magic of the site they
inhabit. They point to a spot downhill where the Wistar
factory building is believed to have stood. They tell of other
pilgrims over past years and exhibit some fragments of glass
they have found in the field. All the while the sun beats hard
upon the cottage whiteness and one feels that if ever the
shades of old Wistarberg could be evoked it would be in
that shining light.

Its legacies, however, are not tied to time or place. One
is the tradition of South Jersey glassmaking as an art which
has carried right through into our own day; the other is the
tangible heritage of that Wistar glassware which survives,
however much it may be the subject of dispute. It is unfortunate that Wistar and most of his successors lacked the
foresight to label their products for future identification. Yet
if Isaac Jones Wistar was correct, Caspar Wistar did that on
at least one occasion. Says Isaac Wistar: "I possess a goblet
made there for his own use, and carrying his monogram."
There is also a legend that this goblet was one of six, the
whereabouts of the other five being unknown. If all of
Caspar Wistar's production had been identified, much argument and confusion would have been spared us.

While the McKearins say that not a single piece of glass
can be attributed with certainty to Wistarberg, the word
"certainty" must be weighed carefully. For there are a

number of known pieces whose provenance does not fall very far short of certain. Two such pieces are illustrated in the McKearins' books. One is a "Seal," 3¼ inches long of a slightly iridescent pale green which was excavated on the site of the Wistar works. Another is a bottle dated 1752, with the seal "Wm. Savery." This belonged to the famous Philadelphia cabinetmaker who, according to family tradition, used it for imported Madeira wine. The odds are heavy that this was made as a specialty at Wistarberg. In Mrs. Knittle's *Early American Glass* there is a photograph of an amber bowl on footed standard and another bowl attributed to Wistar. Also there is a bottle dug out of the bottom of Alloway Creek illustrated in Mary H. Northend's *American Glass*.

Salem County has its own share of Wistarware. Its historical society still keeps on display the exhibit shown at the 1939 World's Fair. In addition, quite a few Salem County families possess pieces which they believe to be Wistarware, some of which have been dug up on the site in past years while others have a provenance going back to Wistar's time. One such is the fine flip glass in the collection of Cleayton Wistar, one of Caspar's many descendants. And there are some notable pieces in museums.

This is not the place, however, to attempt a catalogue listing of Wistarware. Enough to round out the picture of the enterprise which brought economic progress to its contemporaries, left a bequest of beauty to succeeding generations, and established traditions of artistry in blown glass which remain unshaken in a machine age.

When Caspar Wistar stood on the oft-trodden and windswept hill—as he did—regarding the glassworks and the town he had built, he was interested in one thing, making money. None would be more astonished than he to discover that he made history too.

TEA TIME
AT GREENWICH

America's romantic past is usually just around the corner in New Jersey. One need not journey far to find it. For example, follow the New Jersey Turnpike and swing eastward from Salem or take "ye Old King's Highway" through Haddonfield and Swedesboro. Either way only forty-five miles from Philadelphia, in a corner of Smugglers' Woods, there is a tucked-away town which will take the visitor back over the years as swiftly as his car has taken him forward over the miles.

Williamsburg, Virginia, has been called "the city that turned back time." On the Cohansey Creek, deep in fertile Cumberland County, is another such community: Greenwich, New Jersey. There are differences between the two, of course. Greenwich is older. Planned in 1676, its layout as a town antedated that of Williamsburg by fifteen years. Greenwich, too, is much as it stood in the eighteenth century; none of it reconstructed, and only some of it restored. The wonder is that it has come through so much time with so little change.

The "Greate Street" in Greenwich, however, resembles

Duke of Gloucester Street in Williamsburg—straight for a mile and almost identical in width, one hundred feet as against ninety-nine in Virginia's lovely showplace. Huge and magnificent trees cast fascinating shadows on the quiet sidewalks. Stately homes as well as a curious little "Pyrate's House" mark pleasant moments for the passer-by; and inside many of these homes are enormous fireplaces, age-mellowed cupboards, and countless treasures handed down from the early days of gracious living.

Because it was not a provincial capital, Greenwich lacks such glories as a governor's palace and a capitol building. Greenwich did have a chance to become the Cumberland County seat, but that was taken away in 1748 and given to Bridgeton, then Cohansey Bridge, in an election which some said was stolen. While Greenwich has a couple of venerable but sign-beplastered grocery stores, its old craft shops are no more. A few modern structures have crept in, and gasoline pumps stand in grotesque contrast only a few feet in front of one of the most interesting of Greenwich's historic doorways. And whereas restored Williamsburg is now a place as busy as it is beautiful, thronged with visitors, students, and townsfolk, Greenwich is much the reverse. A seeker of peace, quiet, and contentment will find them there; and there, too, one can turn back time.

Turn back time? It is remarkably easy in Greenwich. Set one's fancy free at twilight and it will seem not at all unreasonable to encounter shadows of the living past. Candles instead of electric lights in the windows. Quakers on their way to the old stone meetinghouse on a rise overlooking Greate Street; and if the old house is empty now, it was not so then. Townsfolk are headed for the horse-ferry across the river to Fairfield. No ferry now? What matter? There was once. Near the larger country store, which is quite as old as it looks despite advertising signs, the stage has come in from Cooper's Ferry (Camden); and shaken, weary riders greet kinfolk and then hurry off to refreshment and rest. In the darkening dusk one should not even be surprised to encounter burly buccaneers, headed for business aboard a ship waiting in a nearby curve of the Cohansey.

Greenwich calls to mind other communities—and individuals—who seem to have been destined to rise suddenly from obscurity, enjoy a brief flashing moment in the sun, only to glide slowly back into the previous quietude. Always remote from the main streams of American traffic, Greenwich nevertheless enjoyed its share of colonial water-borne commerce; it shared also the general colonial resentment toward taxation without representation, and expressed that resentment forcefully. If the Cohansey region lacked the planters' aristocracy of Virginia, it echoed, despite Quaker beginnings, the Old Dominion's call to freedom and backed up that call by sending a remarkably large proportion of its sons to service in the Revolutionary cause. Proudest boast of all, Greenwich had a "Tea Party." And the sparks from that party also helped in lighting the torches of liberty for a new nation.

It is not, however, quite time for tea. That will come later. For if Greenwich is proud of its Tea Party, it is almost equally proud of its age. When the British decided to move into New Jersey and take over from the Swedes and the Dutch, it was strictly a commercial proposition. The Quakers who proposed to settle along the Delaware were seeking refuge from persecution—the persecution in New England as well as in Old England—but they were basically real estate promoters. They were out to sell homesites and farms. They were out to make money. That was true of John Fenwick, who in 1675 crossed the Atlantic in the ship *Griffin* to settle Salem and plan Greenwich. It was true also of William Penn, who established Philadelphia, owned a large slice of New Jersey, and as one of Fenwick's executors helped supervise the formal town layout of Greenwich.

John Fenwick seemed to have a magnetic attraction for trouble. Despite the reputed wealth of his second wife, he was heavily in debt on the eve of his departure for America. The title to his lands in New Jersey, based on a royal grant from King Charles II, was involved in complex legal difficulties. Fenwick claimed that a number of his Quaker "friends" in London conspired against him, and among them William Penn. These troubles followed Fenwick to Salem; and soon new ones arose.

Determined to set up his own government, with himself as head, he was arrested upon order of Governor Andros of New York, who claimed jurisdiction over New Jersey also. Fenwick stated on December 8, 1676: "My house was beset, my door broken down, and my person seized in the night time by armed men sent to execute a paper order from the Governor of New York, to whom I was sent prisoner in the depth of winter by sea—his order being to bring me dead or alive—where he tried me, himself being judge, keeping me imprisoned for the space of two years and about three months—albeit that it was not, nor could be proved that I had broken any of the king's laws." [1] Even while he was in prison Fenwick was sued by his own son-in-law among others and deserted by his trusted land surveyors.

Surprisingly, Fenwick managed to sell quite a bit of land amid all these troubles; but it is not surprising that his plans for building a twin town to Salem at "Chohanzich," or Greenwich, were long delayed. On June 25, 1676, in Salem, he had drawn up an agreement with certain of his settlers providing:

> There shall be a neck or piece of land sett out for a town att Chohanzich, and divided into two prts, the one

for the chiefe proprietor, the other to be sett out into towne lotts.[2]

In his will Fenwick directed his executors to carry this plan forward, first selling off the lots belonging to him and then giving every freeholder a lot upon condition that he build upon it. A further interesting proviso was "that Martha Smith my Xtian friend to have a Tenn Acre Lott in the Town of New Salem and two Lotts of land at Cohanzey [spelled thus in the will]."

These provisions were carried out by the executors, among whom were Fenwick's favorite son-in-law, Samuel Hedge, and William Penn. Fenwick's relations with Penn have been puzzling to many. In London he had named Penn as one of those who "combined together to cheat me of my whole estate." Yet in his will Fenwick called Penn "my esteemed Friend" when he named him as one of the executors.[3] In any case, the town of Cohanzey—there are seven other spellings—was laid out in 1684 by Penn, Hedge, and the other two executors, Samuel Smith of Smithfield and Richard Tindall, Fenwick's surveyor.

As already noted, the main street, or Greate Street, was made one hundred feet wide and sixteen-acre lots were run out on each side. Two of the latter were "sett off" to Martha Smith, who with her husband and four children had come over with Fenwick on the *Griffin*.

Even before the town itself was laid out there were settlers in the vicinity, on land bought from Fenwick. One of these was Samuel Bacon, who had arrived with his family in 1682. He liked the prospect from the banks of the river, bought four hundred acres, and called his plantation Bacon's Adventure. Today the general area is known by the less felicitous name of Bacon's Neck, but much of the old plantation is still in the family, owned by Bacon's "nine times great-grandson," Joseph Griscom Hancock. Other original settlers at Greenwich were William and Jeremiah Bacon, Joshua Barkstead, Joseph Browne, James Clark, Richard Danger, Obadiah Holmes, John Ketchum, John March, Enoch Moore, John Nichols, Mark Reeve, Thomas Smith, and James Wasse.[4] Most of these families were members of the Society of Friends.

This new "countrie towne" soon began to grow. A group of Welsh Baptists arrived in 1687, and that same year a group of Presbyterians organized a land development society "for purchase of fertile lands along the Cohansey on which their members could settle."[5] In the early 1690's a group of families came from New England. A number of them had lived in Greenwich, Connecticut, and it has been an unending argument whether Cohansey was renamed Greenwich after the town in Connecticut or after Greenwich on the Thames in England. There is a similar controversy over pronunciation. Most present townsfolk call it "Green-wich"; in nearby Bridgeton it is usually "Gren-witch"; most others use the conventional "Gren-itch." Whatever the pronunciation or origin of the name, the important point is that Greenwich was making healthy progress and was to reach the zenith of its commercial and political importance back in those eighteenth-century days.

Greenwich naturally looked to the sea for the source of that progress and the hopes of its future. Five miles or so down the Cohansey lay Delaware Bay and a short spell farther along was the broad Atlantic. By 1702 Greenwich was recognized as one of New Jersey's three official ports of entry, the other two being Perth Amboy and Burlington. Its now-quiet wharf was a bustling place, with vessels coming and going, some from foreign lands and some from other ports in the colonies. There was a customs office, and merchants had their warehouses nearby.

Shipbuilding was another important aspect of the Greenwich maritime tradition, as it is again today. Greenwich-built vessels followed the ocean trade routes as well as those along the coast, and there was fairly frequent shipping service to and from Philadelphia.

Earliest ship of Greenwich construction in my notes and records was a sloop named the *Swansey*. In 1735 it was owned by James Caruthers and Constant Maskell, both of Greenwich, Maskell also being the skipper. The following year Caruthers and Maskell sold the *Swansey* to one John Carnan, of Bohemia, Maryland, and bought themselves a new locally built vessel, the shallop *Greenwich*.

Two ships appear to have been launched in 1737, both sloops. One was the *Flower*, Benoni Dare, master, and one of the owners along with David Sheppard, Job Sheppard, Charles Davis, Philip Dennis, and John Remington. The other sloop was the *Dolphin*, John Martin, master. He also was one of a group of owners which included Abraham Garrison, Seth Bowen, and Dan Bowen. Of the last named more will be heard later, at the Tea Party.

Other vessels operating out of Greenwich during that period were:

1738

Charming Sally Salisbury, sloop; Constant Maskell, master; Elias Cotting, owner.

Charming Lydia, sloop; Silas Parvin, master and owner.

Phenix, schooner; Ebenezer Miller, master; Joseph Reeve and Ebenezer Miller, owners.

1742

Mary, shallop. Nicholas Croeson, master, and also co-owner with Abraham Stevens. Both men were from Bucks County, Pennsylvania.

1744

Good Intent, sloop; Stephen Stephens, master, and co-owner with Thomas Mulford, of Cape May, Richard Farmer, of Philadelphia.

Speedwell, sloop; Philip Stephens, master; Silas Parvin, of Philadelphia, owner.

1745

Mary, sloop; Pyramus Green, master; Peter Bard, of Philadelphia, owner.

Lydia and Betty, sloop; Reuben Worth, master; Nathan Solley and Silas Parvin, of Philadelphia, owners.

1750–51

Hopewell, sloop; Isaac Smith, master and owner.

Cumberland, sloop; Philip Stephens, master; Anthony Nice and Matthew Parvin, owners.

Princess Louisa, sloop; James McCullough, master; William Blair, William Hodge, Andrew Hodge, all of Philadelphia, owners.

Shirley, brig; Oswell Eve, of Philadelphia, master and owner.

1752

Philadelphia, sloop; Patrick Rooney, master; James Russell, of Maryland, owner.

Sarah & Ann, sloop; Thomas Mulford, master and co-owner with Richard Wood.

Susannah, sloop; Jacob Spike, of Philadelphia, master and owner.

1753–54

Three Brothers, sloop; Samuel Waston, master, and owner with Enos Woodruff and William Watson.

Peggy, sloop; Jacob Spike, of Philadelphia, master and owner.

Sally, sloop; Nathan Solley, master, and owner along with
Isaac Atmore, Samuel Buntin, all of Philadelphia.

Ann, sloop; William Carpenter, Newcastle, Delaware,
master and owner.

1774

Sally, sloop; William Martin, master; John Towers, owner.

1775

Polly, sloop; James Wilson, master and owner. [This vessel was sold July 19, 1774, to Edward Brush.]

This listing does not pretend to be complete. It has been
put together and offered here to show, in part, the extent
of the shipping industry on the Cohansey.

The eighteenth century was also a period of expansion in
religious, social, and community development. On the hill
above the wharf stood what today is the oldest dwelling
in Greenwich, the Reeve-Sheppard House. Its original portion was built in 1686, a middle Georgian wing being added
in 1734. The present frame section dates from 1900. It is a
lovely property, commanding a wide view of the Cohansey.
Close by is the Orthodox Friends Meeting House (1771),
and only a few steps up Greate Street, opposite Market
Square, is the site of St. Stephen's—Church of England—
built in 1729. This church is no longer standing, but the
house used for its rectory (1725) remains in sound condition
and is privately occupied. The most influential church of
those times, the Presbyterian, was located far at the other
end of the town, about two miles away. Organized about
1700, the first building was erected soon afterward. The
present church, dating from 1835, is just across the street.
It was at this site that the famous British evangelist, George
Whitefield, preached no less than four times in 1746, on one

occasion to a great outdoor throng estimated at three thousand persons.

Greenwich enjoyed something of a building boom in that period. Only a short walk from Market Square is the stately Gibbon House, with its handsome exterior in red and blue Flemish bond brickwork, and inside, an exciting ten-foot fireplace and arched antique corner cupboards. The house was put up in 1730 by Nicholas Gibbon, whose family is believed to have built the venerable rectory. Beautifully restored, the Gibbon House is now a private residence. From this point on Greate Street one may see at least seven other fine properties dating from the eighteenth century, and as many more from the early nineteenth, all of them over a century and a quarter old. And far out on the still-pastoral northeast fringe of Greenwich stands yet another important home. Its date is indefinite: perhaps in the 1750's, possibly earlier. It was the farm home of Joseph and Hannah Fithian. Their son, Philip, was to become the most famous and colorful figure in Greenwich history.

Several roads led to Greenwich in those days. As early as 1684 a rugged trail from Salem is recorded; and a right and proper road, four rods wide, was laid out in February, 1707, by way of Quinton's Bridge and Jericho, "into the Town Necke" at the head of Greenwich.[6] This road was extended "over Cohansey Creeke" through Fairfield, and is said to be substantially the same road still in use. Two and a half years later another four-rod road was laid out to Greenwich by way of historic Hancock's Bridge; and since 1697 a road passing near Cohansey Bridge (Bridgeton) is recorded from Fairfield to Burlington, by way of Pine Tavern. Thus both Greenwich and Salem had direct, if rough, communications with Burlington and the other Quaker settlements to the northward in the Delaware Valley.

Extension of the 1707 road from Greenwich wharf over Cohansey creek suggests that there must have been some sort of ferry in operation then. No records of it are available. Indeed the first licensed ferry did not come until 1733. The operator was William Watson, and his grant provided that no one could ferry men, animals, or material things for a distance of two miles above and below the wharf at Greenwich. How Greenwich folk managed after Watson died, in 1742, does not appear; no doubt they crossed the stream somehow. But in 1767 another licensed ferry was established, an agreement having been made with John Sheppard to run it. Sheppard was given a 999-year lease on the ferry rights, and he in turn agreed "to maintain the ferry in good order and keep good and sufficient boats" and posted his property as bond for performance of his part of the agreement. After Sheppard's death, his son continued the ferry operation until 1838, by which time better roads had made use of the ferry infrequent. Young Sheppard was released from his father's bond for a cash payment of $300.

Ferry rates over the Cohansey at Greenwich were fixed in 1798 as follows: [7]

Loaded wagon and two horses	40 cents
Light wagon and two horses	25 cents
Loaded cart and one horse	25 cents
Chair and horse	19 cents
Man and horse	6 cents
Footman	3 cents
Sheep and swine, per head	2 cents
Grain, per bushel	1 cent
Cattle per head	6 cents

From this it is clear that a ferry ride then was lively adventure. One's fellow passengers might be mooing, baa-ing, braying, grunting, mumbling, or even snoring. No wonder some of the Greenwich teen-agers rode the ferry for a lark.

For a time Greenwich even had a ferry to Philadelphia. On October 5, 1774, James Parker advertised in the *Pennsylvania Gazette* that he had "established a stage-boat to ply between Bridgeton and Philadelphia, stopping also at Greenwich." The fare was four shillings, sixpence, and a shilling per hundred weight for baggage. Wind and weather permitting, the boat left Stamper's Wharf, Philadelphia, every Thursday, beginning the return trip on Mondays. Other skippers appear to have been catering to passengers too, as Philip Fithian tells of leaving Philadelphia on August 26, 1773, "on a shallop of Mr. Watson" and arriving "safe at Greenwich a quarter before four" on the following day.[8]

Some preferred the boat ride to the stagecoaches, which were built for neither comfort nor speed and traveled roads made up largely of bumps and ruts. Earliest recorded stage route was that of Michael Lee, in 1771. It ran by way of Roadstown and Shiloh to Cooper's Ferry. Three years later a Michael Hoshell was running a second stage line, apparently in competition. Philip Fithian gives an interesting description of a stage journey to Philadelphia, via Cooper's Ferry, on August 3, 1773:

> Rose at two—Eat some Bread & Butter & set away by half after two—Eleven in the Stage, seven of them Women—We had a dark damp & unsociable Ride til Sunrise. Afterwards the company grew pleasant & cheerful; but we were much thronged—at the Pine Tavern by eight, fifteen miles Moderate driving—Breakfasted—at the Death of the Fox [between Swedesboro and Woodbury] by twelve . . . In town by six. [The fare was five shillings, sixpence].[9]

Greenwich, not Bridgeton, was the main shopping center of Cumberland County in the eighteenth century, and the supermarket of its day was the store of Wood & Sheppard, at the corner of Greate Street and the road to Bacon's Adventure. This firm's business was so extensive as "to make it worthwhile to have bonds printed payable to them." A girl visiting Bridgeton traveled to Greenwich to have her "broken watch crystal replaced" (they were out of stock) and bought other goods during her visit.[10] It was, of course, a general store, which carried everything from food to fertilizer. Later the firm name was changed to Wood & Bacon, and some of their old account books survive.

In one volume of the Wood & Bacon books, dated 1787, the following are some of the customers listed: Joseph Garrison, David Pearson, Thomas Williams, Levi Bond, Peter Andrews, Lewis Mulford, David Ewing, Abner Hall, Richard Wood, Andrew Miller, Charles Allen, John Potts, Samuel Reeve, Enoch Ayars, Silas Bradford, Edward Dennis, and David Fithian. One sale, to Jonathan Bowen on January 17, 1788, consisted of "14 small buttons @ 3d, three large buttons @ 6d, one pr. hose @ eight shillings, 2 skeins of silk and 2 of mohair, @ 2sh." [11] Jonathan obviously was shopping for his wife.

During the early 1800's Wood & Bacon did a considerable business with Cumberland Furnace. Listed for 1816 are large sales of pork, oats, and salt. That same year Ephraim Mulford traveled all the way from Alloway Creek to buy a "grindstone and chizzel," for 14 shillings, sixpence. William Blackman, "Schoolmaster," on the same day purchased six yards of cloth, one and a half yards of baize, two dozen buttons, and "morhair and buttons for rigge." William B. Ewing bought a stove for eighteen dollars. Apparently use of the ferry also could be charged on the firm's books; several such items are listed, including two trips by Dr. Bond—Dr. Levi Bond, an eccentric physician who lived to be ninety-three. Later the store was run by Richard Wood, whose family in 1795 had built the fine "Wood Mansion" close by. Today it is the home of the Cumberland County Historical Society.

Directly across Greate Street from the ancient store is the old stone tavern, now handsomely remodeled as a private dwelling. There were at least three early taverns in Greenwich: one down near the wharf, another at the Ewing-Bacon House at the head of Greenwich (a location once called Othello), and the third this two-and-a-half-story fieldstone building in the center of town. It was built about 1730 and was long a combination of public building, community center, courthouse, and place of refreshment. For twenty years traveling sessions of the Salem County courts sat there, as the distance to Salem was considered inconvenient to litigants; and for eleven months after Cumberland County was created in 1748, by partitioning Salem, it housed the tribunals of the new county. The old tavern was a starting place for the stagecoaches, a meeting place for the townsfolk, and ironically was the polling place for the election that crushed Greenwich's expectations of becoming the seat of new Cumberland County.

Just what happened in that election is not clear to this day, as no records have been located. Bridgeton, then Cohansey Bridge, was a place of only a dozen or so houses. It was not considered a town, certainly not a likely place for a courthouse. Yet a majority of the votes cast were for making Bridgeton the county seat and for erecting there the new courthouse, jail, and other public buildings. Greenwich folk charged the election had been stolen; a mob wrecked the interior of the stone tavern in a fit of frenzy; the freeholders delayed plans for building the courthouse; and some said that big landholders in the Bridgeton area were back of it all. Finally, the excitement simmered down, the courts moved to Bridgeton, and after two years construction of the county buildings was begun.

Most important of these buildings was the jail. There was a jail at Greenwich, probably near Market Square, but a strange affair it must have been. Believed to have been constructed of logs, it was just about as mantight as some modern prisons. Escapes seem to have been easy and frequent. Sheriff and jailkeeper was Ananias Sayre, a leisurely moving chap. On October 5, 1752, he reported that three men imprisoned for debt—Joseph Burgin, William Harris, and Nathan Kook—had escaped and blandly suggested that the county should pay off their creditors. However, Sheriff Sayre was instructed to pursue the missing men, an idea which seems not to have occurred to him. Eventually one of the trio, Burgin, was recaptured, but for the others the freeholders paid to the tune of 10 pounds, 8 shillings, 2 pence.[12] Shortly afterward the freeholders ordered construction in Bridgeton of a pair of stocks, a pillory, and a new jail. This one was of brick. It was finished in 1754, after which the older prison was sold and later torn down. Greenwich, however, did put up a pair of stocks of its own in 1767.

Now perhaps it is time for tea. And what place more appropriate than the Pyrate's House! One should not be surprised to find a Pyrate's House in Greenwich; nor should one scoff at the tradition that a pirate once lived there, in its little north wing built in 1734. The records show that pirates swarmed Delaware Bay in the early seventeen-hundreds, once virtually blockading it; and Greenwich, such a short run up the Cohansey, would have attracted them as a natural hideaway.

Should you enjoy a ghost story over the teacups, the Pyrate's House offers that too. It seems that a buccaneer named John—not even legend supplies his last name—double-crossed some of his plundering shipmates. Whereupon they came ashore, tracked him to the Pyrate's House, found him hiding in the attic, and hanged him there on chains to die. John's ghost, 'tis said, long haunted the place, and on particularly black nights passers-by used to claim they heard a weird clanking of those fatal chains.

The big Greenwich Tea Party, however, began not with the pirates nor their legalized successors, the privateers, but with the men of Smugglers' Woods. Tea smugglers were among the shock troops in the colonial cold war waged against the 1767 Townshend Acts, which put a heavy tax on tea among other commodities. Americans had long been great tea drinkers, especially the women. It was estimated that at least a million of them drank tea twice daily. Per Kalm, the Swedish traveler, found "hardly a farmer's wife or a poor woman who does not drink tea in the morning." [13] Philadelphia women, it was said, were "such slaves to it that they would rather go without their dinners than without a dish of tea." Townshend, crafty statesman that he was, is said to have believed that, however much the men of America might resent his tax, the women would insist on drinking tea and thus provide an entering wedge by which the colonies could be driven to accept taxation without representation.

Townshend's great expectations soon went aglimmering —thanks to the smugglers. British tea imports in the Delaware Valley area dwindled rapidly, and by 1769 almost no British tea was coming in. Yet tea was plentiful. Pennsylvania normally consumed two thousand chests a year, and there was no shortage.[14] Everybody was drinking smuggled Dutch tea, and there are reasons to suspect that not a little of it was finding its way to Jersey as well as Pennsylvania teacups by way of the Cohansey Creek and Greenwich.

By 1773 the British East India Company, whose tea was rotting in warehouses instead of going into colonial teapots, was in serious financial trouble. Short of cash, the company could not pay its bills; its stock had tumbled from 280 to 160; and the British government stood to lose not only the 400,-000 pounds a year it had been receiving from the company but the whole British foothold in India as well.[15]

Lord North was now prime minister, and it was to him that the East India Company's directors turned. All they asked was that the threepence tax on tea be repealed. Then, they argued, the American market would reopen, the tea smugglers would be put out of business, the stored tea could be sold, and the company would be solvent again. But North had what seemed to him a better idea. He proposed, first, to eliminate the British commission houses and permit the East India Company to sell tea directly to the colonies, without paying any middlemen and, second, to ask Parliament to forgo the 400,000 pounds a year the government had been receiving from the company. Thus, argued North, the tea could be made cheap enough to undersell the Dutch and the smugglers, and the threepenny tax could be retained.

North also shared the belief that American women would not give up tea drinking; and he reasoned that with cheaper tea the colonists would again quietly swallow the tax along with their brew. North scoffed at the idea that the Americans prized principle more than price. Suggestions that they might refuse to buy the cheap tea because it was taxed, he brushed aside as ridiculous. In any case, he stood by the royal notion that the Americans must be put in their place —Benjamin Franklin had already discovered that many anti-American schemes came from George III himself. Parliament, too, felt that principle was involved. Had not Lord Clare, in the House of Commons, asserted that one pepper corn in acknowledgment of Britain's right to tax America was of greater importance than millions of pounds without it!

So, on May 10, 1773, Lord North's Tea Act was passed by Parliament, with the "thruppenny" tax kept in force. And at first it seemed that the scheme might work. The East India Company found itself able to sell its tea more cheaply in America than in the British Isles themselves. Instead of twenty shillings a pound the price was cut to ten. Even the smugglers could be undersold. Governor Hutchinson of Massachusetts declared that the Tea Act caused no alarm, and there were reports that many Americans rejoiced in the prospect of slaking their thirst by drinking up, at half price, the tea which had filled to bursting the warehouses of the East India Company. Soon that surplus tea was being stowed aboard vessels headed westward. Consigned to Boston were 298 chests valued at 10,994 pounds; to Philadelphia and New York, 698 chests; to Charleston, South Carolina, 257.[16] Everything was set for Americans to drink the East India Company back to prosperity.

Lord North, however, had underestimated two groups in colonial America: the smugglers and the housewives. The smugglers, hardest hit by the Tea Act, started the ball rolling in a campaign against that legislation.[17] Rumors spread rapidly that the long-stored tea was rotten; physicians declared that the tea might induce "tremors and spasmodic affections"; merchants became alarmed at the prospect of the East India Company's monopolizing the market not only for tea but for spices, drugs, silks, and other commodities. One of the company's immediate goals was said to be suppression of the china factory in Philadelphia, which competed with the china they had for sale.[18]

Significantly, too, the smugglers were in the vanguard when the Sons of Liberty took up the torch and drove home to the colonists the fact that the tax on tea was actually a device to destroy their liberty. Then followed a boycott which was remarkable in its effectiveness, and a still more remarkable example of public self-discipline. Overnight tea drinking had become the thing not to do. Even the smugglers agreed not to smuggle tea.

The women? Lord North had counted heavily upon them, and even heavier was to be the weight of his disappointment. Tea was banned from the dining rooms of the first families of Virginia to the humblest kitchens of Yankee farmers. Just as "Daughters of Liberty" had done much to make the earlier nonimportation agreement a success, so they now turned to other brews, especially coffee, which has been the number one American beverage ever since. Housewives who did serve tea were rebuked and ostracized. Committees of women were set up to punish violators of the boycott, male as well as female.[19] A tea drinker became the equivalent of a traitor; and those Britons who had boasted that the Sons of Liberty would be told a thing or two by their tea-drinking wives were now astonished to find the feminine solidarity against tea as strong as the masculine.

Meanwhile tea ships were headed for America with more of the East India Company's surplus. One, bound for Philadelphia, turned back when the skipper, Captain Ayres, learned that a reception committee was waiting to "heave him keel cut, and see that his bottom be well fired, scrubbed . . . [and] his upper works too [be given] an overhauling."[20] In both Philadelphia and New York merchants held meetings to demand that the East India Company's agents refuse to handle the tea, and when those agents, in various ports, appealed to the royal governors for help, most of the governors played safe and refused to act.

One exception was Governor Hutchinson of Massachusetts, two of whose sons were agents of the East India firm. So, when three tea ships—*Dartmouth, Eleanor,* and *Beaver*

—arrived in Boston harbor, Hutchinson personally undertook to protect them and announced that the tea tax would be collected by troops if necessary. The governor scorned proposals that he order the tea ships to turn back; instead they lay at anchor directly under the guns of two British warships. Soon not only Boston but much of Massachusetts was aroused.

On the night of December 16, 1773, seven thousand people congregated in a drizzling rain. They watched as the three tea ships, which had moved to the inner harbor, prepared to unload. Then a war whoop was heard, and some hundred fifty men, thinly disguised as Indians, made sudden appearance, headed for the wharf, boarded the vessels, broke open the chests of tea, and hurled them overboard. Not only did British sailors lend a hand in the tea dumping, but all this took place within range of the British men-of-war. It was all done quietly. Not a soul was hurt; no other cargo was touched. Such was Boston's Tea Party.

That same month New York's Governor Tryon had the tea ship *Nancy* escorted to the wharf by a British warship, and attempted to land the cargo despite a mass meeting of two thousand citizens. A Tea Party was averted only when the landing effort was abandoned. In March, 1774, however, "New York 'Mohawks' fell upon tea consigned to merchants in the city—and brewed it with salt water." [21] Again in the same month more Boston "Indians" heaved a dozen chests of tea overboard; and on October 18, 1774, at Annapolis, Maryland, a huge crowd, including a delegation from Baltimore, forced Anthony Stewart of that city to set fire to his own vessel, the *Peggy Stewart*, which had come from London with seventeen chests of tea. Last Tea Party of all was at Greenwich, on the night of December 22, 1774. After that it was war.

Greenwich illustrates in microcosm the growth, from early roots, of American independence of mind and attachment to political liberty. As early as 1714 Greenwich citizens were resisting payment of what they considered an unjust tax for the support of crown officials. A petition signed by thirty-four male taxpayers read:

Wee whose Names are under Written do Utterly Denie to pay or Suffer to be taken by Distress or any other ways any money Goods or any other thing by Francis Pagit our so called Constable Because wee Doubt of his Being a Lawful Constable & more especially Because wee have been Illegally Assessed.[22]

In 1715 some thirty-one of these thirty-four signers "all of Cohansey, yeomen" were indicted for resisting the constable and refusing to pay the taxes. Governor Hunter wrote to the Lords of Trade in London:

They are all from New England who have signed it, but whether they be a true sample of the body of the people there, or only a sett of unquiet or reckless men, who could be easy nowhere, and so left that Province for this, I cannot determine.

So unpopular was this tax in Greenwich that when the court named Jonathan Holmes as town constable he refused to take the job and proved so defiant that he was committed to the custody of the sheriff.

Who sparked the idea for a Tea Party in Greenwich? Many believe it was Philip Vickers Fithian, parson extraordinary, circuit rider, chronicler of social customs in Virginia, lover by correspondence, chaplain and dedicated patriot, whose story will be told in the next chapter. Fithian had passed through Annapolis on his way home from Virginia only a few days after the tea burning there, and his

Journals show that he was much impressed. "The people," he wrote, "seem indeed to be full of patriotic fire."

Less than a month after Fithian's homecoming a British brig, the *Greyhound,* Captain Allen, tied up at Greenwich wharf. The *Greyhound* was loaded with tea. Her intended destination had been Philadelphia, but the *Polly* and other tea ships had been turned away there and Captain Allen apparently had been warned by his Delaware Bay pilot that a warm reception might be awaiting him in the Quaker City.

However, commercial skippers as well as smugglers were familiar with the snug haven offered by Cohansey Creek, plus the fact that goods landed there could find their way to Philadelphia by land if not by water. Moreover, there was a Tory in the town ready and waiting to help unload and hide the tea until it could be sold. The Tory was Dan Bowen, a former skipper himself, who lived by Market Square a short way from the wharf. Quietly on the night of December 12 the chests of tea were taken from the *Greyhound* and placed in the cellar of Bowen's place (no longer standing). Supposedly it was all very secret.

Greenwich had no newspaper in 1774, but there never has been need for one to spread local news in small villages and towns. The secret of the tea was soon public property. Fithian wrote on December 18:

> Early last week a Quantity of Tea said to be shipped at Rotterdam was brought & privately stored at Dan Bowens in Greenwich—a pro Tempore Committee was chosen to secure it till the County Committee be duly elected.

This pro tempore committee had been organized in response to the nonimportation pledge signed by the First Continental Congress when it met in Philadelphia the pre-

ceding September. The boycott covered not only tea but
all British merchandise. At the same time a mass meeting
of Cumberland County citizens was summoned, and held
at Bridgeton on December 22, 1774. This meeting chose a
committee of thirty-five to assume charge of the tea, "have
it privately stored, and meet tomorrow to take care of the
same." As Fithian put it:

> The County met at Cohansie Bridge & Chose a com-
> mittee & it was recommended to them to examine into &
> take proper care of the aforesaid Goods.

That very evening a group of young Whigs gathered at
the home of Richard Howell, near Shiloh, about four miles
from Greenwich.[23] Shortly afterward they rode down the
road to Fithian's home, and when they left there they were
disguised, or at least dressed, as Indians.

Before long there were curious doings in Greenwich's
Market Square. A torch-lit file of Indians could be seen
emerging from Dan Bowen's cellar and bearing tea chests
across the street to the green. Soon the whole consignment
of the East India Company was going up in flames, and
reputedly the Indians—no one knows just how many—executed a war dance while the big bonfire lighted up Greate
Street. When the flames died away, leaving only ashes of
tea, the redskins departed as quietly as they had come.

One amusing sidelight on this affair concerns a tea burner
named Henry Stacks. A great lover of tea, he could not bear
to see quite all of it wasted; so he quietly stuffed into his
pockets and into his breeches all the tea they would hold.
Soon he was literally bursting with tea, so much so that he
was caught by his comrades, relieved of the tea, and for
years thereafter known in Greenwich as "Tea Stacks."
Oddly enough a similar incident had occurred at the Boston
Tea Party. One Captain O'Connor "filled his pockets and

also the lining of his coat," according to the recollections of George Hewes, and "we were ordered to take him into custody . . . but he made his escape . . . but had, however, to run a gauntlet through the crowd upon the wharf, each one as he passed, giving him a kick or a stroke." [24]

Destruction of the tea in Greenwich brought quick repercussions. When the county-wide committee met the next day it piously resolved: "first, that we entirely disapprove of the destroying of the tea, it being entirely contrary to our resolves; second, that we will not conceal nor protect from justice any of the perpetrators of the above act."

Quite a few tongues must have been in quite a few cheeks when the vote was taken on that resolution. There on the committee sat at least two of the tea burners: Silas Newcomb and Joel Fithian. Thomas Ewing voted to deplore, but his brother James was one of the burners. Ephraim Seeley also voted for the resolution although he must have known that his sons, Henry and Josiah, were members of the party. The same was true of Daniel Elmer, whose boys, Ebenezer and Timothy, were in the Indian march. As for Philip Fithian, his *Journals* reek with innocence:

> Last night the Tea was, by a number of persons in disguise, taken out of the House & consumed with fire. Violent & different are the words about this uncommon Manoeuvre, among the Inhabitants—Some rave, some curse & condemn, some try to reason; many are glad the tea is destroyed, but almost all disapprove the manner of the destruction.

Nevertheless, there is much evidence to suggest that Fithian was one of the tea burners, if not the instigator of the affair. The Indian costumes are stated to have been put on at his house; his sympathies were no secret; he had talked with the folk at Annapolis; his closest friend, Andrew Hunter, Jr., was present, and so was his cousin Joel; and as for the *Journals* it is understandable that Fithian would not record on paper his role in the Tea Party lest some prying eye should see. Finally, on the fine monument that has been erected on Market Square in memory of the tea burners, Fithian's name appears among the twenty-three carved in granite.

The other burners listed are: Ebenezer Elmer, Timothy Elmer, James Ewing, Thomas Ewing, Joel Fithian, Lewis Howell, Richard Howell, James Booth Hunt, John Hunt, Andrew Hunter, Jr., Joel Miller, Alexander Moore, Jr., Silas Newcomb, Ephraim Newcomb, Clarence Parvin, David Pierson, Stephen Pierson, Henry Seeley, Josiah Seeley, Abraham Sheppard, Henry Stacks, and Silas Whitecar.

Two legal efforts were launched to punish the tea burners. One was a suit brought by the East India Company's Philadelphia agents, John Duffield and Stacy Hepburn, against alleged members of the group: Richard Howell, Moore, the two Newcomb boys, Henry Seeley, and Abraham Sheppard. Twelve hundred pounds' damages were demanded. But a public subscription raised funds for the defense, eminent counsel were engaged, and trial was stalled off until the Revolution ended the royal judicial authority in Cumberland County. The other legal move was a grand jury investigation. This was ordered by Chief Justice Frederick Smyth. Ebenezer Elmer, one of the tea burners, recorded in his diary:

Judge Smith gave very Large Charge to the Grand Jury Concerning the times, & the burning of the tea the fall before. But the Jury Came in without doing anything, & Court broke up.

Judge Smyth sent a jury out a second time, but Sheriff Jonathan Elmer, brother of Ebenezer, had packed this jury with patriots. In fact, the foreman was Daniel Elmer, another of Ebenezer's brothers. So again no action was taken. After Sheriff Elmer's term expired in June, 1775, Governor Franklin appointed David Bowen, supposedly a Tory, as his successor, and now Elmer noted: " 'Twas expected, as Sheriff Bowen had got a Jury of Tories, we should be indicted for Burning Tea." [25]

But he was wrong. This jury, too, refused to find any indictments, and there the matter ended. Legally, that is.

For the tea burners themselves much more was to come. Most of them were to enlist in the Continental Army; a number were to be officers, and two to be chaplains. Four were to become doctors, three to be members of the New Jersey legislature, and one—Richard Howell—a governor of the state. Four were to give their lives in the fight for freedom.

What John Adams said of the Tea Party at Boston is equally appropriate to the Tea Party at Greenwich:

> This destruction of the tea is so bold, so daring, so firm, intrepid and inflexible . . . it must have so important consequences, and so lasting, that I cannot but consider it as an epocha in history.

The important consequences followed in swift succession: first, British punishment through closing the port of Boston in an effort to starve the city into submission, and other measures called the Intolerable Acts by patriots, and the Coercive Acts in England. Then the colonists' retaliation— in the Continental Congress, in the Declaration of Independence, in the Revolution, and in establishment of a free United States of America.

"COHANSIE":
A LOVE STORY

"Of War you have enough in the News; my letters I mean to fill with *Love*." So wrote the brilliant, complex, and volatile Philip Vickers Fithian to his beloved *Laura*, wife of less than a year. The letter was sent from the American camp on Long Island. The date was August 18, 1776, eve of the shattering British victory over the patriot forces with whom Fithian was serving as chaplain. He was to write of love but a few weeks more.

The romance of Philip Fithian and Elizabeth—*Laura*—Beatty is one of the most touching, strange, and beautiful in the annals of colonial America. Surprisingly few people have ever heard of it.

Fithian has gathered posthumous fame as author of two published *Journals* [1] in which his gifts for meticulous observation and human character analysis stamp him as one of the keenest minds of his day. Had he turned to politics instead of religion, his name probably would be found in the history books alongside those of his Princeton classmates, among whom were James Madison, Aaron Burr, and Light-Horse Harry Lee. Instead, he chose to study for the Presbyterian ministry, in which he was to be licensed but never ordained. And it was not his religious missions but his vivid pictures of plantation life in colonial Virginia, so valuable in the Williamsburg restoration, his travels through Smugglers' Woods and the New Jersey Pine Barrens; his accounts of burgeoning development in western Pennsylvania and Virginia, and his comments from camp on the dark beginning days of the Revolution—these were to make their mark on American history a full century and a quarter after his death.

Because of its piquant tenderness and unusual character the love story of Philip Fithian and his *Laura* needs to be told. It is unusual first in the fact that he wooed her for five years, mostly from a distance; and after he married her he left her for nearly seven of the next eleven months. Then he died at camp just seventeen days before their first wedding anniversary, *Laura* apparently having refused to come to his bedside.

Their romance is unusual, too, because the entire story, with negligible exceptions, is seen through Fithian's eyes and told by Fithian's pen, partly through extracts from his *Journals,* partly from his "letters to *Laura*." While Fithian was a prolific writer, we have in contrast nothing at all from *Laura*. No diary. No letters. Other than the picture Fithian gives of her there is little even to suggest what she was like save a few laudatory remarks from some of her other admirers.

Philip Vickers Fithian was born in southwestern New Jersey, at Greenwich—which he always called Cohansie *—on December 29, 1747. His parents were Joseph and Hannah

---

* "Cohansie" is usually spelled Cohansey, but Fithian's spelling is used in this chapter. Originally "Cohansie," for an Indian chief, Chohanzick, embraced a wide area of Cumberland County, but Fithian usually used it as a synonym for the town of Greenwich.

(Vickers) Fithian, whose forebears had come to the New World from England in 1640.[2] Joseph Fithian was a farmer and young Philip grew up accustomed, but scarcely reconciled, to performing the typical chores of a farmer's eldest son. From his middle teens Philip kept a diary, which indicates that he was not cut out to follow his father's furrows. Most of the earlier entries reflect monotony; some show unconcealed discontent. On July 4, 1767, for example, he wrote: "I am wearied with reaping."

Because religion was an uppermost factor in the Fithian home, Philip's chance for more than a minimum education came from two Presbyterian clergymen. One was the Rev. Andrew Hunter, of the historic church at Greenwich, whose nephew—adopted as his son—became Philip's classmate and closest friend. The other was the Rev. Enoch Green, who conducted a small school in connection with his church at Deerfield, roughly twelve miles to the north of Greenwich.

Of the Rev. Mr. Hunter, Philip later recorded that "to his generous Solicitations of my Father, who was not easy to be persuaded of how much importance Learning is, I am wholly indebted for my education." The persuasion became effective on August 11, 1767, since Philip noted that "this morning I had the gracious and agreeable news from my Father that next week I am to go to school to Mr. Green." Six days later his instruction in Latin commenced at the Deerfield parsonage.

At that same parsonage the Fithian romance began. On June 7, 1770, the Rev. Mr. Green married Mary Beatty, oldest daughter of the Rev. Charles Clinton Beatty, who had succeeded the Rev. William Tennent at the Log College at Neshaminy, Pennsylvania. This was the first Presbyterian school in America and forerunner of Princeton University. Mrs. Beatty had died two years earlier, leaving a family of six sons and four daughters. Four of the sons were to play active roles in the Revolution: Erkuries, John, Charles, and Reading. When the Rev. Enoch Green took his bride to the parsonage at Deerfield, her next youngest sister, Elizabeth—to be known as Laura, and also as Betsey and Eliza—went along for a visit. Among the welcomers when the newlyweds arrived was Philip Fithian; and when he saw *Laura* it was love at first sight. On his part, that is. He was then twenty-three and she eighteen. A few weeks later the young Miss Beatty must have been overwhelmed when she received the first of his many "letters to *Laura*." Dated July 15, 1770, it read in part:

> You can scarcely conceive, unless you have in Some Case had the same Feeling, how melancholy, Spiritless and forsaken you left Several when you left Deerfield. A Sullen & Disagreeable Silence succeeded the Conversation which your presence excited. . . .
>
> For my part I cannot walk, nor read, nor talk nor ride, nor sleep . . . I stand foremost in this gloomy Row of the disappointed, for I saw you last of them all, & the transient golden Minutes only fully persuaded me how much real Happiness may be had in your Society.[3]

Having sent off this impassioned missive, Philip waited for a reply. And he kept on waiting! Not until nearly two years later was their acquaintanceship resumed.

Meanwhile, his heart was scarcely bleeding. By November he was addressing a long poem to a "young lady of Cohansie who calls herself Rowena." And one of its warmer lines declared firmly: "You must feel the force of Sovereign Love."

If Fithian's education was belated—he was to enter Princeton at twenty-three—so was his emotional maturity. His developing awareness of the world outside Cohansie and his quick grasp of the political issues which were leading to the Revolution contrast sharply with the sophomoric quality of his earlier love letters. It was the fashion then to write florid prose, usually behind a coy nom de plume. It was the fashion, too, to use extravagant words. As for Philip's poems, most of them were simply long-winded. They may well have bored *Laura*—later he asked her to burn many of them—and they, in turn, contrast with the conciseness of observation in his *Journals* and his increasing care and economy with words.

In the fall of 1770 Fithian went to Princeton, where he found "upwards of 100, including the grammar [preparatory] scholars." Unfortunately he kept no journal during his Princeton days. There are, however, letters, his commencement address, and other papers which indicate that he was a good and serious student. While at Princeton he also found time to dash off letters to girls other than *Laura*. One was "Sally T——, of Penington," to whom he expressed his wish to "enlarge an acquaintance with a young lady whose person and character merit particular esteem." There were three Nancys on his list: Nancy Lawrence, Nancy Riddel, and Nancy Cunningham. There were also several Betseys in his book, a fact which has led some to the incorrect conclusion that he had known Elizabeth Beatty from childhood. Fithian continued writing dreadful poetry at college, sending some of it to "Belinda" and some to "Amanda," the former believed to have been Miss Polly Bullock of Philadelphia.

In June, 1772, Philip met one of *Laura*'s brothers, probably John, in Princeton. This led to his second "letter to *Laura*," in which he observed that "my neglecting to write arose entirely from a fearful apprehension that my correspondence & Myself were both burdensome." He added: "Since you allow me a free Correspondence I shall, in future, write when it is convenient."

It was convenient only a few weeks later. His third letter
was dated Nassau Hall, July 18:

> Without hearing from you I write again & shall be still
> troubling you . . . with Letters 'til you positively punish
> me by denying me the Liberty . . .
> In my illusive Fancy, I lead you by the Hand in a cool
> bright Evening & once more, in that lovely Garden . . .
> hold Conversation in Raptures with you.[4]

He received no reply to that letter either.

Philip graduated in the Class of 1772 [commencement
was in the autumn then] and returned to Cohansie to study
Hebrew and take other instruction preparatory to entering
the ministry. Meanwhile *Laura,* after her father's death in
September of 1772, began to make extended visits to her
sister Mary in Deerfield and her eldest brother, John, at
Princeton. Dr. John Beatty had married a Princeton girl
and had commenced medical practice there.

Laura's visits to Deerfield were Philip's golden opportunities, and he made the most of them. If she would not answer
his letters, she certainly appears to have welcomed his presence. He virtually haunted the Green parsonage. Even
when he was seeing her every other day or so he was still
writing her letters, increasingly impassioned letters. One
was a proposal of marriage. It was dated December 1, 1772:

> You are the Person—The Amiable Object on which,
> after a perfect Acquaintance, I have so far placed my
> esteem, that I cannot easily avoid making proposals to
> you for a nearer Alliance.
> Can you hear me when I tell you this?
> Can you listen to my ardent Wish, & when it seems to
> be in your Power, allow me the Expectation of arriving
> at my Standard of Contentment & Felicity here below?[5]

Philip set a deadline at three the following afternoon "to wait on you with these sentiments—You have this intermediate time to consult with your own Heart." That the answer was no, or at least indefinite, is indicated by the fact that he was proposing to her again on December 15, in a pallid sort of poem. Soon afterward they appear to have reached some understanding or, as he called it, "intimacy." For the moment all seemed serene if not utterly blissful.

When *Laura* visited Princeton, however, the picture changed somewhat, or appeared to. Her indefinable loveliness seemed to sweep the little town like a fresh and balmy breeze. Others began casting sheep's eyes in her direction. This is clear from letters sent to Fithian by some of his Princeton friends. Oliver Reese wrote on December 26, 1772:

> I had almost concluded that your charming *Laura* (who I understand has removed to our parts) had made you forget your friends at prince-ton but your friendly letter has removed my suspicions . . . methinks I could now give you a lecture that would raise your drooping spirits and make you think your *Laura* was your own.[6]

This was the same effervescent Oliver Reese who reported, amusingly, a few months later: "I read much. I study divinity one hour and think of the ladies the next, so that in a short time I expect to be a most eminent Divine."

Andrew Hunter, Philip's closest friend, wrote from Nassau Hall in June of 1773 that "we have had the pleasure of Laura's company here for some weeks past. I hope you will not envy us considering that continual pleasure is too much for such mortals to bear." And in October another friend, William R. Smith, wrote him about the 1773 commencement, and added:

I saw Dr. Beaty and Betsy—I gave your love to them—
and indeed to tell the truth I could not help leaving my
own heart, and love, and all with Betsy—she is really a
sweet soul. I wish ten million and she were mine.[7]

Philip's parents had both died, within the week of February 2, 1772, while he was still at Princeton. Thus after he
completed his studies in Hebrew and Divinity he felt no
family ties strong enough to prevent him from considering
an offer from "Councilor" Robert Carter, of Nomini Hall,
Virginia, to serve as tutor for his five daughters and three
sons. The terms were "thirty-five pounds Sterling, which is
about sixty pounds currency; provide all accomodations;
the undisturbed use of a room; the use of his [Carter's] own
Library; provender for a Horse; and a Servant to wait." [8]
It was a generous offer, difficult to refuse, and after
traveling to Princeton to talk with President Witherspoon,
who had recommended him for the post, Philip accepted.
Soon, however, he began blowing hot and cold. Certain of
his relatives had protested that the Virginians were profane
and wicked (he was to note a few months later that "I am
under no more nor stronger temptations to any kind of
vice, perhaps not so great as at Cohansie"). Philip began to
fret about travel, then about possible illness, and finally
about Laura's popularity in Princeton. But after he received
a blunt letter from Andrew Hunter to the effect that "Dr.
Witherspoon insists on me going to Virginia," he bought a
horse from his uncle, had it shod, packed his clothes, paid a
farewell call on the Rev. Mr. Hunter, and wrote in his
Journals: "My Heart misgives . . . but I must away."
Philip set out on October 20, 1773, leaving Greenwich
at six in the morning and arriving at Nomini Hall, West-
moreland County, about 2:00 P.M. on the 28th. He had
traveled about 260 miles but noted on arrival that "both

Myself and my Horse seem neither tired nor Dispirited."
The complete novelty of life on the plantation of one of the
very first families in Virginia quickly occupied Fithian's
attention when he was not busily occupied in getting his
little school organized. Only after six weeks, judging by
the *Journals,* did he look homeward and begin to worry
about *Laura;* but thereafter the references to her are frequent. On December 4, 1773, he noted: "At Supper I had
the pleasure to toast in my turn Miss Corbin—But I meant
the absent *Laura!*" [9] On December 15 he wrote that "I
cannot help reflecting on my situation last winter, which
was near the lovely *Laura* for whom I cannot have but the
truest, and the warmest Esteem!" Three days later: "In
May next . . . I propose by permission of Providence to
go Home, where I hope to see the good and benevolent
Laura." [10]

Fithian was relatively happy at Nomini Hall, as happy
as his restless mind and nostalgic emotions would permit.
On January 2, 1774, he indulged in some of his increasingly
frequent mind searchings to observe: "I have the opportunity of living with Credit perfectly retired—in a well
regulated family—with a man of Sense."

There was mutual respect between Fithian and the
Carters. He shared their genuine love of music for which
Carter had "a good ear . . . and vastly delicate taste."
There were at Nomini Hall a harpsichord, a pianoforte, a
harmonica (B. Franklin's musical glasses made into an in-
strument), a "guittar," German flutes, and "at Williamsburg . . . a good Organ." Fithian himself played the flute
in their chamber ensemble. He also shared the Carters' attachment to books, and their library, which the indefati-
gable tutor counted and listed, totaled more than fifteen
hundred volumes.

Philip indeed seemed to find time to count, measure, or

describe nearly everything in sight: the number of windows in each wall, the number of panes of glass in each window, the sizes of the outbuildings as well as the mansion, the details of the ladies' stays, and the food consumption of the family, which "one year with another" ran to "27000 pounds of pork; & twenty Beeves . . . 550 Bushels of Wheat, besides corn—4 Hogsheads of Rum and 150 Gallons of Brandy."

More and more did Fithian have to struggle with his Calvinistic upbringing, especially when he was invited to dance. He found pleasure "in the accuracy of a minuet," and while he refused all invitations to join the dancers he expressed the wish "that it had been part of my education to learn what I think is . . . innocent and ornamental."

All this proved no substitute for *Laura.* "I wrote today a letter to *Laura,* I wish it *speed* and *success,*" he said on January 9, 1774. Ten days later he was carving her "much admired Name, upon a smooth beautiful Beech-Tree." A few weeks later he had a dream—"but oh! I dreamed she was treacherous!" And he took his dream seriously enough to record that "if it be true, I must suppress the Greatness of my Disappointment . . . perhaps *Laura* may think that Lovers vows are vain and false." Three days later he was still affected by the dream. "In spite of all my strongest opposing efforts, my thoughts dwell on that Vixen *Laura* . . . like hidden fire they introduce themselves, & seize, & overcome me when I am perhaps pursuing some amuseing or useful Study; or giving precepts & Directions to my little fair Seminary." [11]

It cannot be said that the Virginians were at all lax in their efforts to divert Fithian's mind from *Laura.* They paraded a bevy of belles before him with almost embarrassingly obvious purpose; and while Philip inspected the ladies carefully, and recorded the details of their nature, physique, deportment, and attire, only twice did he evince really active curiosity concerning a candidate.

Laura's closest Virginia rival—and not very close at that— was Miss Sally Panton, an English governess with the Turburville family. Philip noted that "the common voice seems to be against me as to her being Handsome—but her huge *Stays,* low *Head dress;* enormous long *Waist,* a *Dress* entirely contrary to the liking of Virginia ladies, these I apprehend make her in their eyes less personable. . . . Her *Stays* are suited to come up to the upper part of her shoulders, almost to her chin; and are swaithed round her as low as they can possibly be allowing her the liberty to walk at all." [12] The day following these observations Philip chose to add:

> Our young ladies inform me that Miss Panton discovered a strong inclination to be better acquainted with me; which indeed is a curiosity that I cannot say I am altogether destitute of. I shall therefore, when I find it convenient make Miss Panton a visit.[13]

Among these young ladies, for example, was one with the remarkable name of Miss Pinkstone Camel, "a young woman of about sixteen, neat, handsome, genteel & sociable; & in my opinion she possesses as much of these as any young Lady in Virginia whom I have yet seen." Philip was to see quite a few.[14]

Matchmaking went on almost to the close of Philip's stay at Nomini Hall. Probably his most definite invitation to join the first families of Virginia was the presentation of Miss Betsy Lee, a daughter of George Lee, of Mount Pleasant. Here was another Betsy. And Fithian missed none of the details. In her twenty-sixth year, she was a well set maid, of a proper Height, neither high nor low —Her Aspect when she is sitting is masculine and dauntless; she sits very erect; places her feet with great propriety . . . she has a full face, sanguine Complection, her Nose is rather protuberant than otherwise; Her Eyes are exactly such as Homer attributes to the Goddess Minerva; & her arms resemble those which the same Poet allows to Juno. She is truly elegant; her carriage neat & graceful, & her presence soft and beautiful. . . . She was pinched up rather too near in a long pair of new fashioned Stays, which I think are a Nusance both to us & themselves—for the late importation of Stays which are said to be now most fashionable in London are produced upwards so high that we have scarce any view at all of the Ladies Snowy Bosoms. . . .

What made me desirous to see & curious to reconnoitre this young Lady, was a Sentence that was dropt yesterday by a respectable member of our Family, intimating a Desire that I may, on seeing Miss Lee, after having known, by report, her faultless character, be so pleased with her person as to try to make her mine, & settle in this Province—That Kind Body . . . little knows how painful it would be if I was compell'd by any accident of Fortune to spend the remainder of my Days in Virginia. . . . Strong & sweet are the bands which tye us to our place of nativity . . . if a Princess should solicit me to accept, together with Herself, 50000£ a year—I declare, with as great pleasure as truth, that the esteem & Fidelity which I possess for my dear, dear Eliza would make me without reflection, evade & refuse the proposal.[15]

There is a rather touching sequel to this effort in behalf of Betsy Lee. She was to outlive Fithian by more than half a century and to die, at eighty years of age, unmarried.

In the midst of this matchmaking Philip took his yearned-for vacation at home. He arrived there on April 16, 1774, and woke next morning to find that "Cohansie looks as delightsome as ever it used." The following evening he was at the Green parsonage, where he stayed until ten "in company with the amiable Miss Beatty." He spent the afternoon and evening of the 25th with her and rode with her on the 26th. After several more visits and a sentimental letter to her on May 7, there is this significant notation on the 10th:

> Her goodness has at length indulged my importunate Solicitations & in her Society I hope to be happy—I spent the Evening til eleven with her, & in the most entertaining Manner.[16]

Fithian, always so explicit where the Nomini Hall girls are concerned, chose to be a bit vague here. There is no doubt, however, that he had proposed marriage and had been accepted. A whole year later he recalled that *Laura* "was not tedeous, nor backward, in granting my Proposal." There is no indication that he saw her again before returning to Nomini Hall; but he did write her "a chronological letter" on May 12, a "private letter" on May 14, and a plain "letter" on May 22, after he had been examined and accepted by the Presbytery in Philadelphia. Then on May 23 he set off again for Virginia, unhappy, noting at a stop in Maryland that he "slept but little . . . a thousand things perplex me . . . I am unwilling to leave Home—I have already overstaid my time—I have left the girl I love."

Three days later Fithian's spirits were lifted by a warm welcome from the Carters and a supper of crabs and "an elegant dish of Strawberries & cream." Now he noted: "How natural, how agreeable, how majestic this place seems!" A day later, incidentally, he jotted down that they "drank Coffee at four, they are now too patriotic to use tea."

These sharp shifts in mood were to become increasingly characteristic of Philip in his crowded remaining days. One moment he was "more pleased with the Face of the Country [Virginia] than I ever have before"; and the next he was toasting *Laura* longingly "in a Bumpper of old Madaira." He overheard the Carter boys wondering why Mr. Fithian "has not fallen in Love yet with some of our Nomini Girls . . . here he sits from Month to Month (not many Months longer said I to myself) . . . and these reflections were only broken off when the Coachman came in with a wood Tarripin . . . to catch the Bugs and Cockroaches." [17]

During Fithian's vacation he had arranged for a successor, John Peck, who had been graduated from Princeton in 1774 and also was a native of the Cohansie area. The day before Peck's arrival and several days prior to Philip's departure this note was made: "Mrs. Carter to day asked me if Mr. Peck is to be here before my setting out; I answered that he is—And says she, is he grave as you?" As things turned out, the Nomini girls had better luck with John Peck than with Philip Fithian: Peck married Nancy Carter and settled permanently in Virginia.

The day of Peck's arrival, October 15, 1774, was a rough one for Philip:

He comes empty of a letter, & barren of news, at least all he brings seems gloomy; none at all of the great Congress; very little of the present momentous political affairs; that it has been at Cohansie an unhealthy season; that good & useful Mr. Hunter has been ill of a disorder in his head; that Mrs. Reve is gone and left a Brood of infants; that young Tom Jennifer of Port Tobacco, my acquaintance at College too is dead; that matters go in their usual course at Cohansie & Princeton; that *Laura* is not in New Jersey! All his intelligence is similar to this, which is to me harsh & unharmonious as a Ravens ominous Croak! [18]

He was to receive still worse news, presumably from Peck, although that is not so stated. By October 18 Philip was understandably beside himself and his *Journal* records this bitter brew of anger, credulity, and petulance:

[. . . this sad thing I hear of that turn-coat *Laura,* that She loves & courts one Mr. *Rodman* . . . this distresses me exceedingly. But this relieves me, for I have had it always in my View that—Varium & mutabile semper Foemina—Tho I have made a Solemn vow which I have no inclination at all to forego, yet if it shall appear that she has listened to another, my dearest vow is not inviolable; I will retreat from every former Promise, I will not hearken to her womanish solicitations, but I shall in return for her want of goodness treat her with contempt; & sincerely pity, instead of resent, her ineffectual Caprice.[19]

Two days later Fithian was off, furious and in haste, for Cohansie. It is a wonder that in his mood he had time or inclination to record at Annapolis that "Tuesday evening last [October 18] the people of this Town & of Baltimore obliged one Anthony Stewart, a Merchant here to set fire to a Brig of his [the *Peggy Stewart*] lately from London in which was 17 chests of Tea.—The people seem indeed to be full of patriotic Fire." [20]

On October 25 Philip was back in Cohansie—soon to discover that "this sad thing" concerning *Laura* was false; soon to learn that she had indeed remained true.

For Philip the winter of 1774–75 was to be the happiest of his life. It brought him great religious satisfactions, some exciting moments politically, and progress in his romance with *Laura,* which proved gratifying to even so demanding and impetuous a suitor. He was examined by the Presbytery and on December 6 licensed to preach, delivering his first sermon, without notes, at Deerfield on the 18th. Fithian recorded that he was a bit frightened and made "a material blunder in the first Pray'r, desiring of God that the King may become a nursing Mother, & the Queen a nursing Father to the Church."

Fithian preached in his home town of Greenwich on three occasions in January, 1775, mostly to full houses, and on February 3 he began the first of his missionary journeys to Smugglers' Woods and the Pine Barrens. He preached a number of times at the little log meetinghouse at Pleasant Mills, the Clark's Mill meetinghouse near Port Republic, and on one occasion at Brotherton (Indian Mills) "to Mr. Brainerd's Indians—Present about thirty and as many White People." During this journey Fithian wrote to his mentor, the Rev. Enoch Green, that "there is something grand, charming and desirable in this vulgarly despised Egg Harbour . . . I love the simplicity which I see in the manner of the inhabitants . . . the country, the sand, the Pines . . . it is Nature stark naked." [21]

Fithian's political activity in the Greenwich tea-burning episode was covered in the preceding chapter. The depth of his patriotic fervor, however, was shown even more sharply through the prayer written in his *Journals* on the very day he was licensed to preach:

May I have in my own heart much of the meekness and Spirit of the Gospel, & may I have a sense of my duty in these times of distraction & Misery—Furnish me with

an uniform & unbiass'd love for my Country; & give me
courage to engage in every method that has a tendency
to save her from Ruin, even if my life should be in Danger
in the Competition.[22]

Most if not all of that winter *Laura* was in Deerfield,
where since her father's death in 1772 she had virtually
made her home. There are many breaks in the Fithian
Journal during this period, and he mentions *Laura* three
times only, but one of these entries is sufficient to indicate
that he had been her frequent if not almost constant com-
panion while in Cohansie. On Monday, January 30, 1775,
Philip had written: "I spent the afternoon with Mr. Hunter,
& I received from him instructions for my intended Voyage
to Egg Harbour—He gave me correction too about my
intimacy with *Laura,* & such as was not so agreeable as
I should wish—" [23]

Philip was to have his riposte, however, the following
June on his first westward journey. At Cedar Creek, Virginia, he "visited old Mrs. Sarah Vance; a sensible, religious
Woman. She was in her early life acquainted with Mr.
Hunter, of Cohansie, & once they were on the Borders of
being married, before Mr. Hunter went to the Grammar-
School!—But, said the honest Woman, he was born to a
better Fortune. Truly did our venerable Minister carry on
such a Prank in his Youth!—I have not forgot, & must now
record that he frowned on me some months ago for the innocent, and friendly intimacy I have with Laura!—Rev'd Sir,
you must, if you please, from hence forgive me." [24]

Fithian had embarked on this mission tour to western
Pennsylvania and Virginia because there were no vacant
pulpits "in our Bounds." And he left with a certain eagerness born of his confidence that *Laura* now was his and
soon would become his bride. All competition would seem

to have been eliminated. The parting, however, was charged with emotion:

> She wep't, & her powerful Tears quite drowned me in melancholy Rapture—! She was silent; I was literally dumb—She held me by the hand, & I sat reclined, in a mournful posture, by her Side—But at last I must leave her—we parted in Silence & Tears; I stopped a Moment on the Stairs to wipe the Tears & Sorrow from my Face & there made my last Lamentation in the Language of our common Mother, when she was leaving Eden.

> "Must I then leave thee, Paradise?
> " _____ _____ _____ from thee
> "How shall I part _____ _____
> " _____ accustom'd now to heavenly Joys." [25]

Soon both Milton and Cohansie were left behind and Fithian's journey took him to many remote settlements and into many strange households. His frame of mind was now softer than it had been at Nomini Hall; he still had an appraising eye for women, but in comparing them—unfavorably of course—with *Laura*, there were none of the old nagging doubts. A "Whipprewill" reminded him of one which sang for them while they were sitting by *Laura's* window; he still carved her name on beech trees; and he even found one "rural Lass" who was "a very exact Resemblance of my Angel *Laura*." Her name was Jenny Reed. Like Betsy Lee, who piqued his curiosity at Nomini Hall, Jenny lived to a very old age and died unmarried.

Fithian's comments on women, indeed, were now more rhapsodic than in Nomini Hall days. At Warrior's Run, for example, he wrote: "Here I am invited by a Number of Ladies to gather Huckleberries. The Call of Women is invinceable. [*Laura* was to disagree with this!] I must gallant them over the water. Perhaps my Eliza is in the same Exercise this very afternoon in the back woods of Deerfield." [26]

Upon Fithian's return to Cohansie on September 8, 1775, preparations moved quickly forward for the long-anticipated wedding. If Fithian wrote any journals during this period, they have not been found. Indeed, for many years the circumstances of their marriage were mistakenly recorded. It made a good story, that Philip and his *Laura* were finally united in ceremonies at her brother John's home in Princeton, with President Witherspoon of the university officiating and her brother giving her away. Those were to be the circumstances of her second marriage, but as to her first, the records of the Deerfield Presbyterian Church show that on October 25, 1775, Elizabeth Beatty and Philip Vickers Fithian were married there and the officiating clergyman was her brother-in-law and Philip's teacher and friend, the Rev. Enoch Green.[27]

After three short weeks of honeymoon Philip was traveling again, on a second tour of the "frontier settlements," so called although the actual frontier by then had reached much farther westward. Even earlier Fithian had recorded misgivings as to whether his "inclination for rambling into other Provinces, & seeing new and strange Faces & Manners" was stronger than "to fix down at once on some little Farm, in Cohansie, my native, dear Sod?" This leavetaking from *Laura* must have been more dolorous than the previous one. In a letter to her, dated November 9, 1775, he wrote:

Such are you & I—made happy for a moment—Made wretched, by Separation, for Months—In due time we shall meet again—If not here, yet very soon in a heavenly transporting Paradise—! At eight o'Clock every Evening, my dear girl, shall I ask you to retire with me, I will always do it, & we will mutually implore our Almighty Creator, that we may both be preserved & in rapturous Pleasure meet again? Read this letter often. It will remind you of your unchangeable Friend.[28]

Fithian's second missionary journey was less satisfactory than his first. The mounting wave of war, coupled with a few bouts of illness left him distressed, now torn not only between love and his calling but between those two and his impulse to take some active role on behalf of American freedom. Writing from Stephensburgh, on December 2, 1775, he told *Laura:*

> This Colony in every part is in a most pitiable State. Dunmore has issued a diabolical Proclamation declaring Freedom to all Denominations of Servants & Slaves who are able to bear Arms & will repair to His Majesty's royal Standard . . . I have been advised to omit traveling further. I am now undetermined.[29]

By January 14, however, he could note in his *Journal:* "I am now contented. I will return & gladly, to my dear, dear Betsey." But within a week he was in a perplexing dilemma, no novelty to him. Stopping then at North Mountain, near Staunton, Virginia, his question was whether this, "remote & wild as it is," should not be "the Habitation of me and my lovely Betsey." He added: "She told me kindly, long ago, that her Choice, as to the Place & Mode of fixing for Life, is resolved entirely into mine." [30]

Three weeks later Fithian was at home, the dilemma no longer perplexing. Despite comments to the contrary, he had made a home for *Laura* in the old dwelling of his parents which is still standing on the outer fringes of Greenwich. A number of his letters to her bore that address, he wrote in terms of living there, and he left the property to her in his will.[31]

Even a home at Cohansie with *Laura* in it was not enough to hold Philip Fithian very long. Tensions stemming from the Revolution were mounting. One of *Laura's* brothers, Erkuries Beatty, had entered military service in 1775; and her three other brothers, John, Reading, and Charles, all enlisted on the same day, January 5, 1776.[32] To a man of Philip's intense patriotism, aside from his inner restlessness, the call could not long be ignored. On June 20, 1776, he and his childhood chum, Andrew Hunter, Jr., entered the service. They were commissioned chaplains, and both were in units which became part of General Heard's brigade assigned to the defense of New York.

That *Laura* was reluctant to have her husband take this step goes without saying. Her brother John recognized as much in a letter to her on September 10, 1776, in which he said: "I am truly sensible of the disagreeable consequences of leaving wives, when more especially fatigue and danger are our natural companions; but I flatter myself the importance of the contest will sufficiently apologize for our rudeness in leaving you." A final blow came when her sister Mary was left, with her children, in the Deerfield parsonage, inasmuch as the Rev. Enoch Green felt impelled to enter the service also as a chaplain. John Beatty could well say: "Where will you find a family more engaged in the service than ours?"[33]

As summer merged into autumn, none could foresee how completely the stage was set for personal tragedy. Philip became ill almost as soon as he joined the troops. In July he declared that "the vile Water here sickens us all; I am very sick; troubled with a continual Lax, & fearful of a confirmed Flux" but "not a word of being amiss do I say to my dear *Laura*." [34] In September he was well enough to find "something forceably grand in the Sound of Drums & Fifes . . . when they are calling such an Army as ours to contend with another of perhaps equal Force! Whenever they come together the Death of many must be the Consequence." [35] With characteristic determination and consciousness of duty, Fithian visited the many in his battalion that were "sick of Fevers, Fluxes &c." When New York fell to the British he cried: "We are a sinful Nation, O Lord. But is it written in thy Book concerning us that we must always fly before our Enemies?" By September 19 two of the doctors in his own battalion were ill; yet, unwell himself, he walked down "to the Place where the Battle was fought . . . all the Dead are buried, but their Blood is there & 'Garments roll'd in Blood.'"

Four days later Fithian himself was stricken, for the last time. The Rev. William Hollingshead, of Fairfield, "found him lying upon a thin bed raised from the floor only by a little straw covered with a blanket or two . . . reduced to the lowest state one would imagine possible for human nature to support under." A week later his fever had not abated and on October 7 Andrew Hunter left him "about 10 O Clock at Night without any expectation of seeing him alive again." Twelve hours later Philip Vickers Fithian was dead. Weakened by exposure, fatigue, and tension, the prevailing "camp fever," or dysentery, proved beyond his meager powers of resistance.

In his diary Andrew Hunter noted that he had written "to Mr. Fithian's wife at his request, giving an account of his Sickness." In the letter itself Hunter said: "He has given me no orders to request any of his Friends to come to see him, but were I in his situation I should wish to see so near a Friend as a wife . . . There will not be the least danger of the Enemy in the Journey." He added a postscript the

next day: "Mr. Fithian is a little better this morning." [36]
The letter was addressed to Cohansie. *Laura* did not make
the trip. For that fact and for the further fact that he received but three letters from her at camp she has been
severely criticized.

But if *Laura* was remiss, she was to pay for it in com-
pound tragedy. Shortly after Philip's death and burial on
Mount Washington "with as much decency as the nature
of the case would allow," two of her brothers—Reading and
John—were captured by the British; another brother,
Charles, was to die a few weeks later when an accidental
shot from an "unloaded rifle" proved fatal; and finally Enoch
Green arrived home in Deerfield, only to die soon afterward
of the same illness which had taken Fithian. Two husbands
and three brothers, two families left bewildered to shift for
themselves, two empty homes—in Greenwich and Deerfield
—after both Mary and *Laura* took refuge with their brother,
John, in Princeton after he was freed on parole.

The romance of Philip Vickers Fithian and Elizabeth
Beatty is less enigmatic than it seems on the surface, although the hidden aspects provide its special appeal. To
brush off Philip as a flamboyant egotist, *Laura* as a stolid
and unfeeling hausfrau, and their love as one-sided is
superficial and unfair. There is too much evidence to the
contrary, even recognizing that theirs was a union of oppo-
sites, of a complex and mercurial man with a woman whose
very simplicity was second only in attractiveness to her
beauty. And if their story does possess an epic quality, it is
because he provided the heroic element while she, almost
certainly overawed by the cyclonic temperament she had
married, contributed the element of mystery that has been
so tantalizing.

No portrait of either is known to exist. And while Fithian

was detailed indeed in his descriptions of other women, even those in the back country, he provided no word portrait of *Laura,* having been content to call her lovely and amiable, terms which seem to have occurred to most of the other males who from time to time had an eye on her. True, on one occasion Philip wrote bluntly: "You are not handsome, *Laura,* nor is yours a face that will please the tenth Part of your Beholders." [37] But since he was annoyed with her at the time, this description should be discounted even though he went on to praise her intelligence and animated countenance. An astounding compliment, certainly; and it is a wonder she did not set him adrift then and there. However, from other clues, plus bits and pieces from comments and letters including those of her brothers, it is possible to reach a number of conclusions about her.

Laura was blue-eyed, of fair complexion, and a little above medium height. Her features were soft and delicate, and her voice persuasive, musical, and unhurried. Although she was reared in a parsonage, she and her sister Mary were able to lead some of their early boy friends in "as brisk a Country Dance as [they] were able to follow." This was at their Neshaminy home; and both girls were accounted uncommonly merry. Indications that *Laura's* disposition became more subdued may have been due in part to the influence of the Rev. Enoch Green, whose arrival at Neshaminy stopped the country dancing. Her disposition appears to have been mild and even; she was ready to go wherever Philip chose to make their home, even to the rougher regions of western Pennsylvania. Fithian remarked in one of his letters that "we were as near perfect contentment in each others company as mortals can come." She was, of course, domestic in her interests as would become a pastor's daughter. She spun Philip a coat, made him shirts; and later he expressed wonder whether she was "not absolutely sick

of the Confinement of these domestic duties." As for her
affections, despite his jealousies there is no sign that they
ever wavered where he was concerned; she waited five
years for him, and if she had been inclined to a man of
milder disposition she surely had ample opportunities.

There remain the two supposedly damning facts: first,
that he received only three letters from her while he was
in camp, whereas he wrote her no less than sixteen; second,
that when Andrew Hunter suggested that she come up to
see her husband on his deathbed, she did not make the trip.

The matter of the letters was baffling to Philip himself.
He constantly chided her on the subject, long before as well
as after their marriage. On May 12, 1774, he sent her a
rather astonishing inventory of their correspondence and
concluded:

> You may take notice that in the beginning of this Paper
> I made use of the word Correspondence; but I used the
> word improperly; for through the Course of Time in
> which I have written and sent you [fifteen letters] . . .
> for a Balance to them all I have one from you of just
> twelve lines.[38]

Laura wrote him but once while he was at Nomini Hall,
a letter which was five months on the way. There is also
mention of another letter from her, which may or may not
have been the one listed in the inventory. Philip was vague
about that. Thus her three letters to him at camp, in three
months, were one more than she had sent him in the preceding five years.

On August 3, 1776, writing from camp, he rebuked her
again:

> Mr. Hunter & Mr. Caruthers came more than a fort-
> night since I left you, & not a Line by either, since the

week I came away. Blame no Capt. Beatty & Charles any
more. They have a sister that can forget her friends.
And even her most humble Servant—[39]

Philip V. Fithian

Three days later, although overjoyed at finally having
heard from her, he wrote: "Do not, while I am absent from
you, pass over one Opportunity of writing largely to me."
In his very last letter to her, a letter which it must have
pained her to preserve, he said that it was "more than a
month" since he had heard from her, while during that
period he had sent her "seven long epistles," and he mentioned the date of each.

The answer to all this may be clear from the over-all pattern of the correspondence she received from Philip, and
from her brothers for more than twenty-five years after
Fithian's death. That answer is that *Laura* simply could not
express herself in written words and attempts to do so appear to have been painful labor to her. Other than household chitchat she probably could think of nothing to say
and trying to say even that much seems to have raised a
psychological block in her mind. This was something difficult for the highly articulate Fithian to understand. Yet he
suffered from a psychological block too, which was the very
reverse of hers. If he could dash off letters at the mere sight
of a pen, all that free-swinging expressiveness vanished in
Laura's presence. As early as 1767 he was writing a long
letter to his father to ask that he be given higher education;
from its contents it seems clear he could not even ask his
father directly for what he desired. And as late as 1774 he
recalled in a letter to *Laura* that when he had last seen her
he was "dumb," and added that "it is more than probable
that when I see you tomorrow or the Day after, I shall be
the same Block, Motionless, Spiritless & dumb." And while

Philip eventually overcame his difficulty, she did not over-come hers. Accordingly, he thought to remedy it by giving her a virtual course of instructions.

Her reaction, and his counter-reaction, appear in this letter to her dated August 20, 1776:

> You tell me you are not capable of following the Pat-tern I set you; my dear Girl, do not, I pray you, suppose that I meant to lay any Restrictions in any small Degree on your Manner of Writing—Write your native unshakled Thoughts, they will be to me most welcome, they will give the highest Delight—think not while you are writing to him who belongs to your Arms, & wishes ardently to be there the moment his honour will allow it—think not of any thing fine or nice in what you would say—Write as tho' no other Person on Earth could ever see what you wrote, but me; & if Friendship is your Subject, if all the World should see such a Letter, they would justify & praise it. As you would talk, if we were together, without any Regard at all either to Order or Length . . . or any thing else, but to set down a few vagrant Thoughts, when you have a Chance of sending them along; So is the Wish & will be the great Satisfaction of Laura's . . . most affectionate Husband. Philip V. Fithian.[40]

This pattern of one-sided correspondence continued un-broken for years after Philip's death. *Laura* simply did not write letters, and that was that. Her brothers, all of them, scolded her in turn, and in vain. Writing in 1775, Reading Beatty said: "I have not had a Letter from you this good while, surely if you wrote a good many they could not all miscarry." Ten years later he wrote her: "I was thinking of making a comparison between you & a lazy horse . . . I can conceive no reasonable excuse for your long silence."

And in 1800 her brother William was telling her that "in all this time have not heard from you once. I am hurt when I think that a regular post . . . to Bridgetown which is not far distant from you should be a sure and regular conveyance . . . what can it be, want of time or want of inclination or downright indolence." Had they seen Philip Fithian's letter concerning the pattern he set her, they might have understood. *Laura*, in any case, was consistent to her dying day: she did not even write a will!

On the charge that *Laura* ignored the call to her husband's deathbed she seems to be in the clear. It was on September 28, that Andrew Hunter wrote: "Were I in his situation I should wish to see so near a Friend as a wife." However, the letter was not sent that day and on the following day, the 29th, Hunter added the postscript: "Mr. Fithian is a little better this morning." Assuming the letter was sent off on the second day, only nine days still remained before his death; and a careful weighing of the facts makes it very doubtful that *Laura* even received the Hunter letter while Philip was still alive.

The first key fact is that Hunter addressed the letter to Mrs. Betsy Fithian, Cohansie, New Jersey. But nearly two months earlier she had moved from Cohansie to her sister's home at Deerfield. Fithian himself wrote on August 12: "As you have moved to Deerfield I am affraid my Letters will not all reach you." Although Deerfield was but twelve miles distant, communications were haphazard. And even if the letter had reached Cohansie in time for someone there to forward it to her at Deerfield, that person would not normally have been in any hurry about it. For the letter was not marked urgent.

Virtually all this account of Mrs. Fithian has come through her husband's eyes and by way of the strokes of his pen. Of the letters she is known to have written, most were very short and few have survived. We have, however, a direct glimpse of *Laura* during Philip's absence, in the form of a quotation from one of her letters which he repeats in his of August 20: "In the Evenings I am in my Room. I am fond of being alone, for then it is I most enjoy myself & think freely & without Interruption of my dear absent Friend."

We know even less concerning Philip's physical appearance than we do about *Laura*'s. That he was thin is evident in such comments as "my poor Body, thin and bloodless" and "my skinny ghostly body." He was often ill and seems to have possessed little resistance to disease. Perhaps it was knowledge of this that made him think so often of death and speculate on his prospects of returning to *Laura* and to Cohansie.

Of his mind and temperament we know much more. The foregoing surely suggests that Philip Fithian grew up to be an intensely human, kind, understanding, and dedicated man. He was no prude. He had an honest capacity for healthy passion. He was keenly aware of women, but only one, besides *Laura,* seems ever to have made much of an impression upon him. This was the girl called Belinda in his *Journals,* probably Polly Bullock, of Philadelphia, who died of tuberculosis—"a young lady, with whom I had only a short yet a beneficial Intimacy." Later a girl in western Pennsylvania reminded him of Belinda's "lovely Train of Graces." Other women challenged his curiosity but seem not to have tempted him. Yet he was not inhibited in commenting about sex. He chose to record a wedding in a "little Cabbin." A squire, not Philip, performed the ceremony. Philip noted that "the Girl look'd asham'd, tho' lusty . . . pronounced the Ceremony apparently with Reluctance . . . But Oh! her Bosom burned!" Of the groom he had this to say: "In appearance a scurvy, futile, unmeaning Drill

—He seem'd highly pleased, but a vulgar-looking, ragged, Weather-worn Peasant." [41]

With righteous indignation Fithian also noted a scandal at Dunmore, in the Shenandoah Valley:

> An Irishman hired in a Store was taken in an Attempt to spend the Night with a Matron of the Town—The Gallant leaped out from a Window above Stairs quite naked of everything but his Shirt—His Wig, Shoes & Stockings, Hat & Cane, he had left without the Door to secure them against Surprize—His Breeches Waistcoat, & a Cloak, he left behind—With these the angry Husband heated the Stove for his own Satisfaction! Poor Redress.—He ought to have added the sinning Wife! [42]

Fithian's personal and fundamental modesty was put to severe tests during his frontier missions. Time and again he was obliged to bunk in the same room with the entire family. Always he was annoyed; and at Sunbury, Pennsylvania, he remarked: "It seems indelicate, at least new, to strip surrounded by different Ages and Sexes, & rise in the Morning, in the Blaze of Day, with the Eyes of, at least one blinking Irish female, searching out Subjects for Remark." [43]

Nothing, it would seem, escaped Fithian's thirsty curiosity and gifts for observation. This was as true on the frontier as it had been in tidewater Virginia. He could notice while strolling beside Aughwick Creek "two sets of fine Plumbs, one red, or streaked, and very tart on the Tongue" and the other a bright orange color "when rubbed a little" and "very juicy & sweet." He rambled the dry woods of the Kishacoquillis Valley "cropping off the Hazle-nuts, Tops of the fine Wood Mary-Gold; Wood Lily & other wild untended Flowers." Nothing caught his attention more quickly than the tidiness of the homes he attended. Near Huntingdon, Pennsylvania, he breakfasted with Mrs. Forsley, "a smart, neat Woman; her Pewter on the Dresser glistened; her wooden Dishes, Pans & the like, were white & sweet." By contrast was a house in Chilisquaque: "I had been near all over bemeasled with the Fleas,—Fleas biting! —Bugs crawling!—On a hard Board, surrounded with a snoring Family!" [44]

Virtually unlimited was Philip's range of interests. Concern for music and books was evident at Nomini Hall; and even in the heat and chaos of battle on Long Island he could write to *Laura:* "Most of all take care of my Books & Papers, keep them, I intreat you secure; some of them to me are of very great moment." His political awareness dated back to and probably beyond his commencement day address at Princeton. He noted colloquialisms and odd customs, rock formations, the discovery of fossil fragments, and the "mean, dishonest & irreligious" character of Jerseymen who had settled along the Susquehanna. Particularly he concerned himself with the state of public health in the various localities and kept fearful watch upon contagion of the "Bloody Flux," so devastating in those feverish years.

Fithian's was an incandescent intellect. Buffeted as he was by the pressures of a searching mind, it is a question whether for all his religious faith, sincerity, and dedication he could ever have accommodated himself to the normal routine cares of a congregation and the limited life of a country pastor. He scrutinized himself quite as closely as he did other people and the world about him. He was quite aware of his inner conflicts and psychological weaknesses and was also aware that he had no answer for them.

At Nomini Hall, on June 5, 1774, he reflected on the pleasures of the retired life there, only to add: "In spite of my resolution, when I am convinced that my situation is more advantageous here, yet I wish to be there—How exceedingly capricious is fancy! When I am Home I then seem willing to remove, for other places seem full as desirable." [45] That October, on the eve of his return to Cohansie, he confessed: "I am of so strange a constitution that very trifles make me utterly unhappy. A mere conceit, frivolous & unsubstantial often takes away my rest . . . In fact any disappointment, even the most inconsiderable seems to have a general Effect on my Passions & mingle fear & anger, & rage." [46]

Could his two avowed loves, *Laura* and Cohansie, have calmed such an emotional storm center for any extended length of time? It is a question whether even the church could have contained his turbulent spirit. Had Philip returned safe from the war, he almost surely would have become one of the most unorthodox and controversial clergymen of his time or else he would have found another calling and sought new frontiers of the mind as well as of the land. He certainly was not a poet, yet he had a poet's sensitive soul and a poet's prophetic vision. At Cedar Creek in the Shenandoah Valley, on June 1, 1775, he wrote, first, this blistering indictment:

The melancholy Anniversary of a tyrannical Manoeuvre of the infatuated, or rather Hell-inspired British-Ministry, in blocking up the Port of Boston is arrived! —This Day twelve Month their dangerous & cruel Councels began to be executed!—All along the Bladder has been filling with Venom—Now it is distended with Poison —full, ready to crack, to split with Rage!—Feeble and unavailing Efforts! Three Thousand British Forces were sent, & are now to be joined by two thousand More, with 2 hundred Horse—Five thousand hireling Regulars. at Sixpence Ster: per Day, most of them young & unused to

Hardships—Five thousand hireling Britons, against the Millions of America's hardy Sons—The Odds is five thousand against thirty hundred thousand; And all those Myriads fighting for what is dear to them as Life, which they will as soon give up to Power . . .

Then followed this prophetic salute, foreshadowing in its way the singing spirit of Walt Whitman:

O America! Unwieldy Mass of Earth, pleasant & healthful, tho' various in thy Climes—Fertile of every useful Support of Life—On thy Bosom, exuberant of Nourishment, have been raised a wise & gigantic People—They are now flourishing in Learning, & Arts, & chiefly at present, urged on by a misjudging Ministry, are preparing with a Confidence of Success, to rival the whole World in Military Honour—O America! with Reverence I look forward, & view thee in distinguished Majesty—It is not rash to assert, without the Aid of Prophecy, that thy Commerce, & Wealth, & Power, are Yet to rule the Globe! [47]

Finally, Philip Fithian was imbued with a sense of destiny as well as prophecy. In August of 1775 he could write, quite casually:

I had almost forgot to tell the Person who shall read these Papers a couple of hundred Years hence that there is now standing in a Garden in Huntingdon a tall Stone Column, or Pillar, nearly square, which has given to the Town & to the Valley the Name of "Standing Stone Valley." [48]

Soon the couple of hundred years will be up. That tall stone column is gone. Long since. But Philip Fithian's

Papers, dust covered for more than a century, command the attention he envisioned.

Three and a half years after Philip's death, Dr. John Beatty wrote to his brother Reading: "A secret—Sister Betsy is to be married, the second week in next month . . . Mr. Joel Fithian, a widower from Deerfield is the man for *her* Money—a tight match you will say—however it is so—Her partiality for that Country may have been one inducement —a good Fat farmer another . . . & probably a husband at any rate." [49]

That last phrase seems hardly just. Certainly it was not kind to Philip, even though his brothers-in-law probably had difficulty understanding his crackling temperament. The fat farmer was both a cousin of Philip and a close friend who had been involved with him in the Greenwich tea burning. This time Betsey—the *Laura* was doubtless forgotten now—did have her wedding in Princeton, at the home of her brother John; and with President Witherspoon officiating. Two of the other Beatty brothers, Erkuries and George, were present, but had to leave for military duty before the ceremony began, when the groom was two hours late. The marriage took place on March 4, 1780, in the evening, and the couple returned to Cohansie next day for the honeymoon.

If Elizabeth Beatty had wanted a quiet, sedate, and comfortable marriage, she had it now. Joel's temperament was the opposite of Philip's. He was the solid citizen, the successful farmer, ruling elder in the Presbyterian church at Greenwich, and later a member of the New Jersey legislature. There is every indication that the couple were happy and respected in Cohansie. Joel had a son, Josiah, by his first wife. They were to have four of their own, one named for Philip; and the youngest, Dr. Enoch, became Cohansie's leading physician and lived to the remarkable age of one hundred years and six months.

Elizabeth's magnetic attraction continued where letters were concerned: they kept coming in over the years, from brothers and old friends. But, as before, she rarely wrote a reply.

There was peace in the land, peace in her heart, peace in Cohansie. Yet there must have been occasions when she recalled her impassioned lover, the taut emotions of their partings and reunions, and the surcharged hour when he left never to return. Perhaps in an occasional private moment she got out the little knitted bag in which she kept his letters and reread some of them, particularly his very last words to her: "Peace and God's Blessings be with my Betsy, my dear Wife, forever may you be happy."

Elizabeth Fithian lies buried in the old churchyard at Greenwich. Beside her are the remains of Joel. In her *Historical Sketches of Greenwich*, Bessie Ayars Andrews tells of a quiet evening in the late eighteen-hundreds when she and her brother were approaching that churchyard. They were startled to hear a loud and clear voice singing, *"There is a land of pure delight / Where saints immortal reign."* Amid the twilight shadows stood Dr. Enoch Fithian, beside the graves of his parents, his snow-white hair stirred by the soft summer breeze. And he sang the old hymn through, to the very last verse.

If the spirit of Philip still hovered near that unmarked grave on Mount Washington, it surely was listening too—unless, of course, it long since had found its own peace, in Cohansie.

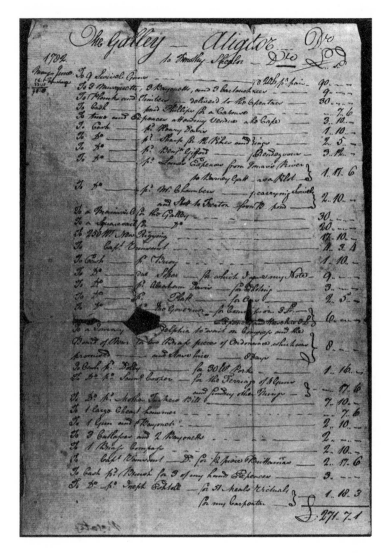

Outfitting a Privateer: Cost account of arming and reconditioning "The Galley—Aligator" as a privateer. Timothy Shaler was the skipper, Joseph Ball the owner. (*Courtesy of The Historical Society of Pennsylvania*)

Ship

Bark

Full-rigged Brig

Hermaphrodite Brig

Top sail Schooner

Fore & Aft Schooner

Sloop

Swivel Gun: This cannon—35⅜ inches long with two-inch bore—is typical of those used by the smaller privateers based along the New Jersey coast. (*Courtesy, The Mariners Museum, Newport News, Va.*)

Privateering: (left) Types of vessels used during the Revolution. (*Courtesy, The Mariners Museum, Newport News, Va.*)

An American Privateer in Action: "The Thorn," Captain Daniel Waters, 16 guns. In 1778 she captured two British vessels in one engagement. (*Courtesy, The Mariners Museum, Newport News, Va.*)

Col. Charles Pettit: By Gilbert Stuart. Original in the collection of Mrs. T. Charlton Henry. (*Photo courtesy of the owner and the Frick Art Reference Library*)

Col. John Cox: Associate of Pettit and Greene in speculation on privateers. (*Reproduction of miniature in* Salons Colonial and Republican *by Anne Hollingsworth Wharton*)

Gen. Nathanael Greene: By Rembrandt Peale (copy after C. W. Peale). Original in the collection of the Maryland Historical Society. (*Photo courtesy of the Frick Art Reference Library*)

William Livingston: First Governor of the State of New Jersey. (*Rutgers University Library*)

William Franklin: Last Royal Governor of New Jersey. Portrait attributed to Mather Brown. From the collection of Mrs. J. Manderson Castle, Jr. (*Photo courtesy of the owner and the Frick Art Reference Library*)

Gen. Charles Lee: Attributed to Cephas Thompson. From the collection of the U. S. Department of Justice. (*Photo courtesy of the Frick Art Reference Library*)

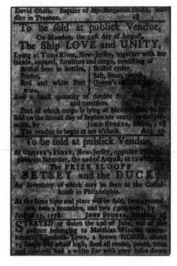

Philip Vickers Fithian: While most of the Fithian Journals are in the handwriting of his brother, Fithian's own signature appears on one document left behind when he departed from Nomini Hall in Virginia. (*Courtesy of the Princeton University Library*)

Privateers at Auction: Advertisement from the *New Jersey Gazette*, August 15, 1778.

Greenwich: Home of Philip Vickers Fithian. Built about 1750. (*Photo by Arthur D. Pierce*)

Declaration und ...

Declaration und erläuterung ...

... Glasmacher ... Hans Wilhelm Wentzel, Simeon ... Caspar und Martin Halter ...

...

4. Feb. 1744 signiert   Caspar Wister

Extract aus dem tagbuch 1741.

1741
Oct 12

... 85 pound ...

Caspar Wistar: Signature and first page of 1741 account book for his glass works at Wistarberg, near Alloway, New Jersey. (*Courtesy of The Historical Society of Pennsylvania*)

EARLY TAVERNS

The Black Horse Inn: Mendham, 1745, still in use as a tavern. (*Photos by Arthur D. Pierce*)

The Indian King: Haddonfield, 1750, restored by the State of New Jersey.

The King George Inn: Mount Bethel, 1692, restored as a tavern in recent years.

The Village Inn: Englishtown, 1732, where Gen. Lee's court-martial was planned, still an inn.

CRADLES OF REVOLT:
THE TAVERNS

"There is nothing which has yet been contrived by man by which so much happiness is produced as by a good tavern or inn," declared the eminent Samuel Johnson. It is a good guess that he soon qualified that opinion. For the American Revolution was clearly cradled in colonial taverns, and Dr. Johnson's contempt for that Revolution was notorious.

On one occasion Johnson remarked that if he were prime minister he would have sent a man-of-war "to level Boston or New York to the ground." [1] Leveled as a result would have been such Boston taverns as the Green Dragon Inn, which Daniel Webster called "the headquarters of the American Revolution." Leveled, too, would have been the famous Province Arms in New York, a popular rallying place for the Sons of Liberty, and the same city's Fraunces' Tavern whose proprietor was both a distinguished host and an intelligence agent for General Washington during the days when the British occupied New York.

In Philadelphia, the London Coffee House kept by William Bradford, who also published the fiery *Pennsylvania*

Journal, was an organizing center for political demonstrations and scene of the burning of the Stamp Act papers. It has even been stated that Thomas Jefferson wrote most of the Declaration of Independence in a tavern, the Quaker City's Indian Queen, but this legend is disputed, the best evidence being that he drafted the charter of liberty in a second-floor room at the house of "a young bricklayer named Graff." [2]

Most famous of all cradles of revolt was the Raleigh Tavern in Williamsburg. There angry Virginians gathered to discuss their grievances. There the House of Burgesses reconvened unofficially after Governor Botetourt, in 1769, dissolved that body for having dared to remonstrate against His Majesty's government. There Jefferson, Patrick Henry, Richard Henry Lee, and other leaders met to sound the call for the First Continental Congress.

While these and other eighteenth-century hostelries have been justly famous, little attention has been paid to the important and often exciting role played by colonial taverns of New Jersey in the nation's struggle for independence. From the seventeenth century New Jersey taverns—the better ones at least—had served as community centers. Public business was transacted, mail distributed, sheriff's sales and auctions conducted. Some court sessions were held in taverns and the landlord himself was frequently a figure of prominence, perhaps the local marshal or judge. Scarce in those times were buildings which could accommodate sizable gatherings. Churches were borrowed for certain secular occasions, but quite a few public events were considered inappropriate for houses of worship. Thus when public unrest was boiling in the decade before 1776 the taverns of New Jersey, like those elsewhere, found aroused colonists criticizing their king, merchants voicing protest over harsh British trade restrictions, travelers bearing news of similar ferment in other colonies. It was in the taverns that petitions were drawn up and signed, the tea boycotts organized, and militia units formed, while more and more thoughtful townsfolk became deeply concerned over the principles at stake as sentiment swung from protest over British restrictions to outright calls for political freedom.

Revolutionary sentiment in New Jersey was long muted and spotty in comparison with that of New England and Virginia. Two major factors were responsible: the objection of most, but not all, of the large Quaker population to a course which was feared might lead to war and the powerful influence of the Church of England.

Burlington was a case in point. Sharing with Perth Amboy the honor of being New Jersey's provincial capital from 1703 to 1776, it was host to a newly elected and rebellious Provincial Congress in June and July of 1776. That session voted to declare itself a Constitutional Convention, and on July 2, two days before the Declaration of Independence, came up with a new constitution for New Jersey. Confronted with an order from Governor William Franklin—Benjamin's illegitimate son—that they declare their allegiance to the king, the Assembly promptly voted to defy the instructions.

On July 15 it formally declared that "the said William Franklin, Esquire, has discovered himself to be an enemy to the liberties of this country; and that measures ought immediately be taken for securing the person of the said William Franklin." [3] The vote was: yeas 42, nays 10. Five days later the governor was arrested and hauled to Burlington in a coach guarded by eighteen men. Earlier Franklin had voiced his fear of being "seized upon and led like a Bear through the Country to some place of confinement in New England." Now that was to come to pass. He was confined in Hartford, Connecticut, for two years, then released to the British in New York, where he became head of the Associated Loyalists.

Many of the best people in Burlington were not at all in sympathy with these activities. The mayor was John Lawrence, an ardent Tory, who later ceremoniously welcomed British and Hessian officers but whose door was closed to patriot legislators. The Rev. Jonathan Odell, Tory rector of St. Mary's Church, who was to play a shabby role in the Benedict Arnold treason plot, was politically and socially active in ostracizing the unwelcome legislators. Another prominent Burlington Tory was Daniel Coxe, who later led in organizing loyalist harassment of his former neighbors and friends. Add the fact that Governor Franklin had lived in Burlington until two years previously and still had many friends there, and it is not surprising that any Burlington folk who did sympathize with the colonial cause were hesitant about expressing their convictions and of challenging the prevailing loyalist social climate.

That is where Burlington's taverns played a major role, for theirs were among the few doors open to the patriots. The city had three first-class establishments in those days: the Blue Anchor, whose site at Broad and High streets is occupied today by the Metropolitan Hotel, Sheppard's Tavern, and the Sign of General Wolfe, known later as the Stage Boat Tavern. These last two were located close to the waterfront.

Most famous of the trio was the Blue Anchor with its appropriately painted sign. Host then was James Edsall, and almost certainly a good proportion of the legislators were quartered there during the session, debated far into the nights in its taproom, and held secret committee sessions in its parlors. Edsall's list of distinguished guests later included Generals Greene, Knox, Reed, and on the British side von Donop and Knyphausen. An early description of the Blue Anchor, built by Richard Smith sometime before 1751, states that "the main front of the original house was two stories and a garret in height, with a porch supported by iron columns along the Broad street front." About 1850 it was known as the Belden House, and in 1858 it was torn down.[4]

Sheppard's Tavern was actually fired upon during the Revolution. Erected by Samuel Burge, it was sold by him in 1774 to Adam Sheppard, coachman of Governor Franklin. The shelling incident took place in May, 1778. British gunboats were heading up the Delaware to destroy American shipping at Bordentown, and they fired several shots into Burlington as they sailed by, apparently *pour le sport*. One cannon ball lodged in a wall and remained there for many years; it is now in possession of the Burlington County Historical Society. Both Sheppard's and the Sign of General Wolfe had been in the line of fire two years earlier. American gunboats fired large and small shot in every direction as Colonel von Donop and his Hessians stopped briefly in Burlington. It was the Hessians, incidentally, whose looting and pillaging swung sentiment in the Burlington area—and in most of New Jersey—to the patriot side. In *Revolution in America* Major Baurmeister wrote: "There was much new evidence of [plundering] in Jersey. It has made the country people all the more embittered rebels."

Only seven miles south of Burlington, in Mount Holly, the county's future capital and second oldest community, there was a different atmosphere in pre-Revolutionary days. Militant sentiments were more openly expressed, particularly at the Black Horse Tavern of Zachariah Rossell. A stage stop on the route from Cooper's Ferry (now Camden) to Middletown, there were always travelers coming and going and exchanging views. Letters were delivered. The tavern newspaper was passed from hand to hand so that all could glean the latest doings of the Continental Congress and fresh details of a war that already was turning from cold to hot in New England. Since a tavern usually had but one copy of a newspaper, it was not surprising to find posted in the taproom notices such as this: "Gentlemen learning to spell are requested to read last week's newspaper."

Zachariah Rossell, long known as "Old Zack," was a colorful character and an ardent patriot. Originally his tavern had been called the Black Horse because its sign bore a painting of King George III in full regimentals riding a big black horse. With the Revolution, the sign was taken down for alteration. One story is that the king was simply obliterated, leaving the big, black horse; another is that His Majesty was replaced by a portrait of George Washington.

Old Zack was active in various capacities during the Revolution, particularly as marshal for Burlington County. He presided at a great number of vendues and sold under the hammer the often-rich prizes of privateers and other captured property. His name appears in numerous newspaper advertisements announcing vendues, sometimes in Mount Holly at the Black Horse and often at "the House of Richard Wescoat at the Forks of Little Egg Harbour" near Batsto and Pleasant Mills. In any case, his tavern was a busy place and Old Zack became so annoyed by some of his patrons that he posted the following verse above his main fireplace:

> All ye who stand before the fire,
> Pray sit ye down; tis my desire
> That other folks as well as you
> Should see the fire and feel it too.[5]

Other leading colonial taverns of Mount Holly were: the Three Tuns on Mill Street, built about 1723 by Samuel

Bryant; the State Arms of Joseph Hatkinson, dating from 1757; Winne's Tavern, on Wood Lane, where von Donop reputedly made his headquarters for a day or so in December, 1776.

Gloucester County was a territorial giant in those times. It included not only the present county of the same name but Camden and Atlantic counties as well. The county seat was Gloucestertown, now simply Gloucester. Situated on the Delaware, it was a pleasant place which reflected the charm of Penn's "green countrie towne" across the river. Its most famous tavern, known simply as Hugg's, was located on the old Salem road at Gloucester Point. It was a sizable establishment for its day and enjoyed special fame and patronage on account of its long hall, or banquet room, on the third floor. Hugg's was a center of activity. Courts were conducted there, and juries quartered. There were town meetings and special functions. Quaker Betsy Ross, nee Griscom, eloped and was married there to John Ross, an Episcopalian, in defiance of her parents. She was expelled from the Quaker faith for marrying "out of meeting." [6] There, too, the early rumblings of the Revolution found quick echo. From 1766 the Gloucester Fox Hunting Club had been meeting at Hugg's for sport and celebration. Many of its members were Philadelphians, and out of those meetings sprang the First Troop of Philadelphia Cavalry. [7]

Even when they were swarming over South Jersey the British apparently met a cold welcome at Hugg's, for redcoats and Hessians alike chose to gather at another tavern, the Two Tuns, better known then as Aunty High Cap's. This nickname derived from a tall cap worn by the landlady with a provocative name—Desire Sparks. "Aunty High Cap's," says John Clement, "was the hostelry where British military rank and discipline were laid aside . . . and full vent given to the manly pastimes so fashionable in that day." Aunty High Cap's has long since disappeared, but Hugg's stood until the 1930's, when it was torn down in spite of strong protests by historical societies and other interested individuals.

Down in Cumberland County at least three taverns were centers of patriot activity. One, the Parvin Tavern in Bridgeton, was maintained by Clarence Parvin, who was prominent among the tea burners at Greenwich. Local militia trained at another Bridgeton tavern, kept by Matthew Potter, and also at John Dare's inn on the Cohansey Creek. In nearby Salem County the "first regularly equipped military organization for defense with barracks" was formed at the Pole Tavern in Pittsgrove. This volunteer company was officered by Captain Jacob and Lieutenant Peter du Bois. Earlier called Champney's Tavern, it gained the name of Pole Tavern because a liberty pole was erected on the green upon the outbreak of the Revolution.

Far to the north, in Princeton, sentiment for independence was stirring long before the formal declaration in Philadelphia or the New Jersey "declaration" in Burlington. In Princeton, again, the taverns provided important forums for public expression, debate, and organization of patriotic groups. The temper of the times in the college community may be gauged from the fact that a company of undergraduate volunteers was formed and sent off in 1775; and, unless college students then were sharply different from college students today, they spent more than a few hours wrestling with the issues of the day in the local taverns, which were admittedly better than average.

The Sign of the Hudibras, at the corner of Nassau Street and College Place, was one of the best. As far back as 1765 the Hudibras—spelled Hudibrass in some old records—had been "noted and well accustomed," although considered expensive. On a cold night in January, 1773, however, the "whole house" was "laid in ashes" by a fire that started from an overturned candle. "All the winter provisions as well as beds and other furniture" were lost despite the college fire engine and "becoming boldness" on the part of the students.[8] Soon the Hudibras was rebuilt, and the new structure, apparently a fine one for its day, had twelve rooms and two kitchens as well as a stable, sheds, and "two excellent gardens well stored with greens, Sallads, Herbs, and all sorts of Garden Stuff." From the windows of this new Hudibras only a year later the guests could see Princeton's counterpart of the Boston Tea Party, when students on the lawn of Nassau Hall burned the entire college supply of tea.

Colonel Jacob Hyer, proprietor of this inn, was a prominent Revolutionary figure and also served as local quartermaster. Earlier Hyer had kept another tavern, the King's Arms. At the Hudibras, however, he entertained many distinguished guests and in 1774 was host to John Adams, the future President, and the whole New England delegation to the First Continental Congress. Hyer, a stalwart figure in or out of uniform, had the gracious smile and sharp, appraising glance that mark the experienced host. He appears to have been secretly close to the higher echelons of the Continental command, for it was he who came forward to give bail when John Honeyman, famous "double spy" who was Washington's most effective and trusted intelligence agent, was arrested for high treason, as a Tory, at Trenton in 1777.[9] Few were in the know where Honeyman was concerned.

Princeton's other top taverns also were located on Nassau Street. A major military thoroughfare during the Revolution, this street witnessed a stirring succession of events. Paul Revere rode through on his way to Philadelphia with word of the Boston Tea Party. In 1776 the king's horses and the king's men marched down Nassau Street and up again, first in pursuit of a fleeing Continental army and then in retreat a few weeks later after Washington's key victories at Trenton and at Princeton itself. In 1781 Washington and Rochambeau were hurrying their armies southward for the clinching triumph at Yorktown. Then, in 1783, a panicky Continental Congress sought refuge in the college community. As might be expected, these events crowded the taverns, and sleeping space in Princeton was often as scarce as hard money.

Overcrowded particularly was the popular Nassau Inn, where committee meetings of the New Jersey legislature were held and where more than a few of the legislators stayed. Erected as a private house in 1756–57, the Nassau was operated as a hotel continuously from 1769 to 1937, in which year it was torn down when Palmer Square was laid out. "Old Nass," as it was affectionately called, had a ballroom which was the scene of many commencement dinners, concerts, dances, and of course political meetings. Known in later years as the College Inn, it is said to have had a sign over the door bearing this invitation:

> Kind traveller, come rest your shins
> At this, the peer of College Inns.[10]

There is a Nassau Inn in Princeton today, on Palmer Square. It is new in construction but nostalgic in architecture. In its Yankee Doodle Taproom are to be found the tabletops of Old Nass carved with students' initials and dates of classes long since graduated.

Sharing equal fame with the Hudibras and Old Nass was the Washington Arms at 68–70 Nassau Street. It was built before 1748 and provided the early background for one of the most fantastic of all New Jersey tavern tales. The very real events began back in 1750 when "there was prowling through the country a man by the name of Tom Bell . . . who greatly excelled in low art and cunning."

It seems that Tom Bell arrived at the Washington Arms one evening dressed in a dark, parson's gray frock and that a prominent Princetonian, John Stockton, mistook him for the Rev. John Rowland, a well-known local divine. Bell moved swiftly to cash in on the resemblance. The story of how he did so is told by the Rev. William Tennent, Jr.,[11] whose father was unhappily involved and whose grandfather built the Little Log College in Neshaminy, Pennsylvania, which was the forerunner of Princeton University. Wrote the Rev. Mr. Tennent:

The next day Bell went into the county of Hunterdon and stopped in a congregation where Mr. Rowland had formerly preached once or twice but was not intimately known. Here he met with a member of the congregation to whom he introduced himself as the Rev. Mr. Rowland. This gentleman invited him to his house, to spend the week; and begged him, as the people were without a minister, to preach for them on the next sabbath, to which Bell agreed. The fake clergyman was treated with every mark of attention and respect, and a private room was assigned to him as a study. The sacred day arrived and he was invited to ride to church with the ladies in the family wagon, and the master of the house accompanied them on an elegant horse. When they had arrived near the church, Bell on a sudden discovered that he had left his notes in his study, and proposed to ride back for them on the fine horse, by which means he should be able to return in time for the service. The proposal was instantly agreed to, and Bell mounted the horse, returned to the house, rifled the desk of his host and made off with the horse.

All this while Rowland and Tennent, as well as two lay associates, Joshua Anderson and Benjamin Stevens, had been far away in Pennsylvania and Maryland on a preaching mission. Upon their return the Rev. Mr. Rowland was charged with the robbery and "the affair made a great noise throughout the colony."

Thanks to the alibi testimony of Tennent, Anderson, and Stevens, Rowland was soon acquitted. However, wrote the Rev. Mr. Tennent, "the spirits hostile to the spread of the gospel were not so easily overcome." And since no further action could be taken against the acquitted Rowland, his three witnesses were now indicted for willful and corrupt perjury.

Of the three "poor Mr. Anderson, living in the county, and conscious of his entire innocence . . . demanded a trial at the first court of oyer and terminer. This proved most seriously injurious to him, for he was pronounced guilty, and most cruelly and unjustly condemned to stand one hour on the court house steps with a paper on his breast whereon was written in large letters 'This is for wilful and corrupt perjury.'"

Had it not been for one more astonishing event the other two defendants might have been convicted also. On the eve of their trial a strange man and his wife appeared. They said they had heard Tennent and Rowland preach in Pennsylvania at the time the robbery took place. Each testified to having had a dream, twice repeated, telling them that Mr. Tennent was in great distress. So they had come to Trenton to be of help. At the last moment yet another witness showed up for the defense: the Princetonian Stockton, who told how he had mistaken Tom Bell for the genuine Rowland in the Washington Arms. As a result Tennent and Stevens were absolved of the perjury charge, and the curious story ended, in effect, where it had begun, at the Washington Arms in Princeton. Tom Bell, however, remained at large.

During the Revolution the Washington Arms was run by Christopher Beekman. There was an attractive green in front and a flagpole around which the Fourth of July was annually and adequately celebrated. Beekman, too, hosted famous guests: Rochambeau, William Bradford, Stephen Girard, Benjamin Rush, and many more. The Washington Arms was another of the buildings demolished in 1937 to clear the area for Palmer Square.[12]

At Kingston, just above Princeton, there was a large colonial tavern, the Sign of the Black Lion. Its proprietor proudly boasted that at times as many as forty-nine stage-coaches could be found waiting outside while four hundred travelers were dining or refreshing themselves inside. For a period the British may have occupied this place, but most of the time both redcoats and Continentals were in too much of a hurry, in advance or retreat, to pause long at the Sign of the Black Lion.

Moreau de Saint-Méry mentioned another Kingston hostelry, "an inn bearing the sign of a mermaid, which was established by its present master in 1744 . . . the water which the people drink comes entirely from an extremely deep well dug about forty years ago." [13]

Next pause on the highway to New York is New Brunswick, which Moreau de Saint-Méry found to have many good inns. One tavern, built about 1741, was first known as the Indian Queen, a common name in that period. Called Bell's Tavern during the Revolution (and later the Parkway), Franklin, Adams, and Rutledge stayed there in 1776 when, as commissioners, they were on their way to meet Lord Howe at a peace parley on Staten Island. The inn was so crowded that Franklin and Adams had to share a bed in a room hardly larger than the bed itself, with one small window. Adams relates an amusing conversation which followed:

> I, who was an invalid and afraid of the air of the night, shut it close. "Oh!" says Franklin, "don't shut the window; we shall be suffocated." I answered that I was afraid of the evening air. Dr. Franklin replied: "The air within the chamber will soon be, and indeed is now worse than that without doors. Come, open the window and come to bed, and I will convince you. I believe you are not yet acquainted with my theory of colds." [14]

Adams was so curious that he opened the window, braved the cold air, and fell asleep while Franklin was still expounding.

Another New Brunswick tavern, Brook Farmer's Red Lion, was evidently a "nest of rebel plotters" prior to independence, as so many others had been, for when the British moved in they took special pains to burn the place and Farmer himself barely managed to escape to Princeton, carrying along his tavern sign with the red lion on it. Earliest recorded New Brunswick tavern, incidentally, was Ann Balding's, opened in 1735 by the wife of a sea captain.

One more haven for freedom fighters was the Harris Tavern, a halfway stop on the road between New Brunswick and Bound Brook. Its patriotic reputation led Major Simcoe and his loyalist rangers to debate a proposal to burn the place as they had burned so many others. For some unrecorded reason it was spared, and in later years was called the Middlebrook Hotel. Though changed a bit by time, this hostelry is still standing.

Three other pre-Revolutionary inns should be mentioned: Cook's Tavern at Hanover, in Morris County, Graham's in Elizabeth, and the house of John Ringo, for whom the town of Ringoes was named.

Ellis Cook, of Cook's Tavern, was a hefty blacksmith turned innkeeper, and another of those landlords who, like Hyer in Princeton, Rossell in Mount Holly, and many more, took an active role in the colonial cause. In 1775 Cook was a member of the Morris County Committee of Observation, the Provincial Council, and the Committee of Safety. Later he was commissioned a lieutenant colonel of the militia, and after the war became a judge of the Morris County courts.[15]

Graham's Tavern was a favorite haunt of the associates of William Alexander, one of Washington's abler generals, better known as Lord Stirling, claimant to a Scottish earldom, a claim which Parliament denied. Lord Stirling fought in every major battle of the Revolution, particularly at Trenton and Yorktown, and had the misfortune to die only a few days before the treaty of peace was finally signed granting the independence for which he had struggled so valiantly and sacrificed his private fortune.

The Ringoes Tavern in Hunterdon County was built about 1720, and as early as 1766 the Sons of Liberty were gathering there to oppose "that worst of all acts called the Stamp Act."

One particularly delightful tavern name sparks special curiosity. It is the Sign of Captain O'Blunder. Who *was* Captain O'Blunder? And what was his blunder? One would give much to know. All I have been able to discover is that the tavern existed, was located in Newton, Sussex County, and that in 1772 its proprietor was one John Allen.

Near Bound Brook there were three taverns noted in pre-Revolutionary days: the Bull's Head, the Sign of the Buck, and the Black Horse. The landlord of the last named rather plaintively told one of his guests that he was not only innkeeper but also weaver, shoemaker, farmer, farrier, gardener, barber, leach, doctor, and, "when I cannot help myself, a soldier." [16] Verily a busy man.

If the tavernkeeper's lot was not always a happy one, to paraphrase Gilbert and Sullivan, the taverns themselves provided more than one kind of headache for public officials. In early days an "ordinary"—as taverns were called prior to the eighteenth century—was considered a necessity and not a luxury. One of New Jersey's earliest statutes on the subject, dating from November, 1668, reads:

> In consideration of the Inconveniences that do arise for want of an Ordinary in every Town, within this Province, It is ordered, that every Town shall provide an Ordinary for the Relief and Entertainment of the Strangers. Provided, that the Ordinary Keeper is to have a Licence from the Secretary and oblige himself to make sufficient Provision of Meat, Drink and Lodging for Strangers; and for Neglect hereof, in any of the Towns, they shall forfeit Fifty Shillings Fine for every Month's Default after Publication hereof.[17]

Most subsequent legislation, however, was concerned not with promoting the establishment of ordinaries but with policing—and taxing—those already established. Acts of 1692, 1693, and 1704 sought in various ways to license ordinaries, control drunkenness, and suppress immorality. The 1704 enactment specified punishment as a six-shilling fine and exposure in the stocks for four hours. Many of the early taverns were simply dives, and by 1728 conditions had become so bad that the legislature enacted new regulations declaring that taverns were "for the accomodating of Strangers, Travellers and other Persons and not for the encouragement of Gaming, Tippling, Drunkenness and other Vices so much of late practiced to the great Scandal of Religion."

Under this new law taverns were to be licensed by justices of the peace, license applications had to be signed by neighbors, and the applicant himself had to post a bond of twenty pounds. Taverns were to be inspected by constables, and rates were to be fixed for liquor, food, and lodging. In 1729, for example, the Salem County Court set the following schedule of prices: [18]

A rub of punch made with double-refined sugar and one and a half gills of rum	9d.
A rub of punch made with single-refined sugar and one and a half gills of rum	8d.
A rub made of Muscovado sugar and one and a half gills of rum	7d.
A quart of flipp made with a pint of rum	9d.
A pint of wine	1s.
A gill of rum	3d.
A quart of strong beer	4d.
A gill of brandy or cordial	6d.
A quart of metheglin	9d.
A quart of cider royal	8d.
A quart of cider	4d.

Equally quaint are some prices fixed for food and lodging by the Gloucester County Court in 1742: [19]

Every breakfast of tea, coffee or chocolate	8d.
Every breakfast of other victuals	6d.
Every hot dinner or supper provided for a single person, with a pint of strong beer or cider	1s, 0d.
Every hot dinner or supper for a company, with a quart of strong beer or cider each	1s, 0d.
Every cold dinner or supper with a pint of strong beer or cider each	8d.
Every night's lodging, each person	3d.
HORSES	
Stabling every horse, each night and clover hay enough	8d.
Stabling each night and other hay enough	6d.
Every night pasture for a horse	6d.
Every two quarts of oats or other grains	3d.

Amendments to tavern licensing laws were made from time to time. In 1768 it was stipulated that six persons of repute had to sign each license application and the tavern-keeper was required to provide a minimum of "two good spare Feather Beds more than is necessary for the Family's use."

New Jersey's early ordinaries fell roughly into three classes: the legitimate first-rate tavern catering to the traveling public; the legitimate house catering chiefly to thirst; and the jug tavern, rough ancestor of the speakeasy, which got its name from the fact that its facilities might well consist of common jugs of firewater for which one paid a penny or so per swig of rum or Jersey lightning (applejack). Whereas ordinaries at first were often log cabins or crude shacks, the better eighteenth-century taverns were well-built structures, mostly of frame construction but in quite a few cases of brick and stone. These better taverns were patterned after the traditional inns of England: in their architecture; in their management; and even in the fact that distinguished American artists such as Gilbert Stuart, Benjamin West, and the Peales painted colorful signs for them as Hogarth, Watteau, Millais, and others had done for the inns in "Merrie England." Here, as in Britain, the landlords were often men of local prominence; as countless British inns boasted that Queen Elizabeth had slept there, American taverns soon were to make similar claims with respect to George Washington.

A main feature of the larger pre-Revolutionary taverns in New Jersey, as already noted, was the large assembly hall or ballroom, supplemented by a parlor and sometimes additional public rooms for committee meetings and private dinners. Next in size was the taproom "with its great fireplace, bare sanded floor, and ample seats and chairs." [20] Other furnishings generally included a writing desk, used by landlord and travelers alike. The bars restored at the Raleigh and Chowning taverns in Williamsburg are typical of those found in many of New Jersey's colonial taverns. They usually were fitted with a barred portcullis, which could be closed by lowering. Behind the bars was the stock of wines, liquors, and beer, and usually a convenient staircase direct to the wine cellar. Often opening from the taproom was the public dining room, with the kitchen to the rear or in a separate building.

Upstairs were the guest rooms, frequently overcrowded, especially in centers of political and social life during "publick times" when courts convened or legislators met. In such emergencies women travelers might be quartered in private homes close by, while the men, often strangers to one another, would bunk two, three, even four to a bed. Any man who objected to a stranger as a bedfellow was regarded as either odd or fastidious. And the seasoned traveler was never too surprised if he had to sleep on the floor.

Actually, sleeping on the floor was by no means the only inconvenience of colonial tavern life. The beds themselves were liable to be uncomfortable and sometimes not too clean. In most, Moreau de Saint-Méry noted, the guest was "expected to sleep between sheets on which traces of former occupants are found with more or less frequency." [21] Sanitary facilities were strictly limited, while in some places laundry service was so restricted that it was not unusual to see distinguished men wearing dirty shirts. Even in Philadelphia as late as 1794 the City Tavern, concededly one of the best, "would have been better rid of vermin that infested the beds." And the London Tavern, a leading hotel at the time the Quaker City was the national capital, was rated as "deficient in comfort at its best." [22]

Food and drink were variables also. Another tavern custom imported from England was the use of "turnspit dogs," forerunners of the modern barbecue. When meat was to be roasted, a dog would be harnessed to a wheel geared up to turn the roasting spit. Various devices were employed to persuade the dog to keep the wheel turning. In some cases hot coals were so attached that if the poor animal stopped his legs would be scorched.[23] While Fido thus learned the hard way to turn the spit, he also learned to hide—or try to—whenever there were signs in the kitchen that the day's menu would boast a roast. Taverns which catered to gourmets offered elaborate bills of fare, and in Delaware Valley frequently followed another fashion of the day by featuring catfish-and-waffle dinners, while turtle feasts then were as popular as snapper suppers are today.

Drinks also varied according to the standards of the establishment. Rum was long the favored base for intoxicating concoctions such as blackstrap (rum and molasses), mimbo (rum and loaf sugar), sling, grog, and toddy. "Stewed Quaker" was a popular Monmouth County drink and consisted of hot cider with a roasted Monmouth Red apple floating on top of the mug or bowl. Jersey applejack was everywhere a specialty of the house and the principal ingredient of a legendary beverage mixture called "Scotchem."

The story of Scotchem concerns a young man who strode up to a bar and barked out an order for a drink of Scotchem. The landlord's son, a novice in the taproom,

mixed a glass of hot water and Scotch whiskey, which the traveler had scarcely tasted ere he roared out: "Don't you know what Scotchem is? Applejack, and boiling water, and a good dash of ground mustard. Here's a shilling to pay for it." The boy stared at the uninviting recipe, but faithfully compounded it, when toot-toot sounded the horn —the coach waited for no man—and off went full coach and empty traveler. The young barkeep looked at the mug of steaming liquid and offered it to an old and crippled trapper who sat in the warm chimney corner of the taproom. "Here, Ezra," the boy said, "you take the gentleman's drink. It's paid for." Ezra was ever thirsty and never fastidious. He gulped down the Scotchem. "It's good," he swaggered bravely, with eyes streaming from the hot mustard, "an' it's tasty, too, ef it does favor tomato ketchup." Forty years later an elderly man entered the bar. The barkeep, a keen-eyed old fellow, glanced sharply at the newcomer, pondered a moment, then opened the closet and drew forth an ancient demijohn of applejack. With boiling water and a dash of mustard he compounded a drink which he placed, unasked, before the traveler. "Here's your Scotchem," he said laconically. The old man solemnly drank his long-paid-for mug of Scotchem. "It's good," he said finally, "and tasty, too, if it does favor tomato ketchup." [24]

THE TAVERNS
GO TO WAR

Once the Revolution became an outright hot war, taverns
were quickly pressed into service by both sides. New Jersey was a major battleground during much of the struggle
and, since it lay athwart the more important highways link-
ing the Middle Atlantic colonies, the military traffic was
enormous. When a troop contingent, Continental or British,
moved into a town, the first step usually was to take over
all the inns and after that such public buildings and private
dwellings as seemed necessary. Many taverns were put to
use as officers' quarters, others as barracks. Still others were
made into military prisons, hospitals, and courtrooms for
courts-martial. In instances where the taverns were not in
military hands they provided places of refuge for the New
Jersey legislature, meeting rooms for the Committee of
Safety, and recruiting and training centers for the militia.

Many tavernkeepers played both sides against the middle
as a means of wartime survival. The British, and especially
the Hessians, sometimes would strip a tavern, carrying off
food, supplies, and even furniture. Comparatively lucky
were such tavernkeepers as John Cox of Moorestown, whose

claim for losses due to troop visitations consisted of "four tons of hay for the use of horses and cattle removing the cannon from Red Bank." [1] Some innkeepers were so adept at carrying liquor on both shoulders that British and Continental forces alike preferred to patronize rather than molest them. Perhaps they had the future in mind; the troops might well be coming back that way. In any event a substantial number of Revolutionary taverns came through the war unscathed, such as New Brunswick's Bell Tavern, the Indian King in Haddonfield, Dickerson's at Morristown, the two Black Horse taverns—at Columbus and Mendham —Bush's Tavern at Ellisburg, and many more.

Many taverns were burned, particularly by loyalist forces wreaking their revenge in this way on innkeepers, often former friends, who were known to be supporting the American cause. Simcoe's loyalist "rangers" put taverns as well as homes and public buildings to the torch. It has been said that Simcoe hated courthouses in particular because to him at least they represented symbols of self-government. In Millstone, once the seat of Somerset County, Simcoe's men burned both courthouse and jail, but were driven off before they could wreck the famous Tunison Tavern there. This place is noted for the fact that in 1780 a new jail was built next door, only to be incorporated into the tavern itself some years later. The tavern at Ringoes survived by similar good fortune in 1778 when a detachment of British raiders was repulsed. [2] Less lucky was Jacob Roberts, whose tavern and house in Camden County were burned while he was serving in the militia. [3]

Although emphasis has been laid upon the more romantic aspects of New Jersey's taverns, history shows that they created problems for the contending forces which counterbalanced, at least in part, the services and benefits that have been mentioned. This applies especially to the "thirst taverns," jug joints, and brothels. Some tavernkeepers would stoop to anything for sixpence. Nicholas Collin, in his journal, tells of one meretricious fellow—a member of his congregation in Raccoon (Swedesboro)—who was so greedy that he took advantage of his own sister's funeral, in cold, wet weather, to peddle liquor to the funeral guests while the church service was going on. This was in 1775. And innkeepers along the Delaware were known to "row out in boats to serve their wares to raftsmen who were floating by." [4] Though the old provincial licensing and control laws remained in effect during the Revolution, their enforcement was inevitably lax, and the unscrupulous tippling houses were quick to take advantage of that fact. This explains why Washington issued the following order:

> The gin shops and other houses where liquors have been heretofore retailed within or near the lines . . . are strictly forbidden to sell any for the future to any soldier in the army.

Liquor was to be a problem for the commander in chief with respect to officers as well as men. After his triumph at Trenton on Christmas night, 1776, Washington ordered that forty hogsheads of rum found among the spoils be staved in and poured on the ground. This was done but not, apparently, until some of his men already had toasted their victory "to a point where their efficiency for further military action seemed doubtful." [5] One estimate has it that approximately a thousand troops were on the sunny side of tipsiness. As for his officers, General Adam Stephen was charged with being drunk at the Battle of Germantown after his men and General Wayne's began firing at each other instead of at the enemy. Stephen was convicted and dismissed from the army. These are but two examples. Others will appear.

Washington himself was no teetotaler and his diary shows that he was a frequent patron of taverns, as were most men of his day. Scores of taverns in and out of New Jersey could claim, with honesty, that G.W. had eaten or slept there. It is recorded that when the First Continental Congress gathered in Philadelphia he had supper and spent the evening at the City Tavern, which was the rallying point for all the delegates. The commander in chief, in fact, appears to have visited, dined, and had drink in most of the taverns in the town—he also visited most of the churches including a Quaker meeting—and his diary mentions dining at Bevan's Tavern, John Byrne's, the Ferry House Tavern, Peggy Mullen's Beefsteak House, also known as the Tun Tavern and a meeting place of the Masonic Grand Lodge; the Vauxhall Tavern of Peggy Mullen's son, the Conestoga Wagon, and probably the outlying Jolly Post Boy.[6] It is no wonder that soon many colonial taverns were being renamed after him.

The commander in chief also chose taverns for his headquarters on many occasions, and the great victory dinner at which Washington took farewell of his officers was held at Fraunces' Tavern in New York. Later, on his triumphal journey to his first inaugural in the same city, receptions and celebrations were held at taverns all along the route. One of these was at the Cross and Key Tavern in Woodbridge, and he was given a tumultuous welcome at the Red Lion in Elizabeth. The Red Lion, built about 1734, originally had been called the Marquis of Granby, but in 1771 its patriotic proprietor changed the name.

Probably Washington's first wartime experience in a New Jersey tavern took place in Hackensack, capital of Bergen County. After the disastrous and disheartening defeats that lost New York the beaten remnants of the Continental forces fled to the Jersey shore and began their rugged retreat to refuge in Pennsylvania. How close the British were upon their heels is suggested by a story of Washington's stay in the tavern of his friend Peter Zabriskie. This tavern, called the Mansion House, was built in 1751 on Hackensack's Court House Square, at that time called the Green. Washington's room, tradition has it, was No. 19, on the second floor. In her *Early American Inns and Taverns* Elise Lathrop notes that "it has the huge fireplace and cupboards of the other bedrooms, the tiles imported from Holland when the house was built, and in addition, in what seems a mere closet, is a secret staircase. Down this staircase it is told that Washington escaped into the dining room and out through a window, while the Hessians were mounting the front stairs. Three or four thousand of these Hessians occupied the town, presenting a 'horrid, frightful sight to the inhabitants, with their whiskers, brass caps and kettle or bass drums.'" It is a colorful tale, but purely a myth. The Mansion House has been marked by a bronze tablet put up by the Bergen County Historical Society. Across the street from the Mansion House was Archibald Campbell's tavern, where Washington is said to have taken some of his meals.

Bergen County in those days included the present Hudson and Passaic counties, and while portions of it were frequent battlegrounds, other richly endowed farming areas were less directly touched by the conflict. So much so that during the terrible winter at Valley Forge, when many of the troops were literally in rags, New Jersey's Governor Livingston made a proposal to seize the petticoats of Bergen County ladies. Wrote the governor:

I am afraid in furnishing clothing to our Battalions, we forget the County of Bergen, which is alone sufficient to supply them amply with winter waistcoats, breeches, etc.

It is well known, that the rural ladies in that part of New Jersey pride themselves on an incredible number of petticoats which, like house furniture, are displayed by way of ostentation, for many years, before they are decreed to invest the fair bodies of the proprietors. Till that period, they are never worn, but neatly piled up, on each side of an immense escritoire, the top of which is decorated with a capacious brass-clasped Bible, seldom read.

What I would therefore most humbly propose to our superiors, is to make prize of these future female habiliments, and after proper transformation, immediately apply them to screen from the inclemency of the weather those gallant males who are fighting for the liberties of their country; and to clear this message from any imputation of injustice, I have only to observe, that the generality of the women in that county, having for above half a century worn the breeches, it is highly reasonable that the men should now, especially on so important an occasion, make booty of the petticoats.

The governor chose to be witty, but he meant what he said.

The American Army's "most important general"—in his own estimation—was most singularly unlucky in taverns. It was the strange destiny of General Charles Lee that three of the most decisive events of his life were to take place in taverns: his capture by the British, the order for his court-martial, and his death.

Charles Lee was vanity in uniform. Eccentric in dress and appetite, "he loved and admired public virtue," Benjamin Rush observed, "but was addicted to many private vices. Obscene, profane . . . his avarice discovered itself in every transaction of his life." Elias Boudinot wrote that "whenever anything on a very large scale struck him, a

partial lunacy took place." [7] Lee's large-scale ambition was
to oust Washington and take command of the army. He was
consumed by a lethal mixture of jealousy and hatred; he
plotted and schemed against Washington with the tenacity
of a termite. Because Lee had willfully disregarded Washington's order to bring his wing of the army to Pennsylvania, the sulky general found himself in Somerset County
on December 12, 1776.

For reasons obvious now but not then, Lee, with only a
very small guard, left his army to go four miles away to the
Widow White's Tavern in Basking Ridge. The attraction
was the widow, whom he seems to have dated in advance.
Her greeting was an affectionate "My general!" Lee apparently spent the night with her while his guards made
merry with the barmaids. Next morning Lee arose in a bad
humor, according to his aide, Captain James Wilkinson.
Yet a not unlikely hangover failed to deter him from writing a letter to General Gates denouncing Washington as
"damnably incompetent." He completed this fine missive
before he started dressing.

Scouting nearby at this time was a small detachment of
five men led by Banastre Tarleton. Tipped off as to Lee's
whereabouts, Tarleton and his men surrounded the tavern
and routed the groggy guards, who dropped their arms and
fled. Tarleton wrote: "I ordered my men to fire into the
house thro' every window and door, and cut up as many
of the guard as they could. An old woman upon her knees
begged for life and told me General Lee was in the house.
This assurance gave me pleasure." [8]

The Widow White, it was said, urged Lee to hide in a
bed. But Tarleton, now certain what fox he had bagged,
opened fire and ordered Lee to surrender lest the tavern
"should be burnt and every person without exception be
put to the sword." Lee threw on his dressing gown. Bare-

headed and still in slippers, he surrendered to a sentry at the front door. Then, tied to a horse, he was taken to New Brunswick, where "the more hilarious among his captors are said to have celebrated by making his horse drunk." [9]

One might dismiss the amatory aspects of this tale were they not confirmed on the spot by Baron von Closen, who was told that a jealous cousin of the widow's had tipped off the British.[10] Moreover, the incident fits Lee's character well, for no sooner was he exchanged than he again demonstrated that he was a far more effective general in a bedroom than on a battlefield.

On the night of his return to the army, at Valley Forge, Washington gave Lee a welcome worthy of a hero. This story comes from Elias Boudinot, who was there:

> All the principal officers of the army were drawn up in two lines . . . all the music of the Army attended. The General, with a great number of principal officers and their suites, rode about four miles on the road towards Philadelphia and waited till Genl. Lee appeared. Gen Washington dismounted and received Genl. Lee as if he had been his brother. He passed thro' the lines of officers and the army, who all paid him the highest military honors, to headquarters where Mrs. Washington was, and there he was entertained with an elegant dinner, and the music playing the whole time. A room was assigned him back of Mrs. Washington's sitting room, and all his baggage was stowed in it.
>
> The next morning he lay very late, and breakfast was detained for him. When he came out, he looked as dirty as if he had been in the street all night. Soon after I discovered that he had brought a miserable dirty hussy with him from Philadelphia (a British sergeant's wife)

and had actually taken her into his room by a back door and she had slept with him that night.[11]

Where the "miserable dirty hussy" had her breakfast is not recorded.

Another New Jersey tavern, the historic inn at English-town, provided the backdrop for Charles Lee's second military disgrace. In the light of history his capture by the British was actually a stroke of luck for the American Army. That army would have been still luckier if the British had kept him. At Valley Forge Lee preached defeatism, despair, and the doctrine that Continental troops never could stand up in battle against British regulars—all the while he was in secret correspondence with Howe's head-quarters in New York, even going so far as to send a letter of congratulation to Clinton when he succeeded Howe.[12] When the British evacuated Philadelphia in June, 1778, and began their long march across New Jersey, Lee fought Washington's plan for a swift attack to split the British force and battle it piecemeal. He succeeded in convincing a number of the American generals, but not Greene, Wayne, and Lafayette.

When a New Jersey offensive was belatedly decided upon, Lee, after sulking a bit, insisted on taking the command from Lafayette. Protocol gave it to him. But when Washington ordered the attack on Clinton's forces as they moved out of Monmouth Courthouse (now Freehold), Lee beat a confused retreat just as a major victory was in sight. Catastrophe was averted when Washington himself rushed in, rallied the troops, and saved the day. Lafayette heard him call Lee a "damned poltroon." Washington had had enough at last.

Lee then proceeded to commit professional suicide with a pen: he wrote Washington two letters so insolent that they could not possibly be overlooked. A high-level conference was called at the Englishtown Inn. There Washington gathered his officers around a table in the dining room and the papers were drawn up calling for Lee's court-martial.

The first session of Lee's court-martial was held in another tavern, that of Hydert Voorhees in New Brunswick.[13] Whether Lee was guilty of treason and had deliberately courted defeat at Monmouth, as some believe, the court-martial was content to convict him of disobedience to orders, misbehavior before the enemy, and disrespect to General Washington. He was suspended for a year, then dropped from the army.

Charles Lee's farewell appearance occurred in a tavern in 1782, at the Conestoga Wagon in Philadelphia, on Market Street near Fourth. The proprietor then was Major Samuel Nichols. There Lee died, "a broken, ruined man, attended only by his former aide, Col. Eleazar Oswald." [14]

Coincidentally, the man for whom Lee had been exchanged was Major General Prescott, British commander in Rhode Island, who had been captured under strikingly similar amatory circumstances. The patriots struck in the middle of the night, hauled Prescott out of a very warm bed, and carried him off reputedly without a stitch upon him. The *London Chronicle* was inspired to comment on the affair with this bit of verse:

> What various lures there are to ruin man;
> Woman, the first and foremost, all bewitches!
> A nymph once spoiled a General's mighty plan
> And gave him to the foe—without his breeches.[15]

When Lee was seized at the Widow White's Tavern, his army was far enough away not to be involved. Soon General Sullivan brought those two thousand troops to join the main forces in Pennsylvania, and preparations for the attack upon Trenton got under way.

There is a divergence of opinion whether the seemingly minor American operations below Burlington were undertaken by coincidence or by plan. But they were taken; and they mattered. When General Israel Putnam, veteran Indian fighter then in command at Philadelphia, began ferrying men and supplies across the Delaware River to Gloucester Point, it was the start of a hit-and-run campaign the result of which was to divert British attention and spread thinner the Hessian troops encamped in Bordentown and Trenton. Joseph White, an artillery sergeant, tells of an affair at a New Jersey tavern during Putnam's operations in December of 1776:

> After crossing the river, we were put into the back part of a tavern; the tavernkeeper refused to take rebel money, as he called it. I went to General Putnam and told him that he had everything that he wanted "but he will not take paper money. He calls it rebel money."
>
> "You go and tell him, from me, that if he refuses to take our money, take what you want without any pay."
>
> I went and told the man what the General said.
>
> "Your Yankee general dare not give such orders," said he.
>
> I placed two men at the cellar door as centries. "Let nobody go down," I said. I called for a light, and two men to go down cellar with me. We found it full of good things, a large pile of cheeses, hams of bacon, a large tub of honey, barrels of cider, and 1 barrel marked cider-royal, which was very strong; also, all kinds of spirit. The owner went to the General to complain.
>
> "The sergeant told me," said the General, "that you refused to take paper money."

"So I did," said he. "I do not like your rebel money."

The General flew round like a top. He called for a file of men. A corporal and four men came. "Take this Tory rascal to the main guard house."

I sent a ham of bacon, one large cheese, and a bucket full of cider-royal to General Putnam. He asked who sent them. He told him the sergeant that he gave leave to take them.

"Tell him I thank him," said he.[16]

In all probability this was the tavern at the Gloucester toll bridge kept by Daniel Cozens, whose wife had inherited both the inn and the bridge from her father, Samuel Shivers. Cozens was such an ardent Tory that he organized a hundred of his neighbors and in 1777 marched them off to join the redcoats. Later the British made him a captain.

Putnam's and other subsequent South Jersey operations were successful enough to lure von Donop and some of his Hessians south from Bordentown: first, to the Sun inn at Black Horse (now Columbus), then later to a skirmish which was perfectly timed, intentionally or not, to prevent von Donop from going to the rescue once the Battle of Trenton was under way.

At Trenton, meanwhile, the Hessians had taken over all the better taverns. In command was Colonel Johann Gottlieb Rall. His officers were quartered in the Blazing Star, run by Frances White; his men utilized the jail (now the site of the Trenton Bank at State and Warren streets). Other regiments commandeered Henry Drake's Bull's Head Tavern, on Second Street, as well as the post office,[17] several churches, the Friends' meetinghouse, and various private dwellings. Principal picket station of the Hessian cantonment was the Fox Chase Tavern of Mrs. Joseph Bond, located on the Maidenhead Road (now Brunswick Avenue).

Seven miles away was the Bear Tavern, on Jacob's Creek, whose lights the chilled Continentals could see as they marched on through sleet and blinding snow that fateful Christmas night.

What followed, of course, is history. The taverns did their part. So did rum, imbibed on a grand scale in celebration of Christmas, a German tradition which Washington had sagaciously taken into account. Colonel Rall himself was one of the chief imbibers and was so drunk on Christmas night that he stuffed into his pocket, unread, a note from a Tory spy warning him that the Continental forces were on their way; he was a brave but pigheaded man, ever contemptuous of the colonial army of "farmers." Rall was mortally wounded in the battle. When Washington and Greene visited him after victory was complete, the note was found in his pocket. On hearing it read the dying man said in German: "If only I had read that [last night] I would not be here now."

Trenton's taverns found their boom days suddenly cut short when the Continental forces quickly recrossed the Delaware. But one week later they were back, and the taverns were bustling once more. The British were returning too. They were led by Lord Cornwallis, hefty, hale, and haughty, who was in none too good a humor since he had been about to sail for England on leave when Rall's debacle necessitated his fast recall. Confronted with a British force substantially outnumbering his own, Washington was willing to risk only a brief engagement, moving his forces to the south side of the Assunpink Creek and wrecking the bridges. There he made his headquarters in Jonathan Richmond's tavern, later shifting to the home of Alexander Douglass, which lay at a more discreet distance from the enemy's fire.

Urged by his aides to force a crossing and attack Washington then and there, even though it was growing dusk, Cornwallis, confident, decided to give his men a night's rest, observing, "We will bag the fox in the morning." In the morning, of course, the fox was gone and with him his entire army. Behind a screen of deceptively maintained campfires, they had taken a bypass route to Princeton and had won another victory there, early on the morning of January 2.

During that brief "Second Battle of Trenton" the Blazing Star Tavern figured in one of the most brutal of the many military murders that marked the campaigning in New Jersey. The Rev. John Rosburgh, chaplain of the Third Battalion of Northampton County Pennsylvanians, was having dinner in the Blazing Star when the advance guard of the British moved swiftly into the center of Trenton, creating great commotion. When the chaplain hurried from the tavern, he found his horse and the patriot troops gone. In trying to reach the American lines he was caught by a party of Hessians. While on his knees praying the sixty-three-year-old clergyman was "bayonetted seventeen times and then cut on the head with sabre slashes." His body was stripped of its clothing, a watch, and money. In the Blazing Star a short time later the Hessian commander loudly boasted of the deed.[18] Is it any wonder Lord Howe's own secretary wrote: "The Hessians are more infamous and cruel than any. It is a misfortune we ever had such a dirty, cowardly set of contemptible miscreants." [19] As bad as the Hessians were the loyalists. Stryker, a careful historian, states that their general, Courtland Skinner, rose in the same Blazing Star tavern that dark evening to applaud the Hessians for the murder of the Rev. Mr. Rosburgh.

Subsequent to his victory at Princeton, Washington was sorely tempted to strike toward New Brunswick, where there was known to be a rich store of British bullion—reputedly 70,000 pounds in gold [20]—and a large cache of supplies. But with Cornwallis in hot pursuit he chose instead to move the army to Morristown for winter quarters, a location where the Watchung Mountains provided strong natural defenses. Washington set up his headquarters in Arnold's Tavern (later known as Freeman's, Hayden's and Duncan's).

Elise Lathrop tells how, at this inn, Alexander Hamilton, then a colonel, probably saved the army from a surprise attack. Hamilton's office also was in the Arnold Tavern, and he quickly became suspicious of a spy who had been hired by Washington. Hamilton believed the man was secretly working for the British, a "double spy." So he laid a trap. "Busying himself while the spy was in the room with what appeared to be an extensive report of the American forces, ammunition, et cetera, but which really represented these as four times greater than they were, the Colonel had himself called from the office, and went out, leaving this report on his desk." When he returned, spy and report both had disappeared. Whether or not the British were deceived by this false information as to American strength, they made no attack upon Morristown that winter. Meanwhile Washington in his hilly hideaway could take a measure of satisfaction in the knowledge that the great British Army which so recently had controlled all of New Jersey was now bottled up in New Brunswick and Perth Amboy.

During the British occupation of Philadelphia, from September, 1777, to June, 1778, New Jersey taverns furnished a grim background for incidents, skirmishes, and even massacres. From a tavern in Salem County loyalists launched their attack on the Hancock House, which is now a state shrine.

Comparable bloody business took place in Shrewsbury, long a Tory stronghold. The historic Allen House was a tavern during part of the Revolution, and a corporal's guard of twelve Virginia Continentals were quartered there for the protection of the village. According to Gustav Kobbé, five loyalists hid among the gravestones of nearby Christ Church and bided their time. One afternoon the Continentals, off guard, left their arms stacked in the tavern while they took a walk in the garden. Quickly the Tories rushed the Allen House, seized the stacked weapons, and bayoneted the unarmed Virginians as they came into the tavern to see what was going on. Three men died, a number were wounded, and the survivors were taken to New York "where they were cast into one of the infamous Sugar House prisons." Adds Kobbé: "The father of the present [1889] Allen House, himself a descendant of the original owner, employed every means to obliterate the blood stains . . . even planing the boards, but the blood had sunk too deep and he laid a new floor over the old one." [21]

At Gloucester County's Chew Tavern, built in 1745 at Chew's Landing, the enemy stopped short of massacre. A Tory spy tipped off the British that Aaron Chew, the proprietor and a lieutenant in the Gloucester militia, had come home on a brief furlough. Soon a detachment of dragoons surrounded the tavern, began firing, threatened to burn the place, and caught Chew and a fellow militiaman, Joseph Albertson, as they attempted to flee. Chew spent two years in a Long Island prison, and even when the war was over he still "expressed his hostility to the British on every occasion." [22]

Stretching across South Jersey in those days was a chain of taverns which served as stations in the transport of supplies and prisoners captured off the coast by privateers. Among these was Falkinburg's Tavern in Clamtown (now Tuckerton), a gathering place for American coastal raiders. Next in the chain was the House of Richard Wescoat at

The Forks of Little Egg Harbor, near Pleasant Mills. A bit
farther on was the Blue Anchor Tavern, constructed in
1740 and kept in 1776 by Thomas Stites. Supposedly it was
named for a party of shipwrecked sailors who came to
anchor there while trying to hike across the state to Philadelphia. Scarcely less important in this traffic was the Long-
a-Coming Tavern—Long-a-Coming is now called Berlin—
operated then by the versatile John Inskeep, who farmed,
ran a sawmill, mended scythes, half-soled shoes, and in an
emergency could pull a tooth.

At Cooper's Ferry there were several taverns in Revolutionary times. One of them was used in June, 1777, for
the commencement of Princeton University, with degrees
awarded to the Class of 1776. The brilliant Dr. John Witherspoon, president of Princeton, was "as high a son of liberty
as any man in America," according to John Adams. Having
evacuated his battered university, he is said to have taken
leave of his students "wondering whether he should ever
teach there again in peace and honor, or whether he should
hang as a traitor before the institution reopened." [23]

Another tavern at Cooper's Ferry was run by Samuel
Cooper, a militant patriot, some of whose letters have been
preserved. In one of them Cooper tells of two other innkeepers, both Tories, going "a foraging as they call it, but
what an honest man calls PLUNDERING." One of these was
John Cunningham, "that kept the Centre," and the other
"Captain Taylor that kept the Bull and Dog." The men set
out in a schooner to seize supplies they expected to sell to
the British in Philadelphia but their expedition was over-
taken by the militia. All but four of the Tories were killed,
and the two tavernkeepers landed in prison in Haddonfield.

Sam Cooper's turn came a few months later. Early in
1778 the Hessian "hell-devils," as he called them, took over
his property. His bedroom and kitchen were "the only place

I have left to make use of, the rest all being taken by officers." Soon put under arrest by Colonel Simcoe, he wrote that "they took my right eye from me." Cooper's right eye was a powerful spyglass with which he had been observing British troop movements and promptly reporting to American authorities. This espionage had been betrayed by his maid, whose current lover was a British sergeant. However, while Simcoe's men were taking Cooper to Howe's headquarters he managed to escape. He found refuge in the house of a friend, who somehow seems to have been on sufficiently good terms with Howe to intercede and obtain permission for Cooper to return to his home on a promise that there would be no more spying. His release, he says, "was a great mortification to many of my old friends, and new enemies" who expected to see him "go to Gaol where many of them said I should have been long ago." [24]

Sam Cooper kept his promise with regard to spying, but he was far from chastened. In another of his letters he gives expression to that deep spirit of dedication and determination which the British never could understand but which made an "impossible" revolution succeed. Cooper's Ferry was thick with redcoats during the British evacuation of Philadelphia. Cooper wrote:

> They can't frighten me nor strike the least terror on me, for I can stand and see them cut, pull Down, burn and destroy all before them and not think more of it than I used to think of seeing a Shingle burnt. When they [the Tories] tell me they will ruin me, I tell them I shall be able to buy one half of them in seven years.

Cooper's tavern and ferry house survived for many years.

In the winter of 1779–80, Washington's forces were back in Morristown, taking over the taverns as usual. This time Washington stayed at the mansion of Colonel Jacob Ford,

Jr., which is today the showplace of the Morristown National Park, with its fine museum and the reconstructed
army encampment nearby at Jockey Hollow.

Over at his tavern, however, Innkeeper Arnold appears
to have been a bit touchy when General Greene moved
into his hostelry. In a letter to Arnold the general said that
he originally had planned "for himself and Mrs. Greene to
stay a few days . . . but upon the Army's being fixt in
the Neighborhood and the General in the town . . . what
was intended only as Lodgings became necessary to hold
as quarters." He continued:

> If you had objected to it I should have been obliged
> to apply to a Magistrate and if he would not have quar-
> tered me and the rest of the Officers . . . I should have
> quartered them myself without the consent of the people.
> This to be sure would have been a Disagreeable circum-
> stance . . . which I never wish to be reduced to; but
> you may Depend upon it the Officers of the Army will not
> lodge in the open fields for fear of putting the Inhab-
> itants to a little Inconvenience.[25]

It was in Alfred Norris's Inn at Morristown that the long-
delayed court-martial of Benedict Arnold was finally conducted. It was there that Arnold loudly proclaimed his
patriotism. It was there that he demanded vindication. And
it was there, all the while, that he was waiting for a British
reply to his letter to General Clinton setting his price for
treason as 10,000 pounds, "whether the contest is finished
by sword or treaty." [26] Later this tavern was known as
Dickerson's, then being kept by a captain of the Revolutionary Army.

Use of taverns for recruiting by the Continental forces
was fairly common throughout the Revolution. That use depended, however, upon two factors: the sympathies, patri-

otic or otherwise, of the innkeeper and whether the British
or the Americans were in control of the area. On some
occasions the recruiting was done right in the taproom, and
with drastic methods reminiscent of those which certain
Scotch lassies—and surely others—were wont to employ to
persuade bashful beaux to propose. An example is found
in a rather plaintive letter from one Samuel Coard to his
erstwhile employer, John Litle, of New Mills (now Pem-
berton). Litle, an ardent patriot, had an ironworks which
produced various products for the American forces. Coard
appears to have been an indentured worker. Under date of
July 2, 1777, he wrote:

> Mr. Litle this to inform you that i was inlisted by
> Joseph Grumly and John Hiland and they both took me
> into a tavern, caled for two quarts of Porter & half a pint
> of Rum, mixed them all together and made me Drunk
> first.
>
> Which I am very Sorry for and me so much Debted to
> you, but if you will pleast to send John Hurly here to
> the General hospital in Trintwon [Trenton] you shall have
> my Whoal Sute of Cloas but I am Wear in them yet. I
> am Shure you could get me of [off] from Captain Cruse
> yet if you pleas for i Shall be hear this month, and if it
> be So i shall for Ever thank you.[27]

The original spelling of this letter has been retained, but
punctuation added. No record is available to show whether
the "inlisted" Mr. Coard stayed in his "Cloas" or stayed in
the army.

Some New Jersey taverns served as places of refuge for
political leaders and government agencies as well as headquarters for the military. The Indian King, at Haddonfield,
kept during most of the Revolutionary period by Hugh

Creighton and his "lovable wife, Mary French," merits special attention because it is one of the finest examples, north
of Williamsburg, of a better-class eighteenth-century tavern,
with the added interest that it is original and not a recon-
struction.

Cornwallis visited the Indian King when the British Army
marched through Haddonfield on its way to New York after
the evacuation of Philadelphia. Many other Revolutionary
figures stopped there: Nathanael Greene, "Mad Anthony"
Wayne, Count Pulaski, the Marquis de Lafayette, and even
John Graves Simcoe shortly before he was captured near
Bordentown and marched through the streets there to public jeering. While there is no record that Washington slept
there, the delightful Dolly Madison did, when she was still
Dolly Payne. Innkeeper Creighton was her uncle, and a
Dolly Madison bed is now on display on the second floor
of the tavern. Dolly, slight of figure, with delicate face, blue
eyes, and jet-black hair, did sleep in this particular bed;
but it was then in the home of a neighbor whom she also
visited in her Haddonfield days. As noted earlier, women
often stayed in private homes when the taverns were
crowded; and the Indian King was usually a busy place.

It was in 1777 that the Indian King made its greatest
contribution to Revolutionary history, when it was both
meeting place and refuge for the New Jersey Legislature.
Trenton and Princeton had become hot battlegrounds, even
more uncomfortable for legislators than for soldiers. Thus
Haddonfield served for a time as the capital of New Jersey.
However, the quiet, charming community was soon to get
its own taste of British and Hessian occupation, but when
the Assembly held its first session there in January, 1777,
the redcoats were heading for New Brunswick.

Several memorable measures were enacted by that first
session,[28] with Governor William Livingston presiding. First,

a Council of Safety was created to deal with Tories and any persons disaffected to or acting against the government. The government, of course, was that of the New Jersey patriots, not that of George III. Earlier a substantial number of Jerseymen loyal to His Majesty had taken up arms, and many others professed neutrality when they were actually serving as British spies and betraying their patriotic neighbors. The Council of Safety was a counter-measure which was to become both feared and respected.

In another enactment, on January 29, 1777, it was decreed that the punishment for high treason was to be the same as in the case of murder, and it was further specified that corporal punishment would not bar the further "forfeiture of the estate of such offender." On May 10 of that year, in another session at the Indian King, the legislators approved the design and preparation of the Great Seal of New Jersey, and on September 20 they took what was—symbolically at least—the most far-reaching step of all when they voted to substitute the word "state" for "colony" in all legal documents. It was the final official break with Great Britain.

The Indian King was built about 1750 by Timothy Matlack, who later became secretary of the Continental Congress. When Matlack sold the property to Mathias Aspden, merchant and shipowner of Philadelphia, there was a tavern on the premises. In 1757 it was sold to Thomas Redman, who later conveyed it to Creighton. The license renewal granted Creighton on September 30, 1776, notes that he had "obtained license for several years past . . . and has given general satisfaction as an Innkeeper." [29] Creighton continued as host until 1790, when he sold to John Burroughs. Later owners were Samuel Denny, John Roberts, Samuel K. Wilkins, Thomas A. Pearce, Samuel Githens, Thomas Humphries, Samuel C. Smith, Joseph C. Shivers, Edward Brick, John Plum, and George W. Stillwell.

After 1850 the inn bore the name the American House. After Stillwell acquired it in 1874 the tavern fell into rapid decline, presumably because Haddonfield had voted to "go dry." Stillwell then attempted to operate his place as a temperance tavern. By 1900, however, the old inn had done duty as a general store, as a boardinghouse, and finally as a neglected shelter for vagrants. In 1903 the Indian King was taken over by the state, restored, its old name revived, and then opened to the public.

Unfortunately, the Indian King for the most part is furnished as a museum and not as a tavern. Nowhere is this more apparent than in the taproom, where there is a piano —but no bar. True, Haddonfield is still dry today, but as far back as 1744 some of its leading citizens were proudly declaring that "a vast quantity of Beer is every season brewed here and exported to Philadelphia and no Beer is in better Credit and Esteem than Haddonfield Beer." [30] The taproom, which has its own separate door to the street, is the first room on the right from the spacious center hall. To the rear is a communicating room which probably was used for serving meals. On the left upon entering is a spacious room typical of the tavern parlor of colonial days and reminiscent, with its impressive fireplace, of the parlor in Williamsburg's Raleigh. At the left rear is another large room, but what its purpose was is problematical. In all there are five rooms on the first floor.

The second floor of the Indian King boasts the long assembly hall where the legislators held those important sessions in 1777. It is still used for meetings, although no pretense of colonial furnishing has been made. In two other rooms on this floor there are museum collections, mostly very much postcolonial. On the third floor of the tavern are eight guest sleeping rooms, making a total of eighteen rooms, plus an attic, a basement, and a wine cellar.

Another building of Revolutionary significance clearly linked with the Indian King is still to be seen directly across the street, which today is called King's Highway. This is a brick structure that served as guardhouse and prison for the Council of Safety, which also held many of its meetings in the tavern. Reportedly this prison, in that same year of 1777, was filled with Tories awaiting trial. No foundation has been discovered, however, for a romantic legend that a secret tunnel ran beneath the main street and connected the prison with the tavern's cellar.

Haddonfield had at least three other Revolutionary taverns. One was once owned by Elizabeth Haddon Estaugh, founder of the community which proudly bears her maiden name; another, at King's Highway and Ellis Street, was built in 1773 by Thomas Perrwebb; and another nearby—the building is still there—was erected in 1777 by Edward Gibbs.

It would not be fitting to close this chronicle without recounting a bizarre post-Revolutionary fracas in a Revolutionary tavern, especially since the story comes from judicial records. The tavern involved was Joseph Hatkinson's, in Mount Holly, later to become part of the Arcade Hotel.

Apparently the fighting spirit was still abroad in Mount Holly a decade later, when two of its residents, neighbors, met one evening at Hatkinson's. One was Gamaliel Clothier, bricklayer by trade; the other was Joseph Butterworth, Jr., a hatter. There had been some differences between the two men over the boundaries of their lands and the fixing of a line for a partition fence. What followed is best told in the quaint but graphic legal language of the brief filed with "His Excellency Richard Howell, Esq., Captain General, Governor and Commander-in-Chief in and Over the State of New Jersey and Territories thereunto belonging, Chancellor and Ordinary in the same":

What Clothier [the bricklayer] had asserted to be true made the said Butterworth [the hatter] very angry provoking Language toward the said Gamaliel Clothier and Clothier told him we are neighbors and had better drop the dispute, but Butterworth being still more abusive and provoking, said Clothier told him that if it was not for the consequences of breaking the Law . . . he would chastise him for his insolence.

Whereupon the said Joseph Butterworth in an angry, threatening manner clenched his Fist and put the same towards the face of the said Clothier to strike & said to Clothier damn the Law . . . I will not take any Law of you upon which the said Gamaliel smote the said Joseph Butterworth with his fist or open hand in the face and the said Combatants immediately clenched together . . .

Butterworth had a Candle and Candle Stock in his Hand when the fray began and thrust the same towards the face of the said Clothier and, a scuffle ensuing, the Candle in the scuffle went out when some of the Company endeavored to part the Combatants. The said Clothier cried out he (Butterworth meaning) is biting my ear off upon which said Combatants were parted and a lighted candle being brought in from an adjoining room . . . the said Butterworth took something out of his mouth and throwed it on the Floor which Daniel Smith one of the Company took up and it appeared to be the bloody piece of said Clothier's right ear, from the top thereof, and we do certify that the said Gamaliel Clothier lost the piece of his Ear in the manner aforesaid. . . .

Signed: Wm. Rosill, Daniel Smith, Benj. I. Budd, Jos. Watkinson, John Ross, Doctor Samuel John, Hutchinson Page, Daniel Shields, Daniel Toy.[31]

SALT OF
THE SEA

It is wise to walk warily when exploring the inviting lanes and byways that tap so many inlets and coves along New Jersey's coast. There is at least a chance that you may come upon, or tread upon, graves containing long-lost bones of a little-known industry which mushroomed early in the American Revolution and as quickly disappeared.

During the 1920's a group of workmen were draining a marsh near Toms River. They were preparing to fill the area with earth for a real estate development. In the process they discovered a stone wall 250 feet long, containing three sluices or gates.[1] Submerged for a century and a half, this masonry was the dam of a saltworks built during the Revolution to extract salt from sea water and help supply the need of the Middle Atlantic colonies for that commodity. The need was urgent.

Philip Vickers Fithian remarked in his *Journals:* "How broad and general is the demand for salt!" And the Rev. Henry Muhlenberg wrote in 1776:

The people push and jostle each other whenever there

is the smallest quantity of salt to be found. The country people complain bitterly because they suppose there are hidden stores in Philadelphia.[2]

Those country people knew what they were talking about; speculation in salt and other scarce commodities had already begun. A year earlier the Continental Congress had sought to head off trouble by passing resolutions urging the respective colonies to encourage the making of salt. But resolutions meant nothing. Colonial New Jersey and Pennsylvania had long depended upon salt imported from other colonies, especially Massachusetts, and from Europe and the West Indies. Now they were isolated from the New England supply by His Majesty's Army in New York; and they were blockaded from foreign sources by the Royal Navy. Salt already was a key factor in economic warfare, and the British never lost sight of that fact throughout the war.

Salt also was a necessity of life, and particularly needed for preservation of meat and fish. Faced with a desperate situation both Congress and the states of New Jersey and Pennsylvania sought to promote salt manufacture by invoking the basic principle involved in privateering: hopes of big, quick, and easy profits.

On May 28, 1776, Congress offered a "bounty of ⅓ of a dollar p'r bushel upon all such salt as shall be imported or manufactured . . . within one year from the date hereof." [3] New Jersey's Council of Safety talked of lending money without interest for the purpose of erecting saltworks within the state, and employees—"one man for every 500 gallons the boiling vessels held"—were exempted from militia service unless their particular county was invaded. Pennsylvania moved still more directly, and its Council of Safety financed construction of the Pennsylvania Salt Works at Toms River.

Soon a real salt rush was under way. Official coaxing, it turned out, was not needed; a much better incentive was the high price salt was bringing at market. Before the war salt had sold in Philadelphia for two shillings a bushel; during the war it brought as much as seven pounds—or one hundred forty shillings—a bushel. Even when New Jersey sought to control salt prices, by an act passed on December 10, 1777, it allowed a price of three pounds fifteen shillings per bushel (thirty-seven times the prewar price) plus six-pence per bushel for every mile the salt was transported from a saltworks to the place of retail sale.

With salt speculation thus given what amounted to a legal blessing, it was only a matter of months before a score or more saltworks, of varying sizes, had sprung up along the New Jersey coast. Some notion of the feverish, get-rich-quick optimism of the times may be gathered from a letter written by Samuel Cooper, of Cooper's Point, to John Litle of New Mills. Litle had an ironworks and made nails, camp kettles, and other products for the Continental Army. The two men were partners in a saltworks at Chestnut Neck. Cooper wrote, in January of 1778:

> My expectations is so great of making a fortune out of the works that I have partly agreed for a Plantation to purchase for ten thousand pounds and I think if they are carried on as they have been till Christmas you & I may venture to begin a ship of at (least) three hundred ton to be Ready for Sea next March. No more, but I shall be Ever obliged to you for the Great fortune which I am like to make by Salt Works.
>
> I hope to see you here tomorror as we intend having a Supper of Oysters & a bottle of the best, for we can

aford it if any body can, since it all comes by Salt Works.

So great was the salt rush to the seashore—all the way from Shrewsbury to Cape May—that on March 28, 1778, the New Jersey Legislature repealed "An Act for erecting Salt-Works and Manufacturing Salt within the State of New Jersey" because of "the great number of private works erecting, as well as already erected, promising an ample supply of salt, so as to render a publick Works unnecessary." [4]

True, the high hopes of these saltmakers were not all to be realized. Some were to profit financially; others were to fail pitifully. Quite a few were to see their works burned and wrecked by the British, the exposed locations of most of them rendering them particularly vulnerable to raids from the sea. But those were still boom times in salt, and prices were holding high—or, to put it less politely, they were outrageous.

There is in the William L. Clements Library a curious letter from "Monmouth County, dated New Year's Day" which gives a sidelight on the New Jersey salt rush from the Tory point of view:

As you mentioned some thing of Salt Pans, I shall just inform you a little about this matter & would have you inform others. There is scarce any but what make Salt, & a great part of them pretend to be friends to the King. Perhaps they may have sent some Provisions to New York and got four times as much as they could get at home, and then they think that they can make salt freely & call themselves Friends to Government, but you will judge that matter whether they are not friends to their own Pocketts. To speak within Bounds there is not less than 2000 Bushells of Salt made every week from Black

Point to Cape May. You may be certain it is so, and more in daily preparing. Three of our old neighbors have got 28 Kettles & 2 Pans which will be going very soon; there is nothing but severe means will do. . . . You know that these works stand near the Water side, that 200 men might destroy them all, which if not done the Country will be supplied. The people come 200 miles for this Salt.

This letter bears no year date and no signature; it also lacks the name of the addressee. Evidently it was sent by a Monmouth County spy to loyalist headquarters in New York, and it well may have inspired the subsequent raids on Monmouth County saltworks. Of special interest in the letter is its over-all estimate of salt production, a figure found nowhere else; and though it comes from a loyalist source, there is no reason to doubt its accuracy within the limits of observation possible to an outsider.

Extraction of salt from the ocean was anything but a new idea in 1776. Manufacture of salt by evaporation of sea water had been carried on in China as far back as 2700 B.C. and in other lands from early times. Massachusetts had such a saltworks in the 1600's, and New Jersey one at Forked River in 1754, run by one Samuel Worden (or Warden).[5] The process, basically, is simple. Some factories simply boiled sea water and recovered the salt residue. Usually, though, the sea water was led into reservoirs through sluice gates at high tide or pumped into catchments, the pumps generally being run by windmills. In such reservoirs the water evaporated naturally, becoming brine; the brine was reduced to salt in iron sun pans or by boiling in vats. Larger saltworks had both pumps and boiling houses. Sun pans used in most of the New Jersey works varied in capacity from 170 to 840 gallons. Salt baskets also are mentioned in the records, and some experts think they may have been used in a purification process.[6]

While many technical details concerning the saltmaking equipment of New Jersey's Revolutionary saltworks remain obscure, it is established that they varied greatly in size and scope. Some were shoestring operations; and a number of the smaller plants, concerning which little is known, were run by squatters. On July 15, 1778, a meeting of the East Jersey Proprietors was called because "a number of persons in the county of Monmouth, having erected salt-works on Barnegat Bay . . . make use of the wood in the vacant lands of the General Proprietors of East Jersey for carrying on the said salt-works." James Parker, president of the proprietors, noted that he understood that "most of these persons have declared their intention to purchase the right to said lands." [7] The session was called to give them that opportunity.

Prospects of abundant profits in the salt business attracted a motley assortment of hopefuls. There were men of prominence, character, and social status, as for example John Neilson of New Brunswick and Aaron Leaming of Cape May. There were bungling promoters such as Thomas Savadge of the Pennsylvania Salt Works, whom we shall meet soon. There were odd individuals and illiterates, as well as professional patriots whose eager-beaver temperaments and talents for sharp practice often embarrassed the American cause and foreshadowed that famous comment of Marshal Villars: "I can take care of my enemies. God save me from my friends!"

One such was David Forman, who had developed a habit of traveling the shady sides of the streets of Monmouth County. Fresh from involvement in an election scandal,[8] Forman, along with a group of partners, joined the salt rush. The location of their enterprise cannot be specified but is believed to have been the one which bore the name of Union Salt Works. And, to the credit of someone in the syndicate, it must be noted that the works became one of the more useful and commercially successful on the upper New Jersey coast. Forman's construction methods, however, were something else again: his labor force proved to be made up largely of a contingent of the Continental Army!

On January 1, 1777, Forman sent a letter to George Washington, informing him that the saltworks project was under way, that he expected it to be of great value in supplying the army with salt, and that the works could be made more extensive and productive if a military detachment were assigned as protection from attack by British sea raiders. An odd light is cast upon the loose setup of the Continental Army by the fact that, although Forman was a brigadier general, he was building a saltworks instead of helping the army during the Battles of Trenton and Princeton. Washington, "who had been favorably impressed by Forman's energy and ability in the militia, transmitted the memorial to Congress without specific recommendation, but with implied approval. Meanwhile, he permitted Forman . . . to retain at the saltworks as a guard, a party of Continental troops which happened to be in the vicinity." [9]

Trouble soon materialized. Forman was charged with using the soldiers to build his saltworks. The complainant was one Trevor Newland, with whom Forman had been engaged in a dispute over land for the works. When the matter was taken to the Council of Safety, Forman declared that Newland was a Tory. But after the Council had heard all the testimony, including that of the captain of the troops, it reported that "the troops so stationed have not been of any use to the Publick; but have been employed

in collecting Materials, and erecting Buildings to promote
the private Interest of Individuals." The Council further
found that the works was not then producing any salt and
for some months would not "furnish a Quantity equal to
the production of divers other Works in the State which
are therefore better entitled to the protection of the
Publick."

The Council requested Governor Livingston to pass its
views along to General Washington. Livingston, however,
ducked the issue because, he said, evidence in his possession indicated that the complainant, Newland, "is not very
friendly to our cause." [10] By mid-March, nevertheless, the
question did come to the attention of Washington, who
wrote Forman as follows:

> To avoid the imputation of partiality and remove all
> cause for censure, both with respect to you and myself,
> I am now induced to direct [that the troops] for the pres-
> ent join and act with Col. Shreve's Regiment, in the
> purposes of the common defence.

Seven months later there were still soldiers at Forman's
saltworks. That is evident from the following letter, dated
October 21, 1777, addressed to Brigadier General Forman,
Salt Works, New Jersey:

> Sir: The enemy yesterday morning threw a large body
> of troops across the Delaware with intention no doubt
> either to storm or to invest Red Bank. . . .
> What I have said is on the supposition that the danger
> to the Salt Works which induced you to go down that
> way is not so great as to require the whole force you
> may be able to get together to guard against it. I do not
> mean to neglect the precautions necessary for their se-
> curity; they are of too much importance; but as the

defence of Red Bank is an object of the greatest moment I wish you to do as much as you possibly can towards it, consistent with a proper degree of attention to the Salt Works.

G. W.[11]

If Forman was wrong in his use of troops to build his saltworks, he was right in his fears of enemy attack. The following April (1778) a British expedition from New York, "a party of about 200 of the King's troops," arrived off Squan (Manasquan) and "marched to some very considerable saltworks erected there by the Rebels, which they entirely demolished." There seems little doubt that this was the Union Works, although there is serious doubt that they were entirely demolished. In fact, they seem to have been rebuilt and back in operation within a remarkably short time, especially considering their extent and the amount of equipment involved.

A good description of the Union Salt Works appeared in the *New Jersey Gazette* on March 24, 1779, when they were offered for sale:

The works consist of a boiling house, about 90 feet long and 33 feet wide, in which are five coppers and four iron pans, the coppers weighing upwards of 3000 lb. . . . four of which pans are round, about six feet diameter and about 12 inches deep, the other about 13 and a half feet long, 6 feet wide and 14 inches deep. The iron pans are made of wrought iron plate near a quarter of an inch thick, two of them are about 12 feet long, 6 feet wide and 14 inches deep; and the other two are each about 16 feet long, 6 feet wide and 17 inches deep; all of which are fixed in the best manner for salt boiling. Adjoining to the boiling house is a convenient storehouse, capable of containing 800 bushels of salt, and contiguous thereto is a pump house in which are two pumps, almost new, by which water from the bay is conveyed wither immediately into the pans, or into a covered cistern holding about 150 hogsheads, at times, when the water is saltest, and from thence let into the pans.

The advertisement offered also a dwelling house (35 by 24 feet), stables, smokehouse, and other buildings, as well as 160 acres of timberland nearby—located on a five-acre tract along the Manasquan River, about a mile inland. Three men signed the advertisement: Nathaniel Lewis, Joseph Newbold, and John Kaign. Forman's name is missing, perhaps because he was back in service with Washington's army or because Forman's was a different works, which seems possible but unlikely. No sale appears to have resulted from the advertisement since the Union Works was in operation as late as November 9, 1779, when it was advertising for woodcutters. After that it faded from the records, and no clue as to its closing date has been found.

The great New Jersey salt rush produced no character more curious than Thomas Savadge, who contracted with the Pennsylvania Council of Safety to build a saltworks at Toms River. Savadge's project differed from other saltworks along the coast because it was officially sponsored and paid for out of public, not private, funds. Named the Pennsylvania Salt Works, it was this enterprise whose ruins were mentioned at the beginning of this chapter; and despite extensive plans and large sums spent, the works was a bitter disappointment, and produced no appreciable quantity of salt.

Optimism came easy to Thomas Savadge, as easy as pessimism did later. First he persuaded the Council of Safety that he could build, in a short time, a works capable of producing 300,000 bushels of salt annually. Then he got himself appointed manager; and thereafter he jollied the Council along for nearly two years without producing any salt at all.

The Pennsylvania Council's contract with Savadge was signed on June 24, 1776, and two days later his "Waste Book"—a sort of daybook [12]—shows orders for lumber, tools, a raft, and bricks from Elijah Clark in Pleasant Mills. That July he made a trip to Batsto, then owned by Colonel John Cox, where he ordered large iron plates for salt pans, while smaller pans were purchased at Lawrence Saltar's forge in Atsion. Cox sublet the order for the plates since Batsto, not then possessing a forge, could not produce the wrought iron required. The subcontractor appears to have been a Benjamin Jackson, and the order [dated over a year later], found in a Cox letter in the State Library in Trenton, calls for "plates to be forged as long as the maggothead will admit of, at least 101 Inches long and 9-10 inches wide . . . & be sure they are straight on The Edges and both Ends of a width." Cox offered to supply the pig iron necessary for forging the plates, which were to be delivered "Either at Mount Holly [which Cox then owned also] or Batsto at your Expence." Cox also agreed that "If should you have more Plates than you can Readily Dispose of I will take them delivered as above at One hundred and twenty pounds per Ton."

The brick ordered from Elijah Clark appear to have been delivered promptly, as the books show that on October 12, 1776, Richard Wescoat was paid for scowing them to Toms River. Two weeks later Savadge reported to the Council of Safety at Philadelphia:

I have nearly compleated a boiling house one hundred and sixty-nine feet long, twenty-nine feet wide; a store sixty feet long, twenty feet wide; compleated two drying

houses, a small kitchen, a lime house, stable finished, mill
work for my pumps in good forwardness . . . Colonel
Cox's . . . people have disappointed me or should have
had part of the works compleated before this. Also a
large quantity of stuff joynted and ready for flooring the
sun pans . . .

The Council of Safety gave Savadge the fullest cooperation. When he urged that the works be provided military
protection, a log fort was built on Toms River with a barracks and a magazine. In November an officer and twenty-
five men were sent there as a guard. In February, 1777, the
Council ordered "that the armed boat *Delaware* under the
command of Captain Richard Eyre be immediately fitted
out and ordered to proceed with all dispatch to the said
works." That same month the Council also dispatched a
company of militia with two cannons. Further official cooperation was provided in the already mentioned action of
the New Jersey Legislature granting limited exemptions
from military service to saltworks employees.

Thanks to the waste book of the saltworks, we know the
names of most if not all its employees as of December,
1776. They were: Timothy Russell, John Johnstone, Robert
Atcheson, Thomas Lotts, Jacob Tilton, Sylvester Tilton,
Nathaniel Bennet, Abel Crossly, John L. Pintard, William
Holstead, Robert Stout, John Havens, Henry Rogers, Gid-
dion Crawford, and George Mount. Most of these men
appear to have lived in the neighborhood, and several were
active otherwise in Monmouth County affairs.

Yet with all this staff and all this time no salt was being
produced. In October, 1776, Savadge had written that his
boiling house was "nearly compleated" and the millwork
for his pumps "in good forwardness." Yet in July, 1777, he
reported: "I have about two weeks work to do at the mill

and pumps which would enable me to get four pans at work and the remainder in a short time." A month later he was writing that "my millwrights have nearly completed the mill and the pump work, when done shall get to work with two or three pans in a few days." It was now more than a year since construction had started, and numerous other private saltworks had been built and were in substantial operation. When November, 1777, came and there was still no salt, the Council of Safety wrote to Colonel Cox at Batsto that "we have at length employed the bearer, Mr. Davidson, to visit the works and furnish us if possible with a distinct account of matters there."

Davidson's report on the situation, if he made one, does not appear in the record. In January, 1778, however, Savadge submitted a report of his own: that two pans at last were completed and that about twenty bushels of salt were on hand. This sounded promising, but for some baffling reason those twenty bushels of salt, if they existed in January, did not show up as a credit on the books until May, five months later. Thus it had taken almost two years to produce twenty bushels of salt. The Council of Safety, understandably, now ordered Davidson to take over the management. But suddenly he became a mysterious figure too. Whether he assumed charge, went back to Philadelphia, or what, is anybody's guess. But Savadge stayed on and on, and he was there when the works—still unproductive—closed down in 1779. Last entry in the waste book is dated April 10 of that year.

From the outset it had been an ill-starred venture, and so it remained to the last. Savadge died in September, 1779, and two months later Colonel Frederick Hagner, acting in behalf of the Council of Safety, put the works up for sale. The following advertisement appeared in the *Pennsylvania Packet*, November 9, 1779:

On Monday the fifteenth day of November inst. will be sold by Public Vendue, the Salt Works belonging to the State of Pennsylvania situate on Barnegat Bay, in the County of Monmouth, in the State of New Jersey, together with the tract of Land containing about fifty acres. . . .

These works have been erected on a very extensive plan, calculated to make a great quantity of Salt, and in a situation the most favorable for the purpose. The buildings are large, commodious, and in good order, consisting of a dwelling-house, boiling-house, drying-house, two store-houses, a windmill for raising the salt water by pumps, and a smith's shop.

On December 31, 1779, the Pennsylvania Salt Works was sold to John Thompson of Burlington County for 15,000 pounds. There is no evidence to indicate that the plant was reopened or that it was in operation when a Tory expedition attacked Toms River on March 24, 1782, wantonly burned much of the town, and "destroyed the salt works."

A second saltworks near Toms River was operated by James Randolph. This was located near Mosquito Cove. Little is known concerning it save the following details given in an advertisement appearing in the *New Jersey Gazette* of March 20, 1782: A vendue of the estate of James Randolph was to be held at the inn of Samuel Forman in Upper Freehold. Offered was:

One plantation at Musqueto Cove, on Toms River, containing 400 acres or thereabouts, the greatest part thereof is excellent salt meadow with a convenient fishing place, salt works, one good frame dwelling house, etc.

It was signed by Benjamin Randolph and Tobias Hendrickson, executors.

Forty-odd miles to the southward was another important Revolutionary salt enterprise: the Friendship Salt Works, situated "in Great Egg Harbour, two miles to the eastward of Absecon bridge." [13] Locating this site would be a major undertaking today, a worthy challenge to even the most ambitious New Jersey explorer. The importance of the Friendship works lies less in the amount of salt produced, which was considerable, than in the fact that it is the only works whose surviving records afford an idea of the human aspects of saltmaking, and what life was like in those remote and isolated industrial hamlets.

The waste book of the Pennsylvania Salt Works reflected the managerial aspects of saltmaking: construction problems, financing complications, sources of supply, and headaches born of sheer bungling. Thanks to the *Journal* of Thomas Hopkins, manager of the Friendship works at Egg Harbor, it is possible to see the other and warmer side of the picture: a glimpse of the workmen at their tasks; aspects of manufacture and maintenance, labor troubles, and, sometimes, the simple problem of finding enough to eat.

As in the ironworks of those days, the Friendship saltmakers labored around the clock. Because production, in the *Journal*, is noted in baskets, whereas salt was sold by the bushel, it is impossible to give an accurate estimate of the value of the output. However, a normal day's production seems to have averaged eleven or twelve baskets, and Hopkins implied dissatisfaction only when the number of "baskets draw'd" fell to six or seven. Unfortunately, Hopkins's *Journal* covered a period of only about two months in the year 1780, and no further information has come to light to show when the Friendship works opened or when it closed. Nor are the owners' names known: Hopkins mentioned owners but never identified them.

Three years earlier, in 1777, Hopkins was a baker in

Philadelphia. Commenting on his efforts to aid Continental prisoners while the British occupied the Quaker City, he says: "Had I gone to work with my Bake Houses for the British I could have Baked from twenty to thirty Hundred of Bisquet pr. Day, for which I could have had 7/6." Instead, he helped the prisoners, who were so hungry that they "had been seen to Pull up the Grass & Eat the Roots." Hopkins appears to have had a just complaint to Congress over failure to reimburse him for "106 Head fatt cattle," flour, clothing, and other provisions for which "I laid out all my hard Cash." With indications that he still was in Philadelphia in 1778 or later, it is quite possible that the *Journal*, which began on August 11, 1780, marked the beginning of Hopkins's management of the Friendship works.

This *Journal* is one of the many manuscript treasures of the Historical Society of Pennsylvania. It is much too long to be fully reprinted here, but with the Society's permission I am offering extracts so edited as to present a rounded picture of life as it was lived at the Friendship Salt Works during a hot, humid autumn in 1780. For clarity, some of Hopkins's highly original spelling has been modernized in brackets.

AUGUST

11—Left home with James White crossed to Coopers Ferry. Proceeded on the Road near to Haddonfield, recollected leaving the Books behind . . . returnd by myself for them. Rose the 12th by daylight, paid our reckoning at Haddonfield 35/5/0 & proceeded to the Blue Anchor where we fed our Horses & got Breakfast . . . then sett off for the Works where we arrivd about Six OClock through Shoals of Musquetoes althe [all the] way who attacked us on every quarter with great Venom. Found one sett of Works

going, Martin & Nicholas Working them, Nicholas
Hart hauling Wood . . . three Wood Cutters came
in & said they could not stand it any longer the
Musquetoes being so very thick . . . drawd 11
Basketts Salt this Evening—

13—Sunday Morng. A very fine Tide. The Water very
good. Opend the gates & filled the Pond . . . no-
body at Work except the two Men at the fires.
Drawd 11 Basketts Salt.

14—Nicholas Hart Halling [hauling] wood. Jos. Allen &
John Young getting their Waggons in Order to go
to Philada. The Wood-cutters refusing to cut induced me to offer them 2/6 p. Cord which they
agreed to . . . after dinner the Wood-cutters returnd & said they would work no more as the
Weather was so hot and the Musquetoes so thick
. . . am fearfull unless we can employ some immediately shall be obd. to stop the Works.

15—The 3 Wood-cutters elopd before Day & stole an Ax
& a Loaf of Bread. Drawd 12 Basketts Salt.

16—No Wood-cutters at work—past Nine OClock the
Pickle [brine] not boil'd down yet owing to green
wood.

17—After Breakfast trimd Casks, 9 OClock went and Examined the watter in the ditch & found it Damed
[dammed] across the Natturall Ponds so that the
watter could not come up from the bay . . . set
the pump to work. . . . Martin Nelson Drunk &
very abusive.

18—Musquetoes & flies very plenty—Martin & Nicholas
at the fires. Agreed with Richard Demey to cut
wood . . . Martin Nelson drunk & Left the Works
from 3 OClock P.M. until 6 OClock & I had to go
help Nicholas to shift pickle . . . Martin so very

quarelsome with Cursing & Daming that I could hardly keep my hand of him. 10 baskets salt.

19—Measured up all the salt that was in the store. Nine Bushells of it was made when I came to the works. Set the pumps at work, fill'd the Cistern, Draw'd 11 baskets salt. The Musquetoes & flies exceeding plenty so that I can scarce write.

22—Nicholas Hart return'd from Halling wood & broke the Little Waggon, the large one being broke down before. One OClock opened the gates to get watter but it prov'd bad, let it out again.

23—Nicholas Hart at work in Garden for want of a waggon. Stopd the leaks in trunk, Dug the Ditch deeper, stopd Leaks in Cistern. 12 OClock P.M. flies & musquetoes in great plenty.

24—Set two pumps at work & from tasting of the watter . . . I am sure that wee use two much fresh watter & I am of the Opinion that if there was a trunk of logs from the Ditch across the Creek & to have the Naturall ponds dug one spitt Deep, & to have waste gates from the Ditch & pond that wee should make as much salt in two Days as wee do in three. After Breakfast Nich. Hart went to cut wood, the wagon not being mended yet . . . musquetoes in Clouds, Enough to eat up [a] horse.

25—Went & bought some fresh beef & salted it. set both pumps at work. Having green wood. Drawd only 10 baskets salt.

27—Cloudy Foggy morning. Set off to go to Little Egg Harbour.

28—Jos. Allen set off for Philada with 5 Casks Salt. Barney splitting wood—Henry at work about house —Martin Drunk.

29—Nicholas Johnson tending fires, Martin being Drunk in the daytime was not up all night & in the Morning went & got more rum & because I talk to him about his going on in such a manner, Instead of its having the Desired Effect he fell to Cursing and Damning. upon which I desired him to go down to the Salt House & mind his Business. He told me that he would go when he pleas'd for that it was none of my business & fell to Cursing of mee. I then took hold of him by the shoulder & push'd him out of Doors. I told him that if he did not behave better that I must & would discharge him. Got a pond good watter . . . did nothing in Evening . . . This day 8 baskets.

30—Martin drunk, gone after more rum. Waggon not mended yet. Mended salt house Roof. 2 OClock . . . set the pump at work, fill'd the Cistern & pond. Draw'd 10 Baskets salt @ 5 OClock P.M.

SEPTEMBER

1—Cloudy . . . wind N.E. full tide . . . the watter weal [wheel] having two spokes broke & braced it all Round, on both sides, set the pump at work. N. Hart got the waggon home.

6—Nicholas & Martin tending, Jos. Allen wood, Barney splitting, Henry cooking, John London & my self minding salt pan, found seven Rivets gone in one place many more Elsware. 6 wood Cutters at work today. Draw'd 12 Baskets salt.

7—Sent Jas Whylie to get fish & Clams, being out of meat. At work mending the pan. Lived on Clams today. Drawd 12 Baskets salt 2 OClock.

8—Very Buzzyly [busily] Employ'd with Jno. London about mending the Large pan. Clear & pleasant, no flies or mosquitoes. Our meat Intirely out, lived on Clams to Day.

9—Finished mending Large pan & got it in its berth this forenoon & paid John London, smith, Five Hundred Dolls on acct, of work done. Several applied to cut wood. Expect them next week.

10—Set the pump at work & found the head of watter low. Examined the Damn [dam] & found the trunk very Leaky—went to Meeting & in the afternoon made Inquiry after beef. The waggon not Return'd from Philada. Draw'd 11 Baskets salt 3 OClock.

11—Nichs. & Martin tending, Barney splitting, Allen Hall, wood—out of meat, went to Jafett Leads [Japhett Leeds] & got a Sheap which wee are to give flour for . . . Jas Whylee got some fish & about 1500 Clams. N. Hart & J. Young got to the works 4 OClock P.M. with 5 Casks Oats. Draw'd 11 Baskets salt.

12—11 Hands Cutting wood to Day . . . fill'd up 5 Casks salt to send by J. Young—heavy Rain hail & Thunder, most part of night. Draw'd 11 Baskets Salt.

13—Got up about 2 OClock, cal'd up Henry to get mee Breakfast, sent Barney to feed the Horse, set of [off] for home 3 OClock through Clouds of Musquetoes, as far as the Blue Anchor . . . arriv'd at Cooper's about 6 OClock . . . & got home about seven OClock in the evening. Left my son Robt. at the works.

24—Left home in Compy. with Jas White . . . cross'd to Cooper's . . . proceeded on the Road to Long Comeing [now Berlin] where we had bated [fed] our Horses, got a Drink & paid our Reckoning 24 Dolls—set out for Blew [Blue] Anchor where wee arrived in the Evening, had our Horses fed, got Supper, went to be [bed] . . . arrose in the morning,

got Breakfast . . . set out for the works where wee
arrived at two OClock P.M. where wee found L. D.
wife & sister E.B. & wife G Harris & my son Robt.
just going to set Down to Diner . . . the next day
the works was set up at Vendue & was bid in for
the owners . . .

OCTOBER

6—Left home about 2 OClock P.M. . . . cross'd the
river to Sam Cooper's . . . arrived at Murrell at
Long Comeing where I fed the horse, got Supper &
went to bed. Arrose at five . . . arriv'd at the works
at 5 OClock where I found my son Robt. who informed me that one set of works was in blast, our
wood gone, the watter very fresh having had a great
deal of rain. I Concluded it best to stop the works
until the watter is better. . . .

9—Bot [bought] a Bull of Jafett Leads for Eight pounds
hard Money. Kill'd him & brought the beef to the
works, weighed aboout four Hundred. . . .

11—This afternoon two of our Horses died with the botts.

13—Barney & Martin splitting wood, Jake cleaning Salt
House & pans. John Young left the works this morning without Acquainting me that he was going away.
. . . My son Robt set of [off] for home after Breakfast.

15—6 OClock Breakfasted & set out for Little Egg Harbour to get Ax's & agreed with Stephen Eyre to
come to work in about one or two weeks. Lodged at
Moss's.

16—Set off from Moss's & breakfasted at Willis's & had
a fateguing walk to the ferry's, paid ferryage Seventy
Dols & got to Jafett Leads, Rested little & set of

[off] for the works and arriv'd at dusk, having walked near 30 miles.

17—Tried the watter in the pond & found it very fresh, let it out, & got a pond of good watter, set one pump at work. Strickland employ'd in getting the other two fit for work.

18—Set the works in black 10 OClock A.M. Rebecca Allen came to keep house for us this Evening. Spoke to Isaac Condeary's son about the Ditch he was a Cutting from the bar near to the Damn [dam]. I told him that if he let out the watter I thought he was in a fair way to bring trouble on them & that the owners would sue them for Damages for Every Day the works were stop'd.

2—Clear, pleasant morning. Went to set the Pumps to work and found a Ditch cut through by the damn [dam] so that we can't pump.

Early that afternoon Thomas Hopkins set off for Philadelphia by way of Murrell's at Long Coming and Cooper's Ferry; while his son Robert, four days later, "left home about noon to go to Burlington after a horse to take down to the works." There, inexplicably, the *Journal* ends. Braddock-Rogers believes there was more of it, but that the rest was destroyed. In any case, the only other available information on this enterprise is an advertisement in the *Pennsylvania Gazette* on September 13, 1780. Announcing the proposed sale of the works by auction, it gives the best description we have of the Friendship Salt Works, although some of the virtues cited in the ad scarcely match up with the rough realities mentioned in Hopkins's *Journal*:

The works consist of 8 wrought iron pans, viz. 1 boiler, 22 by 16 feet, 3 ditto 16 by 12 feet, and 4 making pans, 16 by 7½ feet, all lately set up on new construction far superior to any other on the continent; and are capable of making a very considerable quantity of salt, supposed about a hundred bushels a day. Also a good dwelling house, a salt house, a store house and stables, a large covered cistern, 100 feet long, 22 feet wide and 2 feet deep; the whole erected on a healthy and pleasant point of land . . . and the privilege of cutting wood within one mile of the works. The works are supplied with water from the bay (of the best quality) which is pumped into the cistern. The sale to continue day to day until the whole are sold.

Best works on the continent! A hundred bushels a day! A healthy and pleasant point of land (with no mention of clouds of mosquitoes)! Clearly, advertising writers were no shrinking violets in those days either. As the *Journal* noted, the works were bid on by the owners. Perhaps they were "L.D., E.B., and G. Harris," who were at the works for dinner September 25. But, since the property itself was leased, there is no help in checking through deed or mortgage records, and unless fresh material comes to light somewhere the rest of the Friendship story will remain a mystery.

Three other saltworks were located in the Great Egg Harbor area. Summarized below is the little that is known about them:

FRAZIER KINSLEY'S SALTWORKS: This consisted of "4 large pans and several kettles, supposed to contain three or four thousand gallons . . . salthouse, drying house, dwelling house and stables." This works was offered for sale by Kinsley, "or Peter January in Philadelphia," in the *Pennsylvania Evening Post* of July 21, 1778. No location is given other than Great Egg Harbor. It could have been the Friendship works in its early stages.

NATHANIEL PETTIT'S SALTWORKS: Located "two miles northward of Absequan River" and "about eighteen miles southward of the Forks of Little Egg Harbour," it is mentioned as an "independent saltworks" in a 1778 advertisement for woodcutters and laborers.[14]

KENNEDY & MC CULLOH'S: "Situated about three miles from Great Egg Harbour Bar," this "compleat set of saltworks" was offered for sale "for cash only" on September 3, 1778. The property included stores, dwelling house, four horse teams, an ox team, a stout active Negro man, 100 acres of wood with an unexpired lease having five years to run at twenty-five pounds a year.[15]

Two saltworks are known to have operated in the Little Egg Harbor region. One of these, owned by Samuel Cooper and John Litle, was mentioned earlier in this chapter. It was established in 1777, apparently in the vicinity of Chestnut Neck, and was destroyed during the British attack there on October 7–8, 1778. Early that month Cooper wrote his partner: "I have just learned that there is an expedition going on towards Egg Harbour and I understand you have a quantity of Salt there. I hope you will think as I do and remove it as soon as possible, for Depend on it the works will be Destroyed and there should be no time lost. Salt sells for eight pounds in town."

The Cooper-Litle works must have been a dismal place, since it depressed even "Sam" Cooper. In January, 1788, he wrote: "My Waggon is gone off this morning with 8 Bushels Petatoes for the use of the works and Sundreys for the men which they stand in great need of. For my part I don't know how they have stood it so long in such a cold place and nothing but Green pine wood to Burn. I told Tomme to get oak wood let it cost what it would, for Mark's wife has done more than ever I could Expected considering the bad Wood, and two young Children. The men has likewise stood it admirable concidering wet feet from morning till night and no Rum." [16]

The other saltworks at Little Egg Harbor was on Falkinburg Island, at first owned by Thomas Heston & Co., and sold, in 1779, to Jacob Falkinburg of the family of first settlers in Tuckerton (then Clamtown). It was one of the smaller enterprises, an advertisement in the *Pennsylvania Packet* of April 24, 1779, mentioning one 3,000-gallon wrought-iron pan, cast-iron pans, a salt pond, etc.

Three Cape May County saltworks were located at Townsend's Inlet, Turtle Gut Inlet, and Cape May.[17] The first noted was run by Dr. Robert Harris, who also manufactured gunpowder for the Pennsylvania Committee of Safety. Little else is known of the place save that the British had marked his establishment for destruction, but there is no evidence that any direct effort was made to carry out the threat. Harris, in 1782, was elected a representative from Cape May to the General Assembly.

Except that the Turtle Gut saltworks was run by Levi Hughlingsworth, no information has turned up concerning it.

At Cape May Aaron Leaming set up a saltworks in 1777. His diary for May 23 of that year noted: "Mr. Hand & Mr. Godfrey went on the beach to Set up my Salt Works. 6 Kettles viz. 3 of 32 gall. & 3 of 42 gall. each, about 222 gall. the whole." On July 18 Leaming recorded that "Mr. John Holmes and I having concluded to encrease our Salt Works, Persons Leaming . . . is preparing to set out to buy Kettles. Our aim is to buy 3 tons for him and 2 tons for me and 1 ton for Jesse Hand. For that purpose I gave Persons 125 pounds—to pay in earnest toward the 3 ton for Hand & me the rest must be paid when the Kettles are ready." On

July 27 John Holmes and Persons Leaming had "been gone
9 days to Reading Iron works to buy kettles . . . and they
bot 10 Ton . . . @ 50 pounds per ton." [18]

Another prominent Jerseyman also engaged briefly in the
salt business, Colonel John Neilson of New Brunswick, with
three partners—Major John Van Emburgh, Captain Jacques
Voorhees, and John White, the last of Philadelphia. A saltworks was built at Toms River in 1777, as one of several
speculative ventures of this group. When profits did not
materialize, they leased the works and, finally, sold out
in 1782.[19]

Aside from these fragmentary notes virtually nothing is
known of additional New Jersey Revolutionary saltworks
save their names, owners, and in some instances, approxi-
mate locations. Dr. K. Braddock-Rogers, of the University
of Pennsylvania, gave a list of these in a pioneer article in
the *Journal of Chemical Education* in December, 1938.
Other than the works already mentioned they are:

A "small works at Shrewsbury." Destroyed by the
British in 1778.

Several works set up near the mouth of the Shark
River. Two of these were burned by the British.

Samuel Brown's works at Forked River, burned by a
band of loyalists in 1782.

Ocean View; Rio Grande; Cold Spring—"several works
at each place."

It is plain that the great salt rush did not produce the
rapid riches so many expected. Large or small, the Revolutionary saltworks along the Jersey shore were constantly
menaced by two enemies: the British and the very sea from
which they drew their salt. Contemporary newspapers mention destruction of a number of small saltworks by great
storms and tides; and the record already has shown that

nearly a fourth of the works listed were burned or wrecked by the British and their loyalist helpers.

The *coup de grâce* for New Jersey's saltworks, however, came when the bottom fell out of the salt market. Prices began to decline as more and more salt was manufactured, and they fell further when imports began coming with increasing steadiness both from Europe and from the West Indies, especially Turks Islands. Some of these supplies got through the British blockade, which became weaker as French naval activity diverted British attention; and others were acquired as the result of seizures of British merchant vessels by American privateers. Thus it is no wonder that as early as 1778 many of the saltworks were put up for sale.

During the War of 1812 efforts were made to revive the New Jersey coastal salt industry. Braddock-Rogers lists four such works: the Leeds works on Absecon Island, near Atlantic City; the Bartlett works, near Tuckerton; the Thacher works, in the same vicinity; and the works of Zadock Brown at Absecon. Little is known of these enterprises other than Brown's, which not only survived until 1825, but also, after being destroyed by a storm in that year, was rebuilt and stayed in business until 1840. For the record, Brown's successors in the business were, after 1825, Hosea Frambes and Ryon Adams; after 1836, John Bryant. These works are said to have been located at what is now Maine and Baltic avenues in Atlantic City. They consisted of six big tanks, two rows of three each, and a large windmill pump with cedar log piping to keep the vats filled with salt water. Movable roofs were used to cover the tanks at night and on rainy days. After 1840 Bryant operated another saltworks in South Atlantic City, but its exact location is not known.[20] Commercially, these post-Revolutionary works were not important; historically, they are of nostalgic interest.

THE MURDER OF JOSHUA HUDDY

The twelfth of April, 1782, dawned as a quiet day. The war was about over. American independence seemed in sight.

Riding at anchor off Sandy Hook, with apparent serenity, was His Majesty's man-of-war *Britannia*. Shortly before noon a boat was lowered, and six sailors began rowing for the Jersey shore. In that boat were seventeen others: sixteen loyalists and one patriot, and he was manacled. A landing was made at Gravelly Point, below what is now Atlantic Highlands. There the loyalists improvised a gibbet out of three fence rails and a barrel. And there they hanged Captain Joshua Huddy. It was the cold-blooded murder of a prisoner of war, and the beginning of an international incident.

Joshua Huddy, of the New Jersey militia, had been captured in a loyalist raid on the blockhouse which he had commanded at Toms River. Others captured with him had been exchanged; Huddy was condemned to die. He was condemned without formal charges, without a hearing, without a chance to defend himself. When some patriots later that afternoon found Huddy's dangling, lifeless body, there was pinned to it this notice:

We the Reffugees * having with Grief long beheld the Cruel Murders of our Brethren and finding Nothing but such Measures Daily Carrying into Execution

We therefore Determine not to suffer without taking Veangeance for numerous Cruelties and thus begin and have made use of Capt. Huddy as the first Object to present to your Veiws, and further *Determine* to Hang man for man as long as a Reffugee is left Existing

UP GOES HUDDY

for

PHILLIP WHITE [1]

This manifesto was as dishonest as the crime was dastardly. The Philip White purportedly avenged was a loyalist spy. He had been caught and was killed while attempting to escape. Developing events exploded loyalist attempts to portray him as a martyr.

Leader of the Huddy murder party was Captain Richard Lippincott, a neighbor of Huddy in Shrewsbury prior to the Revolution. An ardent Tory, Lippincott had been arrested in October, 1776, for concealing a British spy. He was jailed in Burlington but had managed to escape, made his way to New York, took an active role in loyalist activities there, and on February 17, 1781, was appointed a captain of the Associated Loyalists, an organization headed by William Franklin, last of New Jersey's royal governors.[2]

General Stryker has called Lippincott an infamous man. Certainly at first he appears to have boasted, perhaps as a form of terrorism, of his part in the hanging of Huddy. Only after it became clear that the British High Command was almost as shocked as the Americans by this barbarous

---

* The terms "loyalist," "refugee," and "Tory" were used synonymously and indiscriminately.

act did Lippincott begin to cringe behind the defense that he was merely carrying out orders.

Events followed in swift succession. On April 14, 1782, a protest "approven by upwards of four hundred respectable Inhabitants" of Monmouth County and signed by a group of their leaders, was presented to "His Excellency George Washington, Esqre., Commander-in-Chief." It noted, first, that "hanging any person, without any, even a pretended tryal, is in itself not only disallowed by all civilized people, but it is considered as barbarous in the extreme." Second, it was stated that "the Law of Nature and of Nations, points to Retaliation as the only Measure which can in such cases give any degree of Security that the practice shall not become general." [3]

One week later Washington wrote as follows to Sir Henry Clinton, British commander in chief:

The inclosed Representation from the Inhabitants of the County of Monmouth, with testimonials to the facts (which can be corroborated by other unquestionable Evidence) will bring before Your Excellency the most wanton, unprecedented and inhuman Murder that ever disgraced the Arms of a civilized people. . . .

Candor obliges me to be explicit. To save the innocent, I demand the guilty. Captain Lippincot therefore, or the Officer who commanded at the Execution of Captain Huddy must be given up. . . . [4]

For Washington that was strong language. Yet it only reflected mounting public indignation as well as fast-surging sentiment in Congress. While awaiting Clinton's reply, Washington took a poll of his generals and commanding officers, and of twenty-five replies all agreed that retaliation was a "justifiable expedient." [5] Clinton, in turn, had called

for an opinion from his Board of Officers, headed by Lieutenant General Robertson. Meeting on April 25, 1782, they
found, unanimously, that "all those concerned with Captain
Lippincot in the Execution of Joshua Huddy . . . should
be immediately apprehended, and with Captain Lippincot
himself, be tried by a General Court Martial." [6]

Franklin and his loyalists were on a spot. They had cried
"Up Goes Huddy for Philip White!" Now they brought forward a witness, one Tilton, to justify the hanging. Tilton
declared that Huddy had captured Philip White "six miles
up in the country, cut off both his arms, broke both his legs,
pulled out one of his eyes, and then damned him and bid
him run."

This atrocity story quick backfired. It was shown that
Huddy could not possibly have had a hand in the death of
Philip White for the reason that Huddy at that time was
in a British prison in New York and had been there the
four previous days. Then came out the full truth about
White himself:

On Saturday, the 30th of March last, he [White] was
surprised by a party of our people, and after he had laid
down his arms, in token of surrendering himself a prisoner, he again took up his musket and killed a son of
Col. Hendrickson; he was however taken by our light
horse, and, on his way from Colts-Neck to Freehold,
where they were conducting him, he again attempted to
make his escape from the guard who called on him several times to surrender; but he continued running, although often crossed and recrossed by the light horse
. . . and finally, when escaping into a bog, impassable
by the horse, he received a stroke in the head which killed
him instantly. The above facts have not only been proved
by the affidavits of our friends who were present, but by

the voluntary and candid testimony of one Aaron White, who was taken prisoner with the said Philip.[7]

Such clear evidence convinced Sir Henry Clinton, who disavowed the hanging as a "barbarous outrage" and ordered Lippincott taken into custody and held for court-martial. This action did not please William Franklin, who protested to Clinton that Lippincott had been "seized and sent to the Provost" before he could complete his defense report on the affair.[8] In still another letter to Clinton, dated April 27, 1782, Franklin made an effort to justify Huddy's murder:

I am desired by the Board [of Associated Loyalists] to inform you that the three prisoners . . . delivered to Captain Lippincot on the 8th Instant were not exchanged according to the Intentions of the Board, but that they were nevertheless disposed of in a Manner which the Board are clearly of Opinion was highly justifiable from the general Principles of Necessity and the peculiar nature and circumstances of the Case. . . .

Randolph and Fleming were both exchanged for Captn. Tilton. Captn. Lippincot . . . mentioned verbally that Huddy was *exchanged* [laying an emphasis on the word] for Philip White. . . .

Your Excellency will please to excuse the freedom of these Observations. They are not intended to give you any offence; but it would ill become us to be silent when we find that one of our Officers is not only seized without the least intimation to us of any such intention, but when from the mysterious conduct which has been observed on the occasion, an universal Alarm has spread among the Loyalists within the Lines, and is likely to be productive of more pernicious consequences among those without. . . .

Wm FRANKLIN [9]

Clinton's reaction to "these Observations" was not long in coming. While he refused to hand Lippincott over to Washington, pending the court-martial, he cracked down firmly on Franklin and his loyalists. The Board minutes for May 2, 1782, note that "the Commander-in-Chief [Clinton] directs that no Expedition or Excursion against the Enemy shall take place under their [the Loyalists] charge without His Excellency's particular Order." [10] In effect this put an official halt to further loyalist raiding of the New Jersey coast as well as an end to further murders in the campaign to "hang man for man as long as a Reffugee is left existing." At top loyalist levels this order was reluctantly obeyed; at lower levels some outrages continued.

Despite Clinton's sharp rebuke, Franklin and his Associated Loyalists, with one exception, persisted in attempting to justify the murderous "exchange" of Joshua Huddy for Philip White. The exception was Daniel Coxe, the old Tory of Burlington, who declared he "never gave any countenance to . . . or had any foreknowledge of" the plan for Huddy's execution.[11] Courtland Skinner was on the court which tried Lippincott, but no support was given there for William Franklin's philosophy. Instead, the court-martial held that Franklin and his Board were primarily responsible for Huddy's execution;[12] and Lippincott was acquitted on that ground, the ground that for all the blood on his hands he had merely obeyed the orders of his superiors.

Soon after Lippincott's acquittal Adam Hyler, the daring privateer captain, staged a bold attempt to kidnap Lippincott. Taking a picked group of men disguised as a British naval press gang, he set out after dark and landed in New York at Whitehall wharf, proceeding at once to the house where Lippincott was known to be living. Lippincott was out, having "gone to a cock-pit." Since it was unsafe to linger, Hyler and his men returned to their boat. It was not, however, a wasted trip. Spotting a sloop from the West Indies lying off the Battery, the privateersmen boarded her, cut her cable, set her sails and with a northeast wind got her to Elizabethtown Point. There, before daylight, Hyler took off forty hogsheads of rum. He then burned the sloop to prevent her recapture.

As a consequence of the court-martial, Sir Henry Clinton, while still deploring the murder of Huddy, firmly refused to surrender Lippincott to Washington; and there seems to have been no suggestion that William Franklin be handed over instead. Franklin, in fact, had fled to England before the court-martial was over.

Washington was not slow to act. Earlier he and his council of officers had determined that if Lippincott were not given up, a British prisoner would be selected by lot and hanged in retaliation. The British, after all, had set the pattern. In the case of Major André, Clinton had chosen to let him hang rather than give up the traitor Arnold. He could have saved André; he preferred to save Arnold. Here was a somewhat similar case. Again Clinton was called upon to choose between a British soldier—in this case wholly innocent—and a scoundrel; and again he elected to save the scoundrel. Worse, with the passage of time Britain was to reward and honor that scoundrel.

Somewhere in the pigeonholes of psychiatry there may be an explanation for that special and implacable hatred which the Loyalists of New Jersey reserved for their former brethren and friends and neighbors. When the Revolution began the Loyalists were at least on solid and legally defensible ground. With wiser policy, much of that ground might have been held. The Loyalists were supporting an established government, i.e., law and order; and at that time New Jersey was one of the Colonies most lukewarm toward the Revolution—after New York, New Jersey had the highest estimated proportion of loyalists.[13]

Bitterness, however, corroded the loyalist cause everywhere, and particularly in the Garden State. Intensity of feeling, of course, was not one-sided; but as we shall see the fury and vindictiveness of New Jersey's loyalists alarmed even the British High Command, which feared what came to pass: loss to the king's cause of the many neutral Jerseymen as well as a substantial number who had been loyal when the conflict began.

The Jerseyman of 1776, whatever his political sympathies, must have been bewildered by the motley character of the Royal Army that confronted him. More than half of it was composed of hirelings from German princes.* Probably a tenth part of the remainder was made up of other Jerseymen, often neighbors and even kinfolk.

It was not generally known in the colonies how unpopular the war was with a great many Englishmen at home and what difficulty His Majesty was having in obtaining recruits. Nor was it common knowledge in New Jersey that Vice-Admiral Keppel had refused to lead the Royal Navy in war against the Americans, that William Pitt had withdrawn his son from the army, that Lord Effingham

---

* While the German troops usually are called "Hessians," only about 60 per cent of them actually came from Hesse-Cassel. Nearly four thousand were from Brunswick, and the rest from four other principalities. Most of these men were professionals, but quite a number were drafted, some mutinied before embarking, and a large number who survived the war refused to return to their native lands but chose to start new lives in the new country.

had resigned his commission when he learned that his regiment was assigned to America, and that Lord Jeffrey Am-
herst rejected both a peerage and a personal appeal from
George III to take command in the American struggle, because he did not choose to fight his old comrades of the
French and Indian struggle.[14]

The average Jerseyman did know that the patriots were
in control of the state government, that William Franklin
was out of the governor's office and William Livingston in.
And he knew above all that the army of His Majesty was an
unexpectedly hostile, strange, and fearsome aggregation
which conducted itself in the manner of a conqueror rather
than that of a liberator. Howe's troops as well as the Hessians, most of whom spoke no English, roamed far and
wide, looting and raping and burning on a scale which the
British commanders apparently could not control, even as
they ruefully admitted that their own forces were creating
embittered rebels.

Then came the Loyalist "Greens," so called for their uni-
forms, with their raiding and the massacres that completed
the alienation of an enormous number of Jerseymen from
their obedience to the crown. In Monmouth, Gloucester,
and Cumberland counties particularly, the character of
Tory operations made more enemies for George III than
even the marauding by the Hessians.

It was the murder of Joshua Huddy that brought the
warped picture of loyalist activity into sharp focus, put an
effective end to much of that activity, and terminated
loyalist influence—never actually great—upon subsequent
British conduct of the war.

Beyond doubt the Huddy murder also prejudiced the
Tory position in the negotiations for peace; and William
Franklin's official responsibility for the crime may well have
been part of the basis for his father's unshakable opposition

to American concessions to the loyalists when the treaty was being drawn up. As Carl Van Doren points out, for a moralist Franklin was strangely implacable on this subject; while Jay and Adams might have yielded rather than break off the peace negotiations, "Franklin could not be moved." [15] Compensation for confiscated loyalist estates was one of the last sticky obstacles to a completed treaty, and even when the British virtually begged for a face-saver, the most Franklin would agree to was a recommendation to the states for restitution of the seized properties. Franklin knew full well that the states would never follow such a recommendation.

Thus the loyalist cause was finally consumed by the fire of its own hatred and bitterness. The loyalists' very vindictiveness lost them countless friends in England as well as in America, friends which wiser methods and more restrained conduct might have kept. From the beginning the loyalists, by taking up arms, made the Revolution a civil war as well as a war for independence; and it is no wonder, as Henry Steele Commager and Richard B. Morris point out in *The Spirit of 'Seventy-Six*, that throughout the colonies patriots regarded them "with a loathing they never felt for British regulars." [16] Worse, the loyalists always seemed to be in the thick of the dirtiest infighting: in the Wyoming and Cherry Valley massacres and in Tarleton's Legion, where their penchant for killing surrendered Continentals came to be known as "Tarleton's Quarter." Yet it was in New Jersey that loyalist zeal reached its zenith of frenzy and it was in New Jersey that the Loyalists' chances for postwar reconciliation met crowning tragedy in the aftermath of the Huddy murder.

Searchers for an explanation of this surcharged sentiment, so seemingly localized, will not find an answer in the important issue of property confiscation. Such confiscation was general, and there was no more proportionately in New Jersey than elsewhere; indeed, quite a few cases of kindhearted leniency could be cited. With respct to physical punishment or maltreatment of Tories, the New Jersey record is on the mild side. There were some applications of tar and feathers. Thomas Randolph, of Quibbletown, a cooper, was "stripped naked, well coated with tar and feathers, and carted in a wagon publickly around town," whereupon he repented and was quickly released.[17] Hundreds of Jerseymen were cited for treasonable activity, but the files show that most were acquitted or released, only a fraction were punished, and I can find no record of any hanging for disloyalty. Again to quote Commager and Morris: "what is perhaps most impressive . . . is not the severity but the relative mildness of the Patriots. There was violence, to be sure, but little bloodshed and few authenticated cases of loss of life." And that statement is applied to the entire thirteen colonies.

In his "Origins of the American Law of Treason," in the William and Mary *Quarterly* for January 1960, Bradley Chapin, Assistant Vice Chancellor of the University of Buffalo, observes: "The pardoning power was used widely and took every form from blanket amnesty to 'shadow of the gallows' pardons. Only a tiny minority of those charged with treason ever experienced the terror of the gallows and the hangman's noose. Drastic purges and violent assizes were not a part of the Revolution. There was no reign of terror. The record is one of substantial justice done."

The conduct of New Jersey's Loyalists stands in sharp contrast. There is simply nothing which may be held against the Patriots that compared with the killings inspired by the little coterie of Loyalists huddled in New York. To cite only the two worst:

The Hancock House Massacre. In March, 1778, twelve

soldiers, off duty, and four civilians were slain in the Hancock House, Salem County, after they had surrendered. Sickler writes that when "the Greens entered the house, the Americans, seeing former friends and neighbors, shook hands with some of them unmindful of their errand"; whereupon the mistaken men were cut down "some begging for their lives as they named the men who were killing them." The orders had been: "Spare no one—give no quarter!" They were carried out.[18]

The Long Beach Massacre. This was carried out at night, in October, 1782. A party of loyalists murdered twenty sleeping men. It should be repeated that there is nothing in the patriot record in New Jersey which could excuse or justify such measures as "retaliation," let alone honorable combat.

Where, then, lies the answer? Some may point to loyalist frustration, stemming, first, from their own failure to recruit Jerseymen to the king's cause on the scale they had anticipated and, second, from Lord Howe's unwillingness to "distribute arms among them without bothering about formal military organization." [19]

Howe had reasons for misgivings as to loyalist judgment as well as loyalist eagerness. When he first occupied New York he was told that "New Jersey is a region overflowing with loyal adherents to the crown who only wait a safe opportunity to declare themselves." [20] At first Howe believed this. He reported home that "I have great reason to expect an enormous body of the inhabitants to join the army from the provinces of York and the Jersies." And he appointed Courtland Skinner (last of New Jersey's royal attorneys general) first a colonel and then a brigadier general with authority to raise five battalions of 2,500 soldiers, the headquarters to be on Staten Island.

By early 1777 Skinner had recruited only 517 men; by

November of that year he could offer only 859, and in May, 1778, the peak total was a mere 1,001—much below the total authorized.[21]

An even deeper source of irritation was Howe's unwillingness to pass out arms among the loyalists "so they could go forth, either individually or in impromptu groups, to terrify sympathizers with the Revolution and to make themselves masters of their districts."[22] Howe felt that such tactics would embitter the struggle beyond reconciliation, and reconciliation was his long-range goal. The rightness of Howe's viewpoint was demonstrated after his successor, Sir Henry Clinton, reversed that policy. By 1779 Skinner was offering a reward of 2,000 guineas for capture of Governor Livingston "dead or alive,"[23] and the events noted above were occurring in bloody succession, with a climax in the murder of Joshua Huddy.

Thus Loyalist frustration undoubtedly was part of the picture. Yet one must look further still for the dark malignancy of spirit behind so many of the undertakings of the loyalists in New Jersey after Clinton had reversed Howe's policy and given them the fuller rein they had wanted. One must look to the head of the Associated Loyalists, William Franklin himself. Somewhere in the psychological background of this complex man lay at least a partial explanation of that odd metamorphosis by which a youthful Whig became more royalist than the king, by which a son devoted to his father became that father's open enemy, and by which an able colonial governor dedicated to respect for law could stand charged, by a British court-martial as well as by Congress, with the murder of Joshua Huddy.

It is difficult to measure the effect upon William Franklin's ego of the fact that he was born a bastard, and presumably never knew the identity of his mother. Some believe she was Deborah Read before or after she began to call herself Deborah Franklin; others have alleged that she was a maid named Barbara who had served in the Franklin household.[24] Benjamin Franklin, however, kept the secret and carried it with him to his grave. Even the date of William Franklin's birth is uncertain.

There is, however, little evidence that his enigmatic origin seriously disturbed William Franklin. Benjamin not only acknowledged the paternity of his natural son—the polite phrase of those days—he gave him all the advantages. When Benjamin went to London he took William along and entered him in the Middle Temple. When Benjamin was awarded the degree of Doctor of Laws by Oxford in 1762, William was awarded an honorary M.A.[25] The elder Franklin was also responsible indirectly for William's appointment as royal governor of New Jersey in the fall of 1762. Lord Bute, over some opposition—John Penn called William not even a gentleman—had the younger Franklin commissioned, apparently believing that the favor might persuade Benjamin Franklin to support the anticolonial policies of George III. It was the reverse that happened: the Tories eventually got the son, but lost the father.

In his earlier years as governor William Franklin not only displayed much of his father's ability in administrative matters but also seems to have lent a sympathetic ear to New Jersey's grievances against Parliament and the crown. As time passed, however, it became clear that the red carpet treatment in London had done its work. More and more Franklin came to think of himself not as an American but as an Englishman. He married a West Indian-born English girl, Elizabeth Downes, who undoubtedly exerted a strong influence upon him. His closest friends in both Burlington and Perth Amboy were stanch in their attachment to British political thought, and he shared their distrust of the people and was ever wary of any rebellious spirit manifesting itself among their elected representatives in the Assembly. It has been pointed out that "there was in Franklin much of the paternal aristocrat. He worked tirelessly for the welfare of his province; yet he wanted any concessions to come from him and to be of his own free will." [26]

As these factors deepened the ideological wedge between William Franklin and his illustrious father, so also did the matter of money. In *Poor Richard's Almanack* Benjamin had observed that "he who goes a borrowing goes a sorrowing; and indeed so does he that lends to such people." The elder Franklin was human enough not to follow his own advice. So miserable and meager was the salary paid William Franklin in the governor's office that every year he was obliged to borrow from his father to make ends meet, with the result Poor Richard foretold. When the crisis came, William turned against the father who had kept him afloat financially and stood by a Ministry which had underpaid him and also had given him scant understanding or help in meeting the problems of his province.

As the colonial cold war tensions mounted, William grew increasingly arrogant and hostile while Benjamin's efforts to influence his son became increasingly fruitless. In 1774 the father wrote his son that "as there is no prospect of your being promoted ever to a better government, and that you hold has never defray'd its expenses, I wish you were well settled on your farm." Understandably, but unwisely, Benjamin reminded William that his office "has not offered you sufficient to prevent your running every year behindhand with me." [27] And when William proposed that Boston should pay for the tea tossed overboard before complaining about the Intolerable Acts, Benjamin wrote sharply that he was "seeing everything with government eyes" and had become a "thorough courtier."

Each letter seemed to drive the two men farther apart,

and William paid no attention whatever to his father's prophetic warning of May, 1775: "In that state of American affairs which, from the present arbitrary measures, is likely soon to take place, you will find yourself in no comfortable situation, and perhaps wish you had soon disengaged yourself." Later Benjamin had two talks with his son. Both were fruitless. The break was final. Less than a year later William Franklin had been arrested by the New Jersey Assembly, under circumstances described in an earlier chapter, and taken to Connecticut. A contemporary newspaper said: "He is son to Dr. Benjamin Franklin, the genius of the day and the great patron of American liberty." [28]

Did William Franklin become increasingly jealous of his father? Of his incontestable brilliance? Of the warm regard in which he was held everywhere, even in wartime London? Did William resent his own inferiority not alone in the regard of Jerseymen but even in the esteem of those to whom he was so ready to kowtow in England? Did this complex lie behind his subsequent recklessness of conduct? Was a festering envy responsible for the bitterness that grew with each succeeding year until it became clear that Benjamin might be on the winning side of the war also? Must Benjamin always be "right" and William always "wrong"?

One further background factor was Benjamin's attachment to William Franklin's own illegitimate son, William Temple Franklin. Born in 1760, of another unidentified mother, Temple (as he was called) became Benjamin's secretary, and the grandson gave the great philosopher much of that devotion which he had vainly hoped for from his son. A crowning blow was the death of Elizabeth Franklin, William's wife, while he was still in military custody in Connecticut.

Against such a background the murder of Joshua Huddy begins to become emotionally explainable; and in its aftermath loyalism soon met its tragic end. Hatred had come full circle. Not only were the loyalists discredited in Britain but Franklin was never afterward trusted with a government post of consequence, although he was given a small pension. Moreover, as already shown, the loyalists had made it virtually impossible, in a practical sense, for the British to win American concessions for them in the treaty of peace. And the only way out—for an estimated 80,000 of them—was exile! [29]

It was by no means as apparent in 1782 as it became later that the Americans had won the real victory in the Huddy case even though those responsible had gone personally unpunished.

The cry everywhere—in New Jersey, throughout the colonies, in Congress—was for swift retaliation. As a consequence, the whole character of l'affaire Huddy was suddenly to change: Huddy himself was to be lost sight of and Washington and Congress were to get themselves into a thorough-going mess.

Washington's war council had voted unanimously for retaliation and had agreed to select, by lot, a British officer to be executed in the event that the British refused to surrender Huddy's murderer; and, despite the court-martial, Lippincott was regarded as the man. Sir Henry Clinton and Sir Guy Carleton, who succeeded him, pledged an end to loyalist outrages but firmly refused to hand over Lippincott.

In an order to General Moses Hazen, at Lancaster, who seems not to have been overly smart in handling the matter, Washington called for "a British captain, who is an *unconditional* prisoner, if such a one is in our possession; if not a lieutenant, under the same circumstances." Hazen held the drawing. Thirteen captains were involved, and thirteen slips of paper were put in a hat. One was marked "unfortunate." That lot fell to Captain Charles Asgill of the Guards, only son of Sir Charles Asgill, Baronet, heir to an extensive fortune and only nineteen years of age. Worse, as Hazen should have known, Asgill was not an unconditional prisoner; he was one of the capitulation prisoners taken at Yorktown.[30]

It looked like Asgill's unlucky day; actually it was Washington's. The commander in chief seems to have had misgivings over Asgill from the start. On June 4, 1782, he wrote Hazen:

"I am much concerned to find that Captain Asgill has been sent on notwithstanding the Information you had received of these being two unconditional Prisoners of War in our possession. I much fear that the Enemy, knowg our Delicacy respectg the propriety of Retaliating upon a Capitulation Officer . . . will put an unfavorable Construction upon this Instance of our Conduct. At least under present circumstances Capt Asgill's Application to Sir Guy Carleton will, I fear, be productive of remonstrance and Recrimination only, which may very possibly tend to place the Subject upon a disadvantageous footg." [31]

Washington could not have been more right; and he soon was to regret his failure to follow his instincts. Asgill had been born for a martyr's role. A handsome young aristocrat, personally popular, and possessed of all the social graces, he soon became a romantic figure of innocence about to be sacrificed to bloodthirsty rebels. Even Alexander Hamilton wrote that "so solemn and deliberate a sacrifice of the innocent for the guilty . . . [will] encourage an opinion that we are, in a certain degree, in a state of barbarism." [32] Benjamin Franklin was not taken in by such self-reproach in time of war. Writing to Richard Oswald in Paris, he laid the facts squarely on the line:

The situation of Captain Asgill and his family afflicts me, but I do not see what can be done by any one here to relieve them. It can not be supposed that General Washington has the least desire of taking the life of that gentleman. His aim is to obtain the punishment of a deliberate murder, committed on a prisoner in cold blood by Captain Lippincott. If the English refuse to deliver up or punish this murderer, it is saying that they choose to preserve him rather than Captain Asgill. It seems to me, therefore, that the application should be made to the English ministers for positive orders directing General Carleton to deliver up Lippincott. . . .

The cruel murders of this kind, committed by the English on our people since the commencement of the war, are innumerable. The Congress and their generals . . . have often threatened retaliation, but have always hitherto forborne to execute it.[33]

Franklin, however, was logical, and this was not a moment for logic!

On May 27, 1782, Asgill had sent the following plea to Carleton:

General Washington having ordered lots to be drawn for the Captains of Cornwallis' capitulated Army that one might be secured as amenable for Captn. Huddy's Death . . . the unfortunate chance fell to me. Conscious of my own innocence & firmly relying that I shall receive every support & Assistance my unhappy circumstance may need from your well known Justice & Humanity, I shall certainly await Your Excellency's Resolves.[34]

Carleton's well-known justice and humanity consisted of standing immovable where Lippincott was concerned, of refusing even to punish him, and of doing nothing whatever for Asgill. As Benjamin Franklin had said, the British chose to preserve the guilty rather than the innocent; and that Asgill was to be saved would be not their doing but a consequence of the clemency of Britain's enemies.

Washington was up against an emotional storm, and soon he was to wish fervently for a way out. The capitals of Europe had become engulfed in a cloudburst of sentimentality. Asgill was lionized. Plays were written with Asgill as the hero. Protest and sympathy seemed to flow from every pen. The murder of Huddy was ignored and forgotten; Europe never had made a fuss about that, anyway. Nor was the slightest attention paid to American forbearance from retaliation after the British had hanged Colonel Isaac Hayne at Charleston the preceding summer. But Asgill? Here was a charming aristocrat, scion of a noble family, whereas Huddy, Hayne and many more were Americans of no social standing.

On July 18, 1782, Lady Asgill, nee Thérèse Pratviel, a French Huguenot, wrote from London a deeply touching letter to the Comte de Vergennes, Louis XVI's foreign minister. If the British refused to save her son,* perhaps the French would try. Portions of her letter follow:

> My son (an only son), as dear as he is brave, amiable as he is deserving to be so, only nineteen, a prisoner under the articles of capitulation of Yorktown, is now confined in America, an object of retaliation. Shall an Innocent suffer for the guilty? Represent to yourself, sir, the situation of a family under these circumstances; surrounded

---

* According to the memoirs of the Baron de Grimm, cited by Stryker, Lady Asgill had "called in person upon the King" who ordered that "the author of the crime . . . should be given up." Influence of loyalists resident in London is mentioned as blocking this order. It seems doubtful, however, that the incident ever occurred; and there is scant indication that the loyalists had sufficient influence to get a royal order countermanded.

as I am by objects of distress, distracted with fear and grief, no words can express my feeling or paint the scene: my husband given over by his physicians a few hours before the news arrived, and not in a state to be informed of the misfortune; my daughter seized with a fever and delirium, raving about her brother, and without one interval of reason, save to hear heart-alleviating circumstances.

Let your feelings, sir, suggest and plead for my inexpressible misery. A word from you, like a voice from heaven, will save us from distraction and wretchedness. I am well informed General Washington reveres your character. Say but to him that you wish my son to be released, and he will restore him to his distracted family and render him to happiness. My son's virtue and bravery will justify the deed. His honor, sir, carried him to America. He was born to affluence, independence and the happiest prospects. Let me again supplicate your goodness; let me respectfully implore your high influence in behalf of innocence, in the cause of justice, of humanity. . . .[35]

It was, of course, an affecting letter, with terrific emotional impact. Yet its subtler implications were not lost on Louis XVI and Marie Antoinette, to whom Vergennes referred the missive. It was time for aristocracy to close ranks. Enemies the monarchs of France and Britain might be, but their courts had a common stake in the preservation of privilege and a common distrust if not fear of those democratic forces which seemed to have been unleashed in America. That there was basis for such distrust and fear became grimly evident a decade later, when Louis and his queen were themselves executed.

In 1782, however, Their Majesties felt quite secure and did not hesitate to put pressure on Washington. Dated July 29, a letter from Vergennes (enclosing a copy of Lady Asgill's) to the American commander in chief was penned with a very thin velvet glove. He noted that Lady Asgill's situation "seems the more worthy of notice on our own part, as it is to the humanity of a nation at war with her own, that she has recourse for what she ought to receive from the impartial justice of her own generals." Then he added:

> Your Excellency will not read this letter without being extremely affected; it had that effect upon the king and Queen, to whom I communicated it. The goodness of Their Majesties' hearts induces them to desire that the inquietudes of an unfortunate mother may be calmed, and her tenderness reassured.

Vergennes's glove now came off:

> There is one consideration, sir, which though it is not decisive, may have an influence on your resolution. Captain Asgill is doubtless your prisoner, but he is among those whom the arms of the King contributed to put into your hands at Yorktown. Although this circumstance does not operate as a safeguard, it however justifies the interest I permit myself to take in this affair.

Then Vergennes virtually dictated that there be no retaliation at all for the Huddy murder:

> In seeking to deliver Mr. Asgill from the fate which threatens him I am far from engaging you to seek another victim; the pardon, to be perfectly satisfactory, must be entire.[36]

This was blunt, almost crude, language for one ally to employ in addressing another. Yet Washington had to swallow, and swallow hard. A year earlier the French had been engaged in promoting, in cooperation with Russia, Spain, and Austria, a peace parley at Vienna on terms which "would have tricked the United States out of its independence . . . in violation of the conditions of the Franco-American Alliance." [37] That scheme having failed, fresh peace negotiations were under way and the American negotiators had excellent reason to fear, and endeavor to prevent, another French attempt at a double-cross. At the same time Franklin was angling for one more French loan to tide Congress over until a peace was signed.[38]

What, then, was Washington to do? Especially in view of Vergennes's dictatorial tone? Yield, of course, but with dignity. So, gracefully, he laid the matter in the lap of Congress. After all, it was Congress which had clamored most loudly for retaliation.

Actually, the French plea had given Washington what he needed: a face-saver in a situation which had become increasingly embarrassing to him and to America. Even before Vergennes's note arrived—it was nearly three months on the way—Washington had looked to Congress with an eye toward clemency. On October 7 he wrote the Secretary of War:

> The case of Captain Asgill is now before Congress . . . and the delay of Congress . . . places me not only in a very delicate, but very awkward Situation with the expecting World. Was I to give my private Opinion respecting Asgill, I should pronounce in favor of his being released from his Duress and that he should be permitted to go to his Friends in Europe.[39]

On October 25 Vergennes's letter came, and on November 7 Congress acted. It voted, unanimously, that "the life of Captain Asgill should be given as a compliment to the King of France." [40] And on November 13, 1782, Washington wrote Asgill:

It affords me singular pleasure to have it in my power to transmit you the enclosed copy of an Act of Congress by which you are released from the disagreeable circumstances in which you have so long been: supposing you would wish to go to New York as soon as possible, I also enclose a passport for that purpose.

I cannot take leave of you, Sir, without assuring you that in whatever light my agency in this unpleasing affair may be viewed, I was never influenced thro the whole of it by sanguinary motives; but by what I conceived a sense of my duty which loudly called upon me to take measures however disagreeable to prevent a repetition of those enormities which have been the subject of discussion. And that this important end is likely to be answered without the effusion of the Blood of an innocent person is not a greater relief to you than it is to Sir, yr. etc.

GEORGE WASHINGTON [41]

Asgill appears never to have replied to this dignified yet warmhearted note, although, with his mother and sister, he could journey to Paris the following year to thank the king and queen for their intercession. [42] Asgill's subsequent conduct, indeed, belied most of the kind things previously said about him. He gave support, by his silence, to lies in the British press concerning his "bad treatment" while in custody in Chatham, New Jersey, particularly to a false tale that a thirty-foot gallows had been erected in front of his prison window with an inscription: "Erected for the Execution of Captain Asgill." [43]

Washington made indignant denial of these calumnies and declared: "I could not have given countenance to the insults, which he says were offered to his person . . . I had every reason to be convinced that he was treated by the officers around him with . . . every civility in their power." The record shows that Asgill was even given parole to go around Morristown as well as Chatham. Two years later Washington, writing to David Humphreys, spoke of "the fallacy of the reports which have been circulated . . . and which are fathered upon that officer as the author." [44]

After his release Asgill hurried to England aboard the ship *Swallow*, arriving at Falmouth on December 15, 1782. He inherited the family riches, became a general in the British Army, and died in 1823.

Meanwhile, Washington had written to Sir Guy Carleton, mentioning first the release of Asgill and adding:

> I am . . . directed to call your attention to that part of your letter of the 13th of August last, in which you say "I have given orders to the Judge Advocate, to make further inquisition, and to collect evidence for the prosecution of such other persons as may appear to have been criminal in this transaction."
>
> In full confidence, that measures have been taken to carry your Excellency's intention into execution, I am to request the favor of you to inform me what probability there is, that the persons who have been really guilty of the action which has been the subject of former discussion, will be brought to a proper account. [45]

Time was to give the answer to this plea for punishment of the murderer of Joshua Huddy: the British government awarded Richard Lippincott a military allowance of half captain's pay for life. He also was granted three thousand acres of land in what is now the city of Toronto. And he lived on that property until he died, at the age of eighty-one! [46]

"GEORGE, BE KING!"

When he ascended the British throne just two hundred years ago, his mother told him: *"George, be King!"* The George was George the Third. And he was to follow his mother's advice, all too soon.

Augusta, a "foolish, ignorant woman" in the English view, had been Princess of Saxony and her ideas of monarchy stemmed from the petty despotism of that court. Her closest adviser—some said her lover—was the handsome, unpopular Scotsman, Lord Bute. George I, the new monarch's great-grandfather, could not even speak English. George II, his grandfather, was chiefly interested in the affairs of Hanover and all too content to let the Whigs rule England. Frederick, his father, was a ne'er-do-well. Thus it is not strange that after a sheltered childhood, George III was subject to his mother's influence, that he made Lord Bute his first Prime Minister, and that he firmly believed he was destined to rule as well as reign.

George the Third's "success" in this respect was made politically possible by the decay of two-party government in England. The Whigs had been in power almost continuously for half a century, and as usually happens under such circumstances, the opposition, or Tory party, disintegrated. There were many non-Whigs in England, but they were disorganized, and it was from those elements that George III carefully chose men who would do his bidding. Ruling at first "without party," George III soon was building a new Tory party quite unlike the old one, a party under his thumb, a party whose self-seekers and placemen nourished his conviction that he could be a constitutional monarch and restore the old power of the Crown at one and the same time.

It is against this background that the events of the Revolution and the often-puzzling anomalies of the British cause must be read, particularly those related in the foregoing chapters. Ever a stubborn man, the King summed up his own character well when he observed that "his memory being a good one, what he did not *forget* he could not forgive." Understanding of this will help to clarify the King's determination to force one repression after another upon the American colonists; the willingness of his handpicked ministers to pursue bitter-end policies to the point of folly; the hiring of the German mercenaries, so unpopular on both sides; the dogged Government attitude in the Asgill case even in the face of petitions from the British officers that Lippincott be given up for an act—Huddy's murder—which was deeply shocking to them. His Majesty's obstinacy resulted in collapse of the French peace proposals on terms denying American independence, a lucky break for the colonists which occurred simply because George III even then thought he could win the war. And by his own admission, he was "the last to consent" to the peace finally signed, a peace forced upon him by the British themselves.

In the past, historical fashion has swung about like a weathervane with respect to George III's responsibility in the American Revolution. That was true even before the Revolution itself. Originally blame for the Mother Country's oppressive measures was put upon Parliament; the king, many thought, was their friend. Not until the colonists took their grievances directly to the throne did they discover the truth which had been slowly dawning upon Benjamin Franklin—that the king himself was author of or sponsor of much of the hated anti-colonial legislation.

After the Revolution, of course, George III was long portrayed as the villain of the piece. Then came a revisionist school to challenge that view. Now the weathervane has swung back close to its original position. Just as the author's friends in England speak of George III as "a German king on a British throne," so have British historians such as Trevelyan, Mumby and others shown that the fight against the American colonies was unpopular in England, and that the king's war "not only gave birth to the independence of the United States, but also determined the future of the British Empire." * British freedoms were at stake too, when as Burke said: "Things could not be otherwise than that Englishmen beyond the seas should claim the full rights of Englishmen." The strength of the British Commonwealth rests upon that foundation today. Just as the victory of Americans for freedom in the Revolution was confirmed, sealed and dedicated when George Washington gave that firm and scornful "No!" to those socially ambitious folk who whispered to him after the fighting was over:

"George, be King!"

* Mumby, Frank Arthur, George III. and the American Revolution; Constable & Company, Ltd., London, 1923.

APPENDIX

A Tavern Guide for Colonial Tourists

Eighteenth-century travelers in New Jersey, whether by carriage, horseback, or stage, had no such tourist guides as those which direct today's motorist to the better eating places, inns, and motels. The following list of historic hostelries, circa 1750–1799, is too late to be of service to wearied journeyers of yesterday. However, it may be of some assistance to the modern motorist seeking adventure, since quite a few of the old taverns, more or less changed, still exist. Some few are still taverns; others are historical showplaces or museums; and a number have been restored as private dwellings.

This list of taverns does not pretend to be complete. It has been compiled from many sources and each date indicates that the tavern was in operation at this time. Where possible, names of owners are given for the dates specified, but since tavern managements changed frequently, the same tavern had quite a few names at varying times. Some taverns listed have been moved from their original sites; others have had later taverns built on the same sites.

Obviously it has been impossible to search the titles or trace detailed history of all these taverns. The list is offered in the hope that it will provide pleasure for those readers who enjoy exploring the Garden State, past as well as present.

KEY

* Signifies places still used as taverns or restaurants.
† Tavern buildings—usually remodeled—now used as museums.
‡ Remodeled for use as private dwellings.
  Where no asterisks appear the tavern is of record only.

*ALLENTOWN: Cunningham's Tavern (1768). Now vacant.

BASKING RIDGE: The Widow White's Tavern (1776), later Veal's Tavern; remodeled as a private house, and since torn down.

BEDMINSTER: Bedminster Tavern (1787), John Malick.

BERGEN WOODS: William Earl's Tavern (1768). Near Weehawkin Ferry.

BETHLEHEM: Hickory Tavern (1766).
Reynolds Tavern (1766).

BLACK RIVER: The Sign of Washington (1794).

BLUE ANCHOR: Sign of the Blue Anchor (before 1740). John Hider earliest known proprietor.

BOONTON: Faesch Iron Works Tavern (1794).

BOUND BROOK: Harris Tavern (1735). Later Middlebrook Hotel.
The Bull's Head.
The Black Horse.
Stanbury's Tavern.
The Sign of the Buck (1772), William Kelley.

BRIDGEPORT (Moorestown Road): Bridgeport Tavern (1785).

BRIDGETON: Parvin's Tavern (1725), Clarence Parvin.
Richard Cayford's Inn (1768).
Potter Tavern (1770). Matthew Potter.

BURLINGTON: Peter Jegou Tavern (1668).
Basnett's Tavern (1687).
Henry Grubb's Ordinary (1687).
Moon Tavern (1732). Later Washington House.
Blue Anchor (before 1751). Richard Smith, James Edsall. The Metropolitan Inn now stands on this site.
Sign of General Wolfe (1764). Later Stageboat Tavern, Peter Boynton.
Sheppard's Tavern (1774). Adam Sheppard. (1808 called Steamboat Hotel).
Alcazar. Traditionally on High Street site of the home of Thomas Olive, first speaker of the New Jersey Assembly.

CAMDEN: (Cooper's Ferry). Cooper's Tavern (1702).
Daniel Cooper's Public House (1748).
Center Tavern (1775).
The Bull and Dog (1776).
(Kaighn's Point). Sign of Adam Keppele (1765). Arthur
Donaldson.
(Newton Creek). Atmore's Tavern (1718). Thos. Atmore.
PENNSAUKEN: Sorrel Horse Tavern (1762). Daniel East-
lack.
* CENTERTON: (Cumberland County). Centerton Inn.
CENTERVILLE: (Old York Road). Centerville Tavern
(1765).
CHATHAM: Timothy Day's Inn (1794).
CHEW'S LANDING: Chew Tavern (1745). Jeremiah
Chew.
Chew's Landing Tavern (1748). Gabriel Davis.
CLARKSBORO: Death of the Fox Inn. (Pre-Revolutionary).
COLESTOWN: Cherry Tree Tavern (1773). Thomas Spicer.
* COLT'S NECK: Colt's Neck Tavern (1717).
* COLUMBUS: The Sun Inn (1776). Later The Black Horse,
and (restored) Columbus Inn.
* CRANBURY: Cranbury Inn (1751). James Predmore.
CROSSWICKS: Cook's Tavern. George Cook.
DUTCH VALLEY: Van House Tavern (1794).
† ELIZABETH: Carteret Arms (1728). Remodeled as a meet-
inghouse.
Sign of the Marquis of Granby (1734). Later the Red Lion.
Sign of the Hogshead (1759), "The Widow Chetwood."
Nag's Head (1760), James Johnson.
Sign of the Duke of Rutland (1766), Colonel Peter Schuyler.
Later the White House Tavern.
Graham's Tavern.
ELLISBURG: Bush Tavern (1773), Isaac Ellis. Later Ellis-
burg Tavern.
ELWOOD: Sailor Boy Tavern.
* ENGLISHTOWN: The Village Inn (1732).
FLEMINGTON: Samuel Fleming's Tavern (1746).

FORKS OF LITTLE EGG HARBOR (near Batsto):
House of Richard Wescoat (1776).

FREEHOLD: House of Robert Campbell (1768).
James Wall's Tavern (1778).
Samuel Forman's Tavern (1779).
Snyder Tavern (1779), William Snyder.

GLOUCESTER: Gerrard's Tavern (1763), William Gerrard.
Hugg's Tavern (1766), Joseph Hugg.
Sign of the Buck (near Westville).
Two Tuns Tavern (1775), Desire Sparks.

‡ GREENWICH: Greenwich Tavern (1730). Now a private
dwelling.

* HACKENSACK: Washington Mansion House (1775).
Archibald Campbell's Tavern (1776).
House of the Widow Watson (1766).

HACKETTSTOWN: Widow Davis's Tavern (1772), on
road to Greenwich Forge.

HADDONFIELD: Estaugh Tavern.
‡ Perrywebb's Tavern (1733), Thomas Perrywebb.
† The Indian King (1750), Timothy Matlack.
Edward Gibbs' Tavern (1777).
Stillwell Tavern (1777), George W. Stillwell.
House of Sarah Norris.

HANOVER (Morris County):   Cook's Tavern (1772), Ellis
Cook.
Tapin's Inn (1794).

‡ HOPE: The Stage Tavern (1773), Ephraim Colver. Now a
bank.

HUNTSVILLE (Sussex):   Thomas Woolverton's Tavern
(1760).

* JOHNSONBURG: Jonathan Pettit's Tavern (1753). Sussex
courts sat there until 1756; now in Warren County.

KINGSTON: Sign of the Mermaid (1744).
Sign of the Black Lion (1770).

* KIRKWOOD: White Horse Tavern (1740), Elizabeth Bates.

LAMBERTVILLE: Coryell's Inn (1732).

LEEDS POINT: Japhett Leeds Inn.

LONG-A-COMING (now Berlin): Long-a-Coming Tavern (1760). Samuel Scull.

MANAHAWKIN: Inn of Captain Randolph.

°MENDHAM: Sign of the Black Horse (1745).

MILLSTONE: Tunison's Tavern (1776), Cornelius Tunison.

‡MONTAGUE: Brick House Inn (1776), Roger Clark (at Dingman's Ferry and Old Mine roads).

MOORESTOWN: Moore's Tavern (1732).

Cox Tavern (1775), John Cox (not Colonel John Cox).

MORRISTOWN: Arnold's Tavern (1760), later Freeman's, Hayden's, Duncan's.

George O'Hara's Inn (1773).

Dickerson—or Norris—Tavern (1774). Where trial of Benedict Arnold was held.

°MOUNT BETHEL: King George Inn (1692). Restored 1953–54 by James and Dorothy Hayden.

MOUNT HOLLY: * Three Tuns Tavern (1725), also called Mill Street Tavern; probably built by Samuel Bryant.

Cross Keys Tavern (1731), Thomas Clark.

* Washington Tavern (1749), John Burr. Hotel still on site.

Black Horse Tavern (1760), Zachariah Rossell.

Hatkinson's Tavern (1760), later The State Arms, John Hatkinson.

Winne's Tavern (on Wood Lane) (1750), Abraham Winne.

MULLICA HILL: The Blue Bell Tavern.

MUSCONETCONG CREEK: Miller's Tavern (1775), Andrew Miller.

NEWARK: Bank's Tavern (1772), James Bank.

Hull's Tavern (1772).

Queen's Head Tavern (1772).

Sign of the Hunt (1794), Archer Gifford.

NEW BRUNSWICK: Balding's Tavern (1735), Ann Balding.

* Indian Queen (1741—possibly 1729); later Bell's Tavern, and the Parkway.

Paul Miller's Tavern (1742); later the Red Lion, Brook Farmer.

Whitehall Tavern (1756), Michael Duff.

The White Hart (1761), Nathaniel Vernon.

Hydert Voorhees Tavern (1776).

NEWTON: The Sign of Captain O'Blunder (1772), John Allen.

Cochran House (1831), stated to be on site of seventeenth-century inn.

° NEW MARKET (formerly Quibbletown): New Market Tavern.

ORANGE: Mumm's Tavern (1798).

PATERSON: House of Abraham Goodwin (1774).

PERTH AMBOY: Long Ferry Tavern (1684).

Crown Tavern (1760). Later the Packer House.

Hull's Tavern (1760).

House of Obadiah Ayres (1761).

PITTSGROVE: Champney's Tavern (1770); called Pole Tavern after 1776.

PLUCKEMIN: Eoff's Tavern (1750), Jacob Eoff.

Bullion's Tavern (1777), John Boylan.

POMPTON: Yellow House Tavern (1781), Joseph Curtis.

PRINCETON: Washington Arms (1748).

Hudibras Inn (1765), Colonel Jacob Hyer.

Nassau Tavern (1768), William Hick; also known as the Sign of the College.

Sign of the Thirteen Stars (1784).

RAMAPO: Seven Stars Tavern (1765).

° REAVILLE: Stage Road Tavern (1755) (Amwell and Old York roads).

RINGOES: House of John Ringo (1720). Later John Snyder's (1784).

ROADSTOWN: Pine Tavern.

SALEM: Hall's Tavern (1691).

Trap Tavern.

SCHOOLEY'S MOUNTAIN: Alpha Hotel (1795).

° SCOTCH PLAINS: Stage Coach Tavern (1737).

† SHARPTOWN: Seven Stars Inn (1765).

SHREWSBURY: ‡ Allen House (1667); briefly used as a tavern.

Sign of the Blue Ball (1768).

SIX MILE RUN (Somerset County): Wood's Tavern (1745), William Wood.

Silver's Inn (1796), Isaac Silver.

* SMITHVILLE (Atlantic County): Smithville Inn (1787), James Baremore. Restored 1951–1958 by Ethel and Fred Noyes.

† SPRINGFIELD: Cannon Ball Inn (1776). Now believed to have always been a dwelling.

TEN MILE RUN (Somerset County): Williamson's Tavern, William Williamson.

TEWKSBURY: John Farley Tavern (1787).

THREE MILE RUN (Somerset County): Kent's Tavern (1766), John Kent.

Waldron's Tavern (1766), Cornelius Waldron.

TOMS RIVER: Daniel Grigg's Tavern.

TRENTON: Sign of the Wheat Sheaf (1744).

Sign of the Highlander on Horseback (1759), Abraham Carpenter.

Royal Oak Inn (1768), Rensselaer Williams.

Jonathan Richmond's Tavern (1775) (below Trenton).

The Blazing Star (1776), Francis Witt.

Bull Head Tavern, Henry Drake.

Fox Chase Tavern, Mrs. Joseph Bond.

Bear Tavern (1776) (above Trenton).

TUCKERTON: Falkinburg's Tavern (1776).

UNIONVILLE: Unionville Inn (1715).

VINELAND (area): The Sign of the Heart Tavern.

WASHINGTON (Warren County): Joseph Wilson's Tavern (1794).

WEST CREEK: William Rose Tavern (1778).

WOODBURY: * Wilkins Inn (1720), Thomas Wilkins. Renovated 1938.

Widow Corman's Tavern (1772) (5 miles below Woodbury).

Joshua Hopper's Inn (1797).

WOODBRIDGE: Woodbridge Inn (1796).
   Cross and Key Tavern.
WOODSTOWN: Nigger's Glory (1755). Douglas and Mary
   Bassett.
WOOLWICH: Inn of Thomas James.

TEXT REFERENCES

CHAPTER I

1. Robert Juet, *Juet's Journal: The Voyage of the Half Moon from 4 April to 7 November 1609* (Newark: New Jersey Historical Society, 1959), p. 27.
2. Leah Blackman, "Historical Sketch of Tuckerton." *Proceedings of the Surveyors Association of West New Jersey,* 1880, p. 415.
3. *Ibid.,* p. 365.
4. Philip Vickers Fithian, *Journal, 1775–1776.* Ed. by Robert Greenhalgh Albion and Leonidas Dodson (Princeton: Princeton University Press, 1934), p. 249.
5. Arthur Pierce Middleton. *Tobacco Coast: A Maritime History of Chesapeake Bay in the Colonial Era* (Newport News, Va.: Mariners Museum, 1953), p. 189.
6. Frederick B. Tolles, *Meeting House and Counting House* (Chapel Hill: University of North Carolina Press, 1948), p. 78 n.
7. Arthur M. Schlesinger, *The Colonial Merchants and the American Revolution* (New York: Frederick Ungar Publishing Co., 1957), p. 45.
8. E. Keble Chatterton, *Kings Cutters and Smugglers* (Philadelphia: J. B. Lippincott Co., 1912), p. 87.
9. George R. Prowell, *History of Camden County, N. J.* (Philadelphia: L. J. Richards and Co., 1886), pp. 37, 63.

10. Blathwayte Papers, Colonial Williamsburg, Inc.

11. Stanley H. Friedelbaum. "Bellomont: Imperial Administrator—Studies in Colonial Administration during the 17th Century," Thesis, Columbia University, 1955, p. 160.

12. Philadelphia Customs House Papers, Vol. 12.

13. Tolles, *Meeting House,* p. 78.

14. William S. McClellan, *Smuggling in the American Colonies at the Outbreak of the Revolution* (New York: Moffat, Yard and Co., 1912), p. 53.

15. John C. Miller, *Origins of the American Revolution* (Boston: Little, Brown and Co., 1943), p. 83.

16. Carl and Jessica Bridenbaugh, *Rebels and Gentlemen* (New York: Reynal and Hitchcock, 1942), p. 7.

17. Miller, *Origins,* pp. 47–48.

18. *Ibid.,* p. 90.

19. Fithian, *Journal, 1775–1776,* pp. 193, 270.

20. Esther Singleton. *Social New York Under the Georges* (New York, 1902), p. 374.

21. James Murray. *Letters of James Murray, Loyalist,* p. 111.

22. Miller, *Origins,* p. 83.

23. *Ibid.,* p. 102.

24. *Ibid.,* p. 8.

25. Alfred M. Heston, *Absegami: Annals of Eyren Haven and Atlantic City, 1609 to 1904.* (Camden: Privately printed, 1904), I, 87.

26. Blackman, *Historical Sketch,* p. 392.

27. *Ibid.,* p. 192.

28. New Jersey Archives, 1st Series, Vol. 7, p. 244.

29. Carl R. Woodward, *Ploughs and Politicks,* p. 61.

30. Schlesinger, *The Colonial Merchants,* p. 49.

31. New Jersey Archives, 1st Series, Vol. 9, pp. 403–04.

32. Miller, *Origins,* p. 266.

33. *Ibid.,* pp. 61–62.

34. John F. Watson, *Annals,* II, p. 421.

35. Joseph S. Sickler, *History of Salem,* p. 123.

36. Philadelphia Customs House Papers, Vol. 10, Historical Society of Pennsylvania.

37. *Ibid.*
38. Sickler, *History of Salem,* p. 127.

CHAPTER II

1. John H. Preston, *Revolution, 1766* (New York: Harcourt, Brace and Co., 1933), p. 250.
2. Edgar S. Maclay, *A History of American Privateers* (New York: D. Appleton and Co., 1910), p. xiii.
3. *Ibid.,* p. 5.
4. William Bell Clark, *Ben Franklin's Privateers* (Baton Rouge, La.: Louisiana State University Press, 1956), pp. 10, 173, 177.
5. Maclay, *History of American Privateers,* p. 5.
6. Dudley W. Knox, *A History of the United States Navy* (New York: G. P. Putnam's Sons, 1936), p. 1.
7. Carl and Jessica Bridenbaugh, *Rebels and Gentlemen* (New York: Reynal and Hitchcock, 1942), pp. 6–7.
8. Knox, *History of U.S. Navy,* p. 3.
9. Maclay, *History of American Privateers,* p. 77.
10. New Jersey Papers, Historical Society of Pennsylvania.
11. Leonard Lundin, *Cockpit of the Revolution* (Princeton: Princeton University Press, 1940), p. 112.
12. New Jersey Society of Pennsylvania, *1932–33 Yearbook,* p. 134.
13. Maclay, *History of American Privateers,* p. 134.
14. Edwin Salter, *A History of Monmouth and Ocean Counties, New Jersey* (Bayonne, N.J.: E. Gardner and Sons, 1890), pp. 298–99.
15. *Ibid.,* pp. 300–02.
16. *Ibid.,* p. 303.
17. *Ibid.,* p. 78.
18. *Ibid.,* p. 427.
19. Harold F. Wilson, *The Jersey Shore,* p. 599.
20. Salter, *History of Monmouth and Ocean Counties,* pp. 208, 211.
21. *Ibid.,* pp. 207–10.

22. Atlantic County Historical Society, *Yearbook*, I, 115.
23. John Tilton Pension Application, Atlantic County Historical Society.
24. Charles S. Boyer, *Early Forges and Furnaces of New Jersey*, p. 179.
25. New Jersey Council of Safety, *Minutes*, Sept. 20, 1777.
26. Ball Papers, Historical Society of Pennsylvania.
27. Atlantic County Historical Society, *Yearbook*, I, 114.
28. Alfred Heston, *South Jersey: A History, 1664–1924* (New York: Lewis Publishing Co., 1924), p. 225.
29. Bernhard A. Uhlendorf, *Revolution in America* (New Brunswick, N.J.: Rutgers University Press, 1957), p. 272.
30. Ibid., p. 308.
31. Maclay, *History of American Privateers*, p. 208.
32. Salter, *History of Monmouth and Ocean Counties*, p. 427.
33. *Ibid.*, p. 428.
34. Lewis T. Stevens, "Cape May Naval Activities in the Revolution," *Cape May County Historical Society Journal*, II, 252.
35. *Ibid.*, p. 253.

CHAPTER III

1. Henry Steele Commager and Richard B. Morris, *The Spirit of 'Seventy Six* (Indianapolis: Bobbs-Merrill Co., 1958), p. 924.
2. J. Franklin Jameson, *The American Revolution Considered as a Social Movement* (Princeton: Princeton University Press, 1926), p. 65.
3. Commager and Morris, *Spirit*, p. 806.
4. Journals of the Continental Congress.
5. E. James Ferguson, "Business, Government and Congressional Investigation in the Revolution," *William and Mary Quarterly*, XVI, 300.
6. Commager and Morris, *Spirit*, p. 988.
7. Francis Wharton, ed., *The Revolutionary Diplomatic Correspondence of the United States* (Washington: Govt. Printing Office, 1889), II, 226.

8. Leonard Lundin, *Cockpit of the Revolution* (Princeton: Princeton University Press, 1940), p. 407.

9. Commager and Morris, *Spirit*, p. 810.

10. John Frederick Schroeder, *Maxims of Washington*, p. 146.

11. Howard Peckham, *The War for Independence* (Chicago: Chicago University Press, 1958), p. 119.

12. Lundin, *Cockpit*, p. 407.

13. Frank H. Stewart Papers, New Jersey State Teachers College.

14. Lewis T. Stevens, "Cape May Naval Activities in the Revolution," *Cape May County Historical Society Journal*, Vol. 2.

15. *Ibid.*, p. 255.

16. Harry Emerson Wildes, *Lonely Midas: The Story of Stephen Girard* (New York: Farrar and Rhinehart, 1943), pp. 39 ff.

17. *Ibid.*, p. 41.

18. Ferguson, "Business Government," p. 309.

19. Greene-Wadsworth Letters, Historical Society of Pennsylvania.

20. *Ibid.*

21. Edgar S. Maclay, *A History of American Privateers,* pp. 211–13.

22. Ferguson, "Business, Government," p. 315.

23. Nathanael Greene Letters, Princeton University Library.

24. Ernest Sutherland Bates, *The Story of Congress: 1789–1935* (New York: Harper and Brothers, 1936), p. 11.

CHAPTER IV

1. Charles S. Boyer, *Annals,* No. 5, p. 11.

2. J. C. Harrington, *Glassmaking at Jamestown* (Richmond, Va.: Dietz Press, 1952), p. 13.

3. *Ibid.*, p. 14.

4. *Pennsylvania Magazine of History and Biography,* V, 384.

5. John W. and Winifred Jordan, *Colonial and Revolutionary Families,* I.

6. Richard Wistar Davids, *The Wistar Family*, Philadelphia, 1896.
7. Wistar Papers, Historical Society of Pennsylvania.
8. Townsend Ward, "The Germantown Road and Its Associations," *Pennsylvania Magazine of History and Biography*.
9. *Pennsylvania Magazine of History and Biography*, XXVI, 91.
10. *Ibid.*, p. 476.
11. *Ibid.*, Vol. 29, p. 121.
12. Frederick B. Tolles, *Meeting House and Counting House* (Chapel Hill: University of North Carolina Press, 1948), p. 165.
13. Isaac Jones Wistar, *Autobiography: 1827–1925* (New York: Harper and Brothers, 1914), p. 18.
14. *Documentary History of New York*, I, 712.
15. Rhea Mansfield Knittle, *Early American Glass*, p. 85.
16. *Ibid.*, p. 87.
17. *Ibid.*, p. 89.
18. Davids, *Wistar Family*, p. 61.
19. *Pennsylvania Gazette*, Nov. 10, 1768.
20. Carl and Jessica Bridenbaugh, *Rebels and Gentlemen* (New York: Reynal and Hitchcock, 1942), p. 325.
21. Wistar, *Autobiography*, p. 20.
22. Salem County Marriage Records.
23. Joseph S. Sickler, *History of Salem County, New Jersey* (Salem, N.J.: Sunbeam Publishing Co., 1937), p. 97.
24. Knittle, *Early American Glass*, p. 92.
25. Tolles, *Meeting House*, p. 131.

CHAPTER V

1. Frank H. Stewart, *Major John Fenwick* (Woodbury, N.J.: Privately printed, 1939), p. 34.
2. Thomas Cushing and Charles E. Sheppard, *History of the Counties of Gloucester, Salem and Cumberland* (Everts and Peck, 1883), p. 510.
3. Stewart, *Fenwick*, p. 55.

4. Cushing and Sheppard, *History,* p. 512.
5. Joseph S. Sickler, *Tea-Burning Town, The Story of Greenwich on the Cohansey in West New Jersey* (New York: Abelard Press, 1950), p. 13.
6. Cushing and Sheppard, *History,* p. 516.
7. *Ibid.,* p. 525.
8. Philip Vickers Fithian, Unpublished Journal, Princeton University Library.
9. *Ibid.*
10. Lucius Q. C. Elmer, *History of Early Settlement and Progress of Cumberland County* (Bridgeton, N.J.: G. F. Nixon, 1869), p. 13.
11. Wood and Bacon Store Records, Historical Society of Pennsylvania.
12. Cushing and Sheppard, *History,* p. 524.
13. Peter Kalm, *Travels into North America,* I, 361.
14. John C. Miller, *Origins of the American Revolution* (Boston: Little, Brown and Co., 1943), p. 267.
15. *Ibid.,* p. 337.
16. *Ibid.,* pp. 339–40.
17. *Ibid.,* p. 344.
18. *Ibid.,* p. 341.
19. *Ibid.,* p. 345.
20. *Newport Mercury,* Dec. 7, 1773.
21. Miller, *Origins,* p. 351.
22. Cushing and Sheppard, *History,* p. 519.
23. Sickler, *Tea-Burning Town,* p. 40.
24. Commager and Morris, *The Spirit of 'Seventy-Six* (Indianapolis: Bobbs-Merrill Co., 1958), p. 6.
25. Cushing and Sheppard, *History,* p. 537.

CHAPTER VI

1. Philip Vickers Fithian, *Journal and Letters: 1764–1774.* Ed. by J. R. Williams. (Princeton: Princeton University Press, 1900), and *Journal, 1775–1776.* Ed. by R. G. Albion and

L. Dodson. (Princeton: Princeton University Press, 1934).

2. Frank D. Andrews, "Biographical Sketch of Philip Vickers Fithian" in *Letters to His Wife* (Vineland, N.J.: Privately printed, 1932), p. 5.

3. Princeton University Library: Unpublished Letter.

4. *Ibid.*

5. *Ibid.*

6. Fithian, *Journal and Letters: 1767–1774*, p. 28.

7. *Ibid.*, p. 43.

8. Princeton University Library: Unpublished Letter.

9. Fithian, *Journal and Letters: 1767–1774*, p. 61.

10. *Ibid.*, p. 64.

11. *Ibid.*, p. 132.

12. *Ibid.*, p. 142.

13. *Ibid.*, p. 143.

14. *Ibid.*, p. 123.

15. *Ibid.*, pp. 192–93.

16. *Ibid.*, p. 163.

17. *Ibid.*, p. 198.

18. *Ibid.*, p. 269.

19. *Ibid.*, p. 271.

20. *Ibid.*, p. 273.

21. Princeton: Unpublished Letter.

22. Fithian, *Journal, 1775–1776*, p. 247.

23. *Ibid.*, p. 249.

24. *Ibid.*, p. 23.

25. *Ibid.*, p. 23.

26. *Ibid.*, p. 61.

27. Frank D. Andrews, *Enoch Green: A Biographical Sketch* (Vineland, N.J.: Smith Printing House, 1933), p. 7.

28. Frank D. Andrews, *Letters of Fithian to His Wife*, p. 14.

29. *Ibid.*, p. 15.

30. Fithian, *Journal, 1775–1776*, p. 174.

31. Cumberland County Wills: *Liber B*, p. 151.

32. Harry B. Weiss and Grace M. Ziegler, *Colonel Erkuries*

Beatty, 1759–1823 (Trenton: Past Times Press, 1958), pp. 8–10.

33. Frank D. Andrews, "Letters to Elizabeth Beatty Fithian, 1772–1802," *Vineland Historical Society Magazine*, (January, 1933–April, 1934), XV, 286.

34. Fithian, *Journal, 1775–1776*, pp. 190–91.

35. *Ibid.*, p. 232.

36. Frank D. Andrews, *Letters of Fithian to His Wife*, p. 47.

37. Princeton: Unpublished Letter.

38. *Ibid.*

39. Frank D. Andrews, *Letters of Fithian to His Wife*, p. 24.

40. *Ibid.*, p. 32.

41. Fithian, *Journal, 1775–1776*, pp. 105–06.

42. *Ibid.*, p. 137.

43. *Ibid.*, p. 67.

44. *Ibid.*, p. 68.

45. *Ibid., Journal and Letters: 1767–1774*, p. 175.

46. *Ibid.*, p. 268.

47. *Ibid., Journal, 1775–1776*, p. 20.

48. *Ibid.*, p. 116.

49. "Letters of the Four Beatty Brothers," *Pennsylvania Magazine of History and Biography*, XLVI, 209.

CHAPTER VII

1. A. Edward Newton, *This Book-Collecting Game* (Boston: Little, Brown and Co., 1928), p. 89.

2. Henry Steele Commager and Richard B. Morris, *The Spirit of 'Seventy-Six* (Indianapolis: Bobbs-Merrill Co., 1958), p. 271.

3. George DeCou, *Burlington: A Provincial Capital* (Burlington, N.J.: Library Co. of Burlington, 1945), p. 137.

4. Frank H. Stewart, *Notes on Old Gloucester County, New Jersey* (Camden: New Jersey Society of Pennsylvania, 1917), III, 234.

5. Charles S. Boyer, *Indian Trails and Early Paths* (Camden, N.J.: Camden County Historical Society, 1938), p. 79.

6. Edwin S. Parry, *Betsy Ross, Quaker Rebel* (Philadelphia: John C. Winston Co., 1930).

7. Boyer, *Indian Trails,* p. 84.

8. *Pennsylvania Packet,* Feb. 1, 1773.

9. William S. Stryker, *The Battles of Trenton and Princeton* (Boston:Houghton Mifflin Co., 1898), p. 88.

10. V. Lansing Collins, *Princeton Past and Present* (Princeton: Princeton University Press, 1946), p. xvii.

11. Archibald D. Alexander, "History of the Log College" in *Biographical Sketches of the Founder and Principal Alumni of the Log College* (Princeton: J. T. Robinson, 1845), pp. 190–94.

12. Collins, *Princeton Past and Present,* p. xvi.

13. Moreau de Saint-Méry, *American Journey: 1793–98,* p. 106.

14. John Adams, *Works,* III, 55.

15. New Jersey Archives, IX, 235.

16. Elise Lathrop, *Early American Inns and Taverns* (Robert McBride and Co., 1926), p. 129.

17. Harry B. Weiss and Grace M. Ziegler, *Legislation Affecting Rural Life in Colonial New Jersey* (Trenton: Past Times Press, 1957), p. 31.

18. Alice Morse Earle, *Stage Coach and Tavern Days* (New York: The Macmillan Co., 1900), p. 118.

19. Boyer, *Indian Trails,* p. 47.

20. Earle, *Stage Coach,* p. 42.

21. Moreau Saint-Méry, *American Journey,* p. 107.

22. Claude G. Bowers, *Jefferson and Hamilton,* p. 119.

23. Earle, *Stage Coach,* p. 55.

24. *Ibid.,* pp. 105–07.

CHAPTER VIII

1. Charles S. Boyer, *Indian Trails and Early Paths* (Camden, N.J.: Camden County Historical Society, 1938), p. 76.

2. *Historic Roadsides in New Jersey,* p. 54,

3. Frank H. Stewart, *Notes on Old Gloucester County, New Jersey* (N.J. Society of Pennsylvania), Vol. 2, p. 40.

4. Hubert G. Schmidt, *Rural Hunterdon* (New Brunswick, N.J.: Rutgers University Press, 1915), p. 205.

5. Alfred Hoyt Bill, *The Campaign of Princeton, 1776–1777* (Princeton: Princeton University Press, 1948), p. 59.

6. Joseph Jackson, "Washington in Philadelphia," *Pennsylvania Magazine of History and Biography*, LVI, 17.

7. Henry S. Commager and R. B. Morris, *The Spirit of 'Seventy-Six* (Indianapolis: Bobbs-Merril Co., 1958), p. 275.

8. *Ibid.*, p. 502.

9. Carl Van Doren, *Secret History of the American Revolution* (New York: Viking Press, 1941), p. 34.

10. Baron Ludwig Von Closen, *Revolutionary Journal: 1780–1783* (Chapel Hill: University of North Carolina Press, 1958), p. 114.

11. Elias Boudinot, *Journal* (Philadelphia: Bourquin and Co., 1894), pp. 76–78.

12. Van Doren, *Secret History*, p. 34.

13. William S. Stryker, *The Battle of Monmouth*, p. 34.

14. Jackson, "Washington in Philadelphia," p. 125.

15. Commager and Morris, *Spirit*, p. 705.

16. *Ibid.*, p. 790.

17. William S. Stryker, *The Battles of Trenton and Princeton* (Boston: Houghton Mifflin Co., 1898), pp. 94, 101.

18. *Ibid.*, pp. 266–67.

19. Howard Peckham, *The War for Independence* (Chicago: Chicago University Press, 1958), p. 47.

20. *Ibid.*, p. 56.

21. Gustav Kobbé, *The Jersey Coast and Pines* (Short Hills, N.J.: G. Kobbé, 1889), p. 29.

22. Boyer, *Indian Trails*, p. 97.

23. Leonard Lundin, *Cockpit of the Revolution* (Princeton: Princeton University Press, 1940), p. 157.

24. New Jersey Papers, Historical Society of Pennsylvania.

25. Nathanael Greene Correspondence, Princeton University Library.

26. Van Doren, *Secret History*, p. 210.

27. New Jersey Papers, Historical Society of Pennsylvania.

28. Frank H. Stewart, New Jersey Society of Pennsylvania, *Yearbook 1929*, p. 61.

29. Boyer, *Indian Trails*, p. 70.

30. George R. Prowell, *History of Camden County* (Philadelphia: L. J. Richards and Co., 1886), p. 618.

31. Burlington County Deed Books, *Liber D*, p. 214.

CHAPTER IX

1. K. Braddock-Rogers, "Saltworks of New Jersey During the American Revolution," *Journal of Chemical Education*, XV, 486 ff.

2. Struthers Burt, *Philadelphia: Holy Experiment* (New York: Doubleday, Doran and Co., 1945), p. 283.

3. Journals of the Continental Congress, 1774–1789.

4. Acts of the Council and General Assembly of New Jersey.

5. Edwin Salter, *A History of Monmouth and Ocean Counties, New Jersey* (Bayonne, N.J.: E. Gardner and Sons, 1890).

6. Braddock-Rogers, "Saltworks," p. 588.

7. New Jersey Archives, 2d Series, XI, 322.

8. Leonard Lundin, *Cockpit of the Revolution* (Princeton: Princeton University Press, 1940), p. 289.

9. *Ibid.*, p. 290.

10. *Ibid.*, pp. 289–290.

11. Frank H. Stewart archives.

12. Pennsylvania Salt Works Papers, Historical Society of Pennsylvania.

13. *Pennsylvania Gazette*, Sept. 13, 1780.

14. New Jersey Archives, 2nd Series, II, 326.

15. *Pennsylvania Packet*, Aug. 6, 1778.

16. Letters of Samuel Cooper, Historical Society of Pennsylvania.

17. Lewis T. Stevens, *The History of Cape May County*.

18. Diary of Aaron Leaming, 1751–1777, Historical Society of Pennsylvania.

19. Harry B. and Grace M. Weiss, *The Revolutionary Salt Works of the New Jersey Coast* (Trenton: Past Times Press, 1958), p. 26.
20. John F. Hall, *Daily Union History of Atlantic City*, p. 155.

CHAPTER X

1. Carleton Papers, 4443. Colonial Williamsburg.
2. E. Alfred Jones, *The Loyalists of New Jersey* (Newark: Historical Society, 1927): p. 130.
3. Carleton Papers, 4394, Colonial Williamsburg.
4. John C. Fitzpatrick, *Writings of George Washington*, XXIV, 147.
5. *Ibid.*, XXIV, 136.
6. Carleton Papers, 4469, Colonial Williamsburg.
7. *New Jersey Gazette,* April 24, 1782.
8. Carleton Papers, 4473, Colonial Williamsburg.
9. *Ibid.*, 4485.
10. *Ibid.*, 4707.
11. *Ibid.*, 4815.
12. William S. Stryker, *The Capture of the Block House at Toms River* (Trenton: Naar, Day and Naar, 1883), p. 22.
13. Lorenzo Sabine, *Loyalists of the American Revolution* (Boston: Little Brown and Co., 1864), II, 20.
14. Catherine Drinker Bowen, *John Adams and the Revolution* (Boston: Little, Brown and Co., 1950), p. 516.
15. Carl Van Doren, *Benjamin Franklin* (New York: Garden City Publishing Co., 1941), pp. 690–91.
16. H. S. Commager and R. B. Morris, *The Spirit of 'Seventy-Six* (Indianapolis: Bobbs-Merrill Co., 1958), p. 327.
17. *Ibid.*, p. 341.
18. Joseph S. Sickler, *History of Salem County* (Salem: Sunbeam Publishing Co., 1937), p. 158.
19. Troyer S. Anderson, *Command of the Howe Brothers During the American Revolution* (New York: Oxford University Press, 1936), p. 312.
20. *Ibid.*, p. 309.

21. William S. Stryker, *The New Jersey Volunteers* (Trenton: Privately printed, 1887), p. 4.

22. Anderson, *Command of the Howe Brothers*, p. 312.

23. Stryker, *New Jersey Volunteers*, p. 17.

24. Van Doren, *Benjamin Franklin*, p. 91.

25. Catherine Fennelly, "William Franklin," *William and Mary Quarterly*, July, 1949, p. 362.

26. *Ibid.*, p. 367.

27. *Ibid.*, p. 380.

28. Van Doren, *Benjamin Franklin*, p. 549.

29. Howard Peckham, *The War of Independence* (Chicago: Chicago University Press, 1958), p. 199.

30. Stryker, *The Capture of the Block House at Toms River*, p. 25.

31. Fitzpatrick, *Writings of Washington*, XXIV, 318.

32. Commager and Morris, *Spirit*, p. 888.

33. Francis Wharton, *Revolutionary Diplomatic Correspondence of the United States* (Washington: Govt. Printing Office, 1889), V, 617.

34. Carleton Papers, 4665.

35. Wharton, *Diplomatic Correspondence*, V, 635.

36. *Ibid.*, V, 534.

37. Samuel Flagg Bemis, *Diplomacy of the American Revolution* (Bloomington: Indiana University Press, 1957), p. 186.

38. *Ibid.*, p. 241.

39. Fitzpatrick, *Writings of Washington*, XXV, p. 241.

40. Elias Boudinot, *Life and Letters*, Vol. 1, pp. 249.

41. Fitzpatrick, *Writings of Washington*, Vol. 25, p. 337.

42. William S. Stryker, *The Capture of the Block House at Toms River*, p. 31.

43. *Ibid.*, p. 30.

44. Fitzpatrick, *Writings of Washington*, XXIX, p. 125.

45. *Ibid.*, Vol. 25, p. 359.

46. Sabine, *Loyalists*, p. 20.

MANUSCRIPT SOURCES

Joseph Ball Papers. Historical Society of Pennsylvania.

Blathwayt Papers. Colonial Williamsburg, Incorporated.

Sir Guy Carleton (British Headquarters) Papers (Photostats). Colonial Williamsburg, Incorporated.

Letters of Philip Vickers Fithian. Princeton University Library and the Vineland Historical Society.

Nathanael Greene—Charles Pettit Correspondence. William L. Clements Library, Princeton University Library, and The Library of Congress.

Nathanael Greene: Letters. Princeton University Library, Historical Society of Pennsylvania.

Diary of Aaron Leaming. Historical Society of Pennsylvania.

New Jersey Papers. Historical Society of Pennsylvania.

Philadelphia Custom House Papers. Historical Society of Pennsylvania.

Waste Book of the Pennsylvania Salt Works. Historical Society of Pennsylvania.

Frank H. Stewart Papers. New Jersey State Teachers College, Glassboro.

Tilton Family Papers. Atlantic County Historical Society.

Caspar Wistar Papers. Historical Society of Pennsylvania.

Wood and Bacon Account Books. Historical Society of Pennsylvania.

Credits for permitted use of published material dealing with Philip Vickers Fithian are as follows:

Philip Vickers Fithian: Journal and Letters, 1767–1774. Edited for the Princeton Historical Association by John Rogers Williams. Princeton: The University Library, 1900.

Philip Vickers Fithian: Journal, 1775–76. Edited by Robert Greenhalgh Albion and Leonidas Dodson. Princeton: Princeton University Press, 1934.

Journal and Letters of Philip Vickers Fithian. Edited by Hunter Dickinson Farish. Williamsburg, 1957. By permission of Colonial Williamsburg, Inc. Copyright 1957 by Colonial Williamsburg, Inc.

Philip Vickers Fithian: Chaplain in the Revolution, 1776. Letters to his Wife, with a Biographical Sketch by Frank D. Andrews. Vineland, N.J., 1932. By permission of the Vineland Historical Society.

BIBLIOGRAPHY

ALEXANDER, ARCHIBALD, DD. *Biological Sketches of the Founder and Principal Alumni of the Log College*. Princeton, N.J.: J. T. Robinson, 1845.

ALEXANDER, ROBERT CROZER. *Ho! For Cape Island*. Cape May, N.J.: Privately printed, 1956.

ANDERSON, TROYER STEELE. *The Command of the Howe Brothers during the American Revolution*. New York: Oxford University Press, 1936.

ANDREWS, BESSIE AYARS. *Reminiscences of Greenwich*. Vineland, N.J.: Privately printed, 1910.

ANDREWS, FRANK D. *Enoch Green: A Biographical Sketch*. Vineland, N.J.: Smith Printing House, 1933.

———— (ed.). *Letters of Philip Vickers Fithian to his Wife*. Vineland, N.J.: Privately printed, 1932.

BATES, ERNEST SUTHERLAND. *The Story of Congress: 1789–1935*. New York: Harper and Brothers, 1936.

BEMIS, SAMUEL FLAGG. *The Diplomacy of the American Revolution*. Bloomington, Ind.: Indiana University Press, 1957.

BILL, ALFRED HOYT. *The Campaign of Princeton: 1776–1777*. Princeton, N.J.: Princeton University Press, 1948.

BLACKMAN, LEAH. *Historical Sketch of Tuckerton*. Proceedings of the Surveyors Association of West New Jersey, 1880.

BOUDINOT, ELIAS. *Journal*. Philadelphia: Bourquin and Co., 1894.

BOWEN, CATHERINE DRINKER. *John Adams and the American Revolution*. Boston: Little, Brown and Co., 1950.

BOYER, CHARLES S. *Early Forges and Furnaces in New Jersey*. Philadelphia, Pa.: University of Pennsylvania Press, 1931.

————. *Indian Trails and Early Paths*. Camden, N.J.: Camden County Historical Society, 1938.

BRIDENBAUGH, CARL. *Cities in the Wilderness*. New York: Alfred A. Knopf, 1955.

BRIDENBAUGH, CARL AND JESSICA. *Rebels and Gentlemen*. New York: Reynal and Hitchcock, 1942.

BURKE, THOMAS. *English Inns*. London: Collins Press, 1943.

BURT, STRUTHERS. *Philadelphia: Holy Experiment*. New York: Doubleday, Doran and Co., 1945.

CAZENOVE, THEOPHILE. *Cazenove Journal, 1794*. Ed. by Rayner W. Kelsey. Haverford, Pa.: Pennsylvania History Press, 1922.

CHATTERTON, E. KEBLE. *Kings Cutters and Smugglers*. Philadelphia: J. B. Lippincott Co., 1912.

CLARK, WILLIAM BELL. *Ben Franklin's Privateers*. Baton Rouge, La.: Louisiana State University Press, 1956.

COLLINS, V. LANSING. *Princeton Past and Present*. Princeton, N.J.: Princeton University Press, 1946.

COMMAGER, HENRY STEELE, AND MORRIS, RICHARD B. *The Spirit of 'Seventy-Six*. Indianapolis, Ind.: Bobbs-Merrill Co., 1958.

COTTER, JOHN L., AND HUDSON, J. PAUL. *New Discoveries at Jamestown*. Washington, D.C.: United States Department of the Interior, 1957.

CRAIG, H. STANLEY (compiler). *Salem County (N.J.) Marriage Records*. Merchantville, N.J.: H. S. Craig, 1928.

CUSHING, THOMAS, AND SHEPPARD, CHARLES E. *History of the Counties of Gloucester, Salem and Cumberland*. Philadelphia, Pa.: Everts and Peck, 1883.

DAVIDS, RICHARD WISTAR. *The Wistar Family*. Philadelphia, 1896.

DECOU, GEORGE. *Burlington: A Provincial Capital*. Burlington, N.J.: Library Company of Burlington, 1945.

DONALDSON, THOMAS. *The House in Which Thomas Jefferson Wrote the Declaration of Independence*. Philadelphia, Pa.: Avil Printing Co., 1898.

DRINKER, ELIZABETH. *Extracts from the Journal of Elizabeth Drinker: From 1759 to 1807*. Ed. by Henry D. Biddle. Philadelphia: J. B. Lippincott Co., 1889.

EARLE, ALICE MORSE. *Stage Coach and Tavern Days*. New York: The Macmillan Co., 1900.

ELMER, LUCIUS, Q. C. *History of the Early Settlement and Progress of Cumberland County*. Bridgeton, N.J.: George F. Nixon, 1869.

FARJEON, JEFFERSON. *The Compleat Smuggler*. Indianapolis, Ind.: Bobbs-Merrill Co., 1938.

FITHIAN, PHILIP VICKERS. *Journal and Letters: 1767–1774*. Ed. by

John Rogers Williams. Princeton, N.J.: Princeton University Library, 1900.

FITHIAN, PHILIP VICKERS. *Journal, 1775–1776.* Ed. by Robert Greenhalgh Albion and Leonidas Dodson. Princeton, N.J.: Princeton University Press, 1934.

———. *Journal and Letters: 1773–1774.* Ed. by Hunter Dickinson Farish. Williamsburg, Va.: Colonial Williamsburg, Inc., 1957.

FORBES, ESTHER. *Paul Revere and the World He Lived In.* Boston: Houghton Mifflin Co., 1943.

FRIEDELBAUM, STANLEY H. *Bellomont: Imperial Administrator.* Thesis, Columbia University. Copyright by the author, 1955.

GREENE, GEORGE WASHINGTON. *Life of Major General Nathanael Greene.* 3 Vols. New York: Hurd and Houghton, 1871.

HALL, JOHN F. *The Daily Union History of Atlantic City and County.* Atlantic City, N.J.: Daily Union Printing Co., 1900.

HARRINGTON, J. C. *Glassmaking at Jamestown.* Richmond, Va.: Dietz Press, 1952.

HESTON, ALFRED M. *Absegami: Annals of Eyren Haven and Atlantic City, 1609 to 1904.* 2 Vols. Camden, N.J.: Privately printed, 1904.

——— (ed.). *South Jersey: A History, 1664–1924.* 2 Vols. New York: Lewis Publishing Co., 1924.

HOFFMAN, PHILIP H. *History of The Arnold Tavern.* Morristown, N.J.: The Jerseyman, 1903. Pamphlet.

HUNTER, FREDERICK WILLIAM. *Stiegel Glass.* New York: Dover Publications, 1950.

JAMESON, J. FRANKLIN. *The American Revolution Considered as a Social Movement.* Princeton, N.J.: Princeton University Press, 1926.

JOHNSON, AMANDUS. *The Journal and Biography of Nicholas Collin: 1746–1831.* Philadelphia: New Jersey Society of Pennsylvania, 1936.

JONES, E. ALFRED. *The Loyalists of New Jersey.* Newark, N.J.: New Jersey Historical Society, 1927.

JUET, ROBERT. *Juet's Journal: The Voyage of the Half Moon from 4 April to 7 November 1609.* Newark, N.J.: New Jersey Historical Society, 1959.

KNOX, CAPTAIN DUDLEY W. *A History of the United States Navy.* New York: G. P. Putnam's Sons, 1936.

KOBBÉ, GUSTAV. *The New Jersey Coast and Pines*. Short Hills, N.J.: G. Kobbé, 1889.

LABAREE, LEONARD W., AND BELL, WHITFIELD J., JR. (eds.). *Mr. Franklin*. New Haven: Yale University Press, 1956.

LANE, WHEATON J. *From Indian Trail to Iron Horse*. Princeton, N.J.: Princeton University Press, 1939.

LATHROP, ELISE. *Early American Inns and Taverns*. New York: Robert M. McBride and Co., 1926.

LUNDIN, LEONARD. *Cockpit of the Revolution*. Princeton, N.J.: Princeton University Press, 1940.

MACLAY, EDGAR S. *A History of American Privateers*. New York: D. Appleton and Co., 1910.

MASON, FRANCIS NORTON (ed.). *John Norton and Sons, Merchants of London and Virginia*. Richmond, Va.: Dietz Press, 1937.

McCLELLAN, WILLIAM SMITH. *Smuggling in the American Colonies at the Outbreak of the Revolution*. New York: Moffat, Yard and Co., 1912.

McKEARIN, HELEN AND GEORGE S. *Two Hundred Years of American Blown Glass*. New York: Crown Publishers, 1950.

MELLICK, ANDREW D., JR. *Lesser Crossroads*. Ed. by Hubert G. Schmidt. New Brunswick, N.J.: Rutgers University Press, 1948.

MIDDLETON, ARTHUR PIERCE. *Tobacco Coast: A Maritime History of Chesapeake Bay in the Colonial Era*. Newport News, Va.: Mariners Museum, 1953.

MILLER, JOHN C. *Origins of the American Revolution*. Boston: Little, Brown and Co., 1943.

NEWTON, A. EDWARD. *This Book-Collecting Game*. Boston: Little, Brown and Co., 1928.

NORTHEND, MARY HARROD. *American Glass*. New York: Dodd, Mead and Co., 1926.

PARRY, EDWIN S. *Betsy Ross: Quaker Rebel*. Philadelphia: John C. Winston Co., 1930.

PECKHAM, HOWARD H. *The War for Independence*. Chicago: Chicago University Press, 1958.

PRESTON, JOHN HYDE. *Revolution, 1776*. New York: Harcourt, Brace and Co., 1933.

PROWELL, GEORGE R. *History of Camden County, N.J.* Philadelphia: L. J. Richards and Co., 1886.

ROBERTS, KENNETH AND ANNA M. *Moreau St. Méry's American Journey, 1793–98*. New York: Doubleday and Co., 1947.

SABINE, LORENZO. *Loyalists of the American Revolution.* Boston: Little, Brown and Co., 1864.

SALTER, EDWIN. *A History of Monmouth and Ocean Counties, New Jersey.* Bayonne, N.J.: E. Gardner and Sons, 1890.

SAVAGE, HENRY LYTTLETON (ed.). *Nassau Hall: 1756–1956.* Princeton, N.J.: Princeton University Press, 1956.

SCHEER, GEORGE F., AND RANKIN, HUGH F. *Rebels and Redcoats.* New York: World Publishing Co., 1957.

SCHLESINGER, ARTHUR M. *The Colonial Merchants and the American Revolution.* New York: Frederick Ungar Publishing Co., 1957.

––––––. *Prelude to Independence: The Newspaper War on Britain 1764–1776.* New York: Alfred A. Knopf, 1958.

SICKLER, JOSEPH S. *Tea-Burning Town, The Story of Greenwich on the Cohansey in West New Jersey.* New York: Abelard Press, 1950.

––––––. *The History of Salem County, New Jersey.* Salem, N.J.: Sunbeam Publishing Co., 1937.

SINGLETON, ESTHER. *Social New York under the Georges.* New York, 1902.

STEWART, FRANK H. *Notes on Old Gloucester County, N.J.* 3 Vols. Camden, N.J.: New Jersey Society of Pennsylvania, 1917.

––––––. *Major John Fenwick.* Woodbury, N.J., Privately printed, 1939.

STRYKER, WILLIAM S. *The New Jersey Volunteers.* Trenton, N.J.: Privately printed, 1887.

––––––. *The Battles of Trenton and Princeton.* Boston: Houghton Mifflin Co., 1898.

––––––. *The Capture of the Block House at Toms River.* Trenton, N.J.: Naar, Day and Naar, 1883.

THOMPSON, ROBERT T. *Colonel James Neilson.* New Brunswick, N.J.: Rutgers University Press, 1940.

TOLLES, FREDERICK B. *Meeting House and Counting House.* Chapel Hill, N.C.: University of North Carolina Press, 1948.

UHLENDORF, BERNHARD A. *Revolution in America:* Letters and Journals of Adjutant General Major Baurmeister of the Hessian Forces (Uhlendorf trans. and ed.). New Brunswick, N.J.: Rutgers University Press, 1957.

VAN DOREN, CARL. *Benjamin Franklin.* New York: Garden City Publishing Co., 1941.

VAN DOREN, CARL. *Secret History of the American Revolution.* New York: Viking Press, 1941.

VON CLOSEN, BARON LUDWIG. *Revolutionary Journal: 1780–1783* (trans. and ed. by Evelyn M. Acomb). Chapel Hill, N.C.: University of North Carolina Press, 1958.

WARD, TOWNSEND. "The Germantown Road and Its Associations," *Pennsylvania Magazine of History and Biography,* Vols. 5 & 6, 1881.

WATSON, JOHN FANNING. *Annals of Philadelphia and Pennsylvania in the Olden Times.* 3 Vols. Philadelphia: E. S. Stuart, 1898.

WEISS, HARRY B., AND ZIEGLER, GRACE M. *Some Legislation Affecting Rural Life in Colonial New Jersey.* Trenton, N.J.: Past Times Press, 1957.

———. *Colonel Erkuries Beatty, 1759–1823.* Trenton, N.J.: Past Times Press, 1958.

WEISS, HARRY B. AND GRACE M. *The Revolutionary Salt Works of the New Jersey Coast.* Trenton, N.J.: Past Times Press, 1959.

WHARTON, FRANCIS (ed.). *The Revolutionary Diplomatic Correspondence of the United States.* Washington, D.C.: Government Printing Office, 1889.

WILDES, HARRY EMERSON. *Lonely Midas: The Story of Stephen Girard.* New York: Farrar and Rinehart, 1943.

WISTAR, ISAAC JONES. *Autobiography: 1827–1905.* New York: Harper and Brothers, 1914.

INDEX